AN ANCIENT JEWISH CHRISTIAN SOURCE ON
THE HISTORY OF CHRISTIANITY
Pseudo-Clementive *Recognitions* 1.27–71

Society of Biblical Literature

TEXTS AND TRANSLATIONS
CHRISTIAN APOCRYPHA SERIES

edited by
Jean-Daniel Dubois
Dennis R. MacDonald

Texts and Translations 37
Christian Apocrypha Series 2

*AN ANCIENT JEWISH CHRISTIAN SOURCE ON
THE HISTORY OF CHRISTIANITY
PSEUDO-CLEMENTINE RECOGNITIONS 1.27–71*

An Ancient Jewish Christian Source on the History of Christianity

PSEUDO-CLEMENTINE *RECOGNITIONS* 1.27–71

by
F. Stanley Jones

Scholars Press
Atlanta, Georgia

An Ancient Jewish Christian Source on the History of Christianity

PSEUDO-CLEMENTINE *RECOGNITIONS* 1.27–71

by

F. Stanley Jones

© 1995
Society of Biblical Literature

Library of Congress Cataloging-in-Publication Data
Jones, F. Stanley.
    An ancient Jewish Christian source on the history of Christianity :
Pseudo-Clementine Recognitions 1.27-71 / F. Stanley Jones.
        p. cm. — (Texts and translations ; 37. Christian apocrypha
series ; 2)
    Includes bibliographical references and index.
    ISBN 0-7885-0118-6 (alk. paper)
    1. Recognitions (Pseudo-Clementine)—Criticism, interpretation,
etc. 2. Jewish Christians—History—Early chruch, ca. 30–600.
I. Title. II. Series: Texts and translations ; no. 37.
III. Series: Texts and translations. Christian apocrypha series ; 2.
BR65.C55R434 1995
270.1—dc20   95-17085
                                  CIP

Printed in the United States of America
on acid-free paper

For

Students and Colleagues

in Göttingen, Long Beach, and Paris

CONTENTS

PREFACE

More than a few teachers, colleagues, students, and friends in the United States and Europe have fostered the growth of this study. They are too many to be listed here, especially with the necessary qualifications that would appropriately relieve them of any possible detrimental imputations. Each may remember his or her particular effort to encourage me to greater diligence, and to each individually I now express my heartfelt thanks. The research was facilitated furthermore by numerous libraries. It was also supported by several institutions: Vanderbilt University, the Association pour l'étude de la littérature apocryphe chrétienne, the American Council of Learned Societies, California State University, Long Beach, and the Pseudo-Clementine Project of the Institute for Antiquity and Christianity. My sincere gratitude extends to all these persons and institutions. While it is my hope to have attained to some of their expectations in this study, I have to ask for their indulgence of the shortcomings that remain.

The reader might legitimately desire an extensive commentary to the remarkable section of the *Pseudo-Clementines* dealt with in this study. I have collected material for such a commentary for well over a decade. Redaction of this collection, which underlies the present investigation and is partially integrated into it, must await an appropriate time. Until then, the indices, ably drawn up by M. Francie Kisko, M.A., who also assisted with the preparation of the final copy, may serve as a guide.

For a comprehensive overview of the *Pseudo-Clementines*, I refer the reader now to my presentation of these writings in Robert W. Funk's forthcoming *New Testament Apocrypha*. There it is argued that the time has come to abandon a hypothesis that has long dominated and mired Pseudo-Clementine research, namely, the hypothesis that a writing entitled the *Kerygmata Petrou* was a (determinative) source for the *Pseudo-Clementines*. The following study, however, stands on its own, with or without this hypothesis. A complete synoptic English translation of the *Pseudo-Clementines*, which would allow this unique ancient Christian novel to step forth for the modern reader in its original glory, is a desideratum I would like to supply someday.

D. R. MacDonald and J.-D. Dubois have conscientiously and graciously monitored the path of this work into the present series. My parents, Catherine and Malcolm, generously attended to the Californian home and proofread the text when a sabbatical permitted study of Pseudo-Clementine manuscripts in London, where Britt, my companion and wife, assisted with remarkable alacrity. The book is dedicated to students and colleagues at the three universities where I have been privileged to offer courses.

LIST OF ABBREVIATIONS

B   Pseudo-Clementine basic writing or its author

E   older Greek epitome of the Pseudo-Clementine *Homilies*

H   Pseudo-Clementine *Homilies* or their author

R   Pseudo-Clementine *Recognitions* or their author

I

INTRODUCTION:
REVIEW OF MODERN RESEARCH

Introduction

The *Pseudo-Clementines* are the corpus of extant witnesses to an ancient Christian novel that recounts Clement of Rome's conversion to Christianity, his travels with Peter, and the romantic recovery of the long-lost members of his family. This novel has been preserved in two main versions, the *Recognitions* (hereafter R) and the *Homilies* (hereafter H). Since these two fourth-century renditions share much material and often agree literally with each other, it is commonly assumed that they both derive from an earlier third-century form of the novel, called the "basic writing" (hereafter B).[1]

---

[1]On the history of this theory, see F. Stanley Jones, "The Pseudo-Clementines: A History of Research," *The Second Century* 2 (1982): 8-14 (reprinted in *Studies in Early Christianity*, ed. Everett Ferguson, vol. 2, *Literature of the Early Church* [New York and London: Garland, 1993]); this article also contains a general history of research into the *Pseudo-Clementines*; see there p. 2, n. 1 for references to other surveys. It is important to gain an overview of the entire Pseudo-Clementine

The *Pseudo-Clementines* are significant for the study of ancient Christianity because they contain traditions of ancient Syrian Jewish Christianity that have not survived elsewhere. Since evidence reflecting the Jewish Christian wing of the ancient church is scarce in comparison with the abundant documentation for the other main branch, gentile Christianity, the *Pseudo-Clementines* offer valuable material for proper historical understanding of the development of early Christian religion. The present study examines a section of R that has often been thought to contain very primitive Jewish Christian material. While the larger goal of this investigation is to contribute towards filling the need for a well-founded history of Jewish Christianity, the following will mostly be concerned with only laying the groundwork for one aspect of such an undertaking. To ease reading, the plan and results of the study will now be summarized.

Chapter 1 reviews the last 150 years of scholarship and thereby discloses the possibilities for interpretation of the two sets of evidence, namely, the witness of Epiphanius on the *Anabathmoi Jakobou*, a writing often thought to be related to R 1.27-71, and observations arising from the application of internal literary criteria to R 1. It is seen, above all, that the theory that R 1.27-71 derives from a special source has been quite common. Despite an abundance of divergent opinions concerning the precise compass and nature of the source, in recent times one scholar's view has become dominant without having been thoroughly examined. The history of research also reveals that the Syriac translation of the lost Greek text of R 1.27-71 has been unduly neglected in favor of Rufinus's Latin rendering.

Chapter 2 addresses this last problem of evaluating the two extant ancient translations of the lost Greek. Its goal is to formulate some broad guidelines that enable responsible movement back from the existing Latin and Syriac versions towards the original Greek. To do

---

corpus before approaching specific problems; this rather obvious point deserves some emphasis in view of certain recent examinations of R 1 (discussed below) that are clearly hampered by a lack of acquaintance with larger Pseudo-Clementine issues.

this, Rufinus's theory of translation and his comments on his rendering of the *Pseudo-Clementines* are investigated. Then, recently discovered Armenian fragments and other acknowledged criteria are employed to reach the conclusion that while each of the two translations has its own peculiar shortcomings, they were both carried out in a fairly conscientious manner and are of approximately the same accuracy.

To save the Syriac version from further neglect, chapter 3 provides the first complete modern translation of the Syriac of R 1.27-71.[2] To enable ready comparison with the Latin, a new translation of this version has been provided in parallel columns alongside the Syriac. Furthermore, an English rendering of the Armenian fragments has been included.

Chapter 4 addresses the question of whether R 1.27-71 is based on a special source, a widely held thesis in previous research. The literary place of this passage in R and in the lost basic writing is identified, and the redaction of each author is isolated. Since the views of the remaining material differ from what is elsewhere attributable to the basic writing, this material seems indeed to derive from a special source. The limits of this source are identified as R 1.27.1-44.1, 53.4-71.6. Examination of this material reveals that its author employed the Greek Old Testament, the Book of Jubilees, Matthew, Luke, Acts, Hegesippus, Justin, and possibly the *Gospel of the Ebionites*. While some Jewish Christian themes are shared with the *Anabathmoi Jakobou*, evidence for dependency on this writing is insufficient. Disclosure of the original structure of the source shows that the writing was composed under the name of Matthew.

Chapter 5 concludes that the author is a Jewish Christian of about 200 C.E. He values astrology, sees Christianity as true Judaism, and is concerned with the Christian inheritance of the land of Israel. He

---

[2]Jozef Verheyden, review of *The Ascents of James: History and Theology of a Jewish-Christian Community*, by Robert E. Van Voorst, in *Ephemerides Theologicae Lovanienses* 66 (1990): 418, bemoaned the fact that Van Voorst left out portions of the passage and pointed out the need for the present *complete* version: "It is a pity that the Author limited himself . . . . The reader would benefit from a continuous translation of the whole section."

possibly writes as a Jewish Christian presbyter or bishop in Jerusalem or Judaea.

With this summary of the plan and results of the study complete, this first chapter may now introduce the problem of Pseudo-Clementine R 1.27-71 by a historical survey of previous research. The review will be strictly limited to the section that is the subject of this study and intends to be primarily objective, but it will also have a critical aspect. Thus, on the one hand, the statements of a previous scholar will be merely presented in the terms and context in which they were originally made. On the other hand, attention will be directed specifically to insights that either have been particularly influential in subsequent research or that seem (to the present author) to bring a matter to a head.

Historical Survey

HILGENFELD TO LEHMANN

A youthful Adolf Hilgenfeld, in a book that inaugurated his prolific career at the age of twenty-four, was the first to draw R 1.27-72 into prominence in Pseudo-Clementine studies. R 1.21.7-9, 74.3-5, 3.32.4-7, 52.5, 74.4-75.11 (passages stating that Peter had sent to James books recording his proclamations) convinced Hilgenfeld that the author not only employed an older writing but also assumed knowledge of this writing among his readers.[3] The ideas of this source, which Hilgenfeld designated the *Kerygma Petrou*, were said to be preserved "fairly purely" in R 1.27-72.[4]

With reference to the list of "ten books" that had been sent to James (R 3.75.1-11), Hilgenfeld made the noteworthy observation that directly preceding R 3.75 R had reported of presentations by Peter on ten days and that the content of the seventh book corresponds to the point at which Peter stops in his recapitulation of his teachings at the

---

[3]Adolf Hilgenfeld, *Die clementinischen Recognitionen und Homilien, nach ihrem Ursprung und Inhalt dargestellt* (Jena: J. G. Schreiber; Leipzig: Chr. E. Kollmann, 1848), 45-52.

[4]Ibid., 52.

end of the seventh day at the conclusion of R 1.[5] The "distinctive" chapters R 1.44-54 present the main content of the first book.[6] The other parts of R 1.27-72 derive largely from books one, five, six, and seven.[7] The content of the rest of the *Kerygma Petrou* can similarly be reconstructed from the "table of contents" in R 3.75.[8] This writing was not dialogical in form, and Clement played no role in it.[9] Hilgenfeld dated the *Kerygma Petrou* to the first century because Paulinism is still the only Christian heresy and because the memory of the first Jewish revolt against Rome is still fresh.[10] The writing should be located in Rome because all the Petrine writings presumably derive from the Roman congregation, because Paul's letter to the Romans reveals the Essene character of this congregation, and because the later reworkings of the *Pseudo-Clementines* occurred in Rome.[11]

Hilgenfeld's many other individual insights into particular passages of R 1 will be taken into consideration in the following chapters. Worthy of special mention here, however, is that Hilgenfeld thought the section had been retouched by a number of later hands.[12] Some of his conjectures actually found documentary support in the subsequently published Syriac version.

In the following year, Hilgenfeld's study was subjected to a thorough review by Karl Reinhold Köstlin.[13] Köstlin differed from Hilgenfeld in particular regarding the growth of the Pseudo-Clementine literature. He promoted the view that the material in R 1-7 (and the parallels in H) presupposes only one source, the *Periodoi Petrou*, and

---

[5]Ibid., 51-52.

[6]Ibid., 70.

[7]Ibid., 82.

[8]Ibid., 82-92.

[9]Ibid., 92.

[10]Ibid., 93-94.

[11]Ibid., 94.

[12]Ibid., 79-81, 91.

[13]Karl Reinhold Köstlin, review of *Die clementinischen Recognitionen und Homilien, nach ihrem Ursprung und Inhalt dargestellt*, by Adolf Hilgenfeld, in *Allgemeine Literatur-Zeitung* (Halle), 1849, cols. 577-78, 585-608, 612-16.

that the *Homilies* were also based on this writing.[14] He did, however, leave open the possibility that book one of R was somehow related to an Ebionite source, namely, "the Ebionite πράξεις ἀποστόλων, in which, according to Epiphanius 30.16, there was particular mention of the ἀναβαθμοί and ὑφηγήσεις 'Ιακώβου against the temple and sacrifice (as in R 1.36-71)."[15] But Köstlin emphasized that R 1 was conceived from the beginning as a part of the *Periodoi*: the justification of the apostles' break with the Jews and the extensive treatment of the genesis of paganism, along with the idea that Christ is the hope of the nations, point to conversions of gentiles and to Clement and the fate of his family.[16] The implication of this view is that one cannot speak of R 1.36-71 as deriving *in toto*, or even to a large extent, from a source older than the Clementine *Periodoi*. To bolster this position Köstlin also drew attention to the elements in the section that indicate that the author stands at great historical distance from the events he is describing.[17] Thus, the destruction of the temple by Titus is said to lie in the "mythical" past.[18]

Five years later Gerhard Uhlhorn gave Hilgenfeld credit for drawing attention to the peculiar nature of R 1.22-74, but Uhlhorn saw himself forced to evaluate these chapters completely differently: instead of being the oldest part of the *Pseudo-Clementines*, this section was actually added by R. The proof for this view was found in the chronological references. The dates in this passage are at variance with the references before and after this section in the *Pseudo-Clementines*.[19] Thus, in R 1.7.3 Christ is still alive, whereas at least seven years and forty-nine days have passed from the time of Christ's death according to the account in R 1.22-74; R 1.72-74 state that

---

[14]Ibid., col. 615.

[15]Ibid., col. 603-4; citation from col. 604.

[16]Ibid., col. 604.

[17]Ibid., cols. 604-6.

[18]Ibid., col. 604.

[19]Gerhard Uhlhorn, *Die Homilien und Recognitionen des Clemens Romanus nach ihrem Ursprung und Inhalt dargestellt* (Göttingen: Verlag der Dieterichschen Buchhandlung, 1854), 313. Unfortunately, R 9.29.1 is not discussed by Uhlhorn.

Peter arrived in Caesarea just one day before the planned disputation with Simon, whereas R 1.13.4 and R 7.33.3 presume a longer stay in Caesarea before the arrival of Clement (the words *docente Zacchaeo* in R 2.1.2 present R's attempt to cover up the discrepancy).[20]

While R is thus given the responsibility for introducing this section into the *Pseudo-Clementines*, the peculiarity of the passage was said to betray that it was taken from a source, or from several sources. The same conclusion finds support in the fact that R 1.71.4 speaks of Peter in the third person.[21] The sundry references to the steps of the temple and to the apostles ascending to the temple, the prominent function assigned to James, and the polemic against the temple and sacrifice were cited by Uhlhorn in support of his assumption that the *Anabathmoi Jakobou* was the source at least of the disputation in Jerusalem. This writing seems to have been created in analogy to the well-known story of the death of James.[22]

An effort to synthesize the results of Hilgenfeld and Uhlhorn was undertaken fifteen years later by Johannes Lehmann.[23] With regard to R 1.22-74, Lehmann decided that Hilgenfeld had hit the mark and thus that Uhlhorn was on the wrong track. Lehmann offered evidence that H 2.22 was dependent on R 1.54, 57, 58, 69[24] and considered

---

[20]Ibid., 314-15.

[21]Ibid., 365-66.

[22]Ibid., 367. Albrecht Ritschl, *Die Entstehung der altkatholischen Kirche: Eine kirchen- und dogmengeschichtliche Monographie*, 2d ed., rev. (Bonn: Adolph Marcus, 1857), 264, was evidently convinced by Uhlhorn that the *Anabathmoi Jakobou* was a source of the *Pseudo-Clementines*. Uhlhorn later abandoned the view that R 1.23-71 was added first by R. See Gerhard Uhlhorn, "Clementinen I," in *Realencyklopädie für protestantische Theologie und Kirche*, ed. Albert Hauck, 3d ed., rev. and enl. (Leipzig: J. C. Hinrichs, 1898), 4:177.

[23]Johannes Lehmann, *Die clementinischen Schriften mit besonderer Rücksicht auf ihr literarisches Verhältniss* (Gotha: Friedrich Andreas Perthes, 1869). On this book, see especially Theodor Zahn, review of *Die clementinischen Schriften mit besonderer Rücksicht auf ihr literarisches Verhältniss*, by Johannes Lehmann, in *Göttingische gelehrte Anzeigen*, 1869, 905-17, and Paul de Lagarde, review of *Die clementinischen Schriften mit besonderer Rücksicht auf ihr literarisches Verhältniss*, by Johannes Lehmann, in *Symmicta* (Göttingen: Dieterichsche Verlagsbuchhandlung, 1877), 2-4, 108-12.

[24]Lehmann, *Die clementinischen Schriften*, 333-35. Particularly convincing is the case for the dependency of H 2.22.5 on R 1.54.4, 57.4.

this alone as sufficient to disqualify Uhlhorn's view.[25]   Lehmann
nevertheless also addressed Uhlhorn's specific arguments. He asserted
that Uhlhorn's observations on discrepancies of chronology actually
made it unlikely that R added R 1.22-74, for in this case the chronology
of the supplement would certainly have been made to accord with the
rest of the work. R simply adopted the material of R 4-10 and R 1.1-
13 without becoming aware of the contradiction.[26] Uhlhorn's view
that this section was drawn from the *Anabathmoi Jakobou* is considered even more improbable, for the content of this writing does not
match R 1. R 1.22-74 have Peter, not James, speaking against sacrifice; these chapters are concerned mainly with the proof that Jesus is
the Messiah; and they mention Paul only at the end of the section and
attack him only surreptitiously. Thus Lehmann remained with Hilgenfeld's thesis that R 1.22-74 constituted the core of the old Ebionite
Kerygma Petrou. The mention of Peter in the third person in R 1.71.4
clearly shows that one is dealing with a source.[27] Lehmann saw in
this section, which was said to be full of Ebionite views,[28] the kernel
of Ebionite ideas that are found fully developed in H.[29]

LIPSIUS TO MEYBOOM

The next contribution to the study of R 1.27-71 was made in the
context of investigations into the legends attached to the figure of
Peter. Richard Adelbert Lipsius argued that the *Kerygmata Petrou* were
dependent on an older source, Ebionite *Acts of Peter*, that is clearly
reflected in R 1.44-71, which formed the opening section of this
writing. Chapters 22-43 and 72-74 were added by the *Kerygmata*,

---

[25]Ibid., 341.

[26]Ibid., 344. As did Uhlhorn, so Lehmann, too, failed to take notice of R
9.29.1.

[27]Ibid., 344-45.

[28]Ibid., 454. As examples he mentioned the temporary meaning of sacrifice, the
view of the kingship as tyrannic, and the hard judgment on the building of the
temple.

[29]See his presentation ibid., 454-58. Here the notion of Christ as *Christus
aeternus* is said to be the kernel of the doctrine of the true prophet; the view that
the prophets are of secondary importance as compared with the law (R 1.68.4-
69.1) is considered to be the first step toward their total rejection; and R 1.47.3
is said to be the basis for the development of the doctrine of false pericopes.

whereas the original source continued with a parody of Paul's conversion, mission, arrest, and stays in Caesarea and Rome. This vicious lampoon may be reconstructed from other, originally anti-Pauline passages in the *Pseudo-Clementines* (particularly H 17.13-20) and from the *Acta Petri et Pauli*.[30] While there is no need to report further details of Lipsius's bold, arresting, and influential reconstruction of this source, which was said to have been dependent on Acts[31] and written a considerable time before the middle of the second century,[32] it should be noted that Lipsius saw no reason to connect this writing with the *Anabathmoi Jakobou*.[33]

Lipsius's work was followed by a period of reservation with regard to the supposed source of R 1.27-71. Thus, Bonn professor Joseph Langen briefly drew attention to the possibility that the disputation in the temple might reflect a source used by R; he mentions the theories of Uhlhorn and Lipsius about the nature of this source.[34] The remarks

---

[30]Richard Adelbert Lipsius, *Die Quellen der römischen Petrus-Sage kritisch untersucht* (Kiel: Schwers'sche Buchhandlung, 1872), 27-46, 82-95.

[31]Ibid., 28, n. 1. Lipsius here tacitly reversed the opinion he expressed in his review of *Die clementinischen Schriften mit besonderer Rücksicht auf ihr literarisches Verhältniss*, by Johannes Lehmann, in *Protestantische Kirchenzeitung für das evangelische Deutschland* 16 (1869): 481. See, however, also idem, "Petrus nicht in Rom," *Jahrbücher für protestantische Theologie*, 1876, 627.

[32]Lipsius, *Die Quellen der römischen Petrus-Sage*, 17, 82.

[33]Lipsius, "Petrus nicht in Rom," 626-27; cf. idem, review of *Die clementinischen Schriften*, by J. Lehmann, col. 477, idem, *Die Quellen der römischen Petrus-Sage*, 27-28, n. 2, 45-46, and idem, *Die apokryphen Apostelgeschichten und Apostellegenden: Ein Beitrag zur altchristlichen Literaturgeschichte*, vol. 2 (Braunschweig: C. A. Schwetschke und Sohn [Wiegandt & Appelhans; M. Bruhn], 1884-87), 2:244-45. Adolf Hausrath, *Neutestamentliche Zeitgeschichte*, pt. 4, *Das nachapostolische Zeitalter*, 2d ed. (Heidelberg: Fr. Bassermann, 1877), 131-53, adopted Lipsius's thesis and offered a concise and lucid summary of it.

Derivation of the section from the *Anabathmoi Jakobou* was also denied by George Salmon, "Clementine Literature," in *A Dictionary of Christian Biography, Literature, Sects and Doctrines*, ed. William Smith and Henry Wace (London: John Murray, 1877), 1:568-69, because R 3.75.7 attributes the origin of this section to another work.

[34]Joseph Langen, *Die Klemensromane: Ihre Entstehung und ihre Tendenzen aufs neue untersucht* (Gotha: Friedrich Andreas Perthes, 1890), 130, n. 1. See also p. 87, where Langen is somewhat more positive about R having used a source "Disputation of the Twelve Apostles in Jerusalem."

of Oxford patristic scholar Charles Bigg are similar.[35] The renowned Cambridge professor, later Bishop of Durham, John Barber Lightfoot was somewhat more impressed with Uhlhorn's thesis and suggested that the story of the martyrdom of James, to which Hegesippus is indebted, formed the grand finale of the *Anabathmoi Jakobou*, earlier portions of which (the first of the "Ascents") are preserved in R 1.[36] His colleague Fenton John Anthony Hort initially indicated only that the basic writing took material in R 1 from a source, which may have been the *Anabathmoi Jakobou* and which belonged to the end of the second century or the beginning of the third.[37] Later, Hort tended more toward the view that Hegesippus and R 1 were both dependent on the *Anabathmoi Jakobou*.[38] Groningen's H. U. Meyboom was more reserved about finding a source in R 1 and decided that amid these doubts the best course forward is abstinence from speculation.[39]

H. WAITZ

R 1.27-71 similarly play only a minor role in Hans Waitz's pivotal investigation of the *Pseudo-Clementines*. Waitz, a pastor in Darmstadt, argued that the section was a part of B and that its original location was during the delay of the disputation with Simon for one day. He

---

[35]Charles Bigg, "The Clementine Homilies," in *Studia Biblica et Ecclesiastica: Essays Chiefly in Biblical and Patristic Criticism*, by members of the University of Oxford (Oxford: Clarendon, 1890), 2:183-84, n. 5.

[36]John Barber Lightfoot, *St. Paul's Epistle to the Galatians with Introductions, Notes, and Dissertations*, 10th ed. (London and New York: Macmillan, 1890; reprint ed., Lynn, Mass.: Hendrickson Publishers, 1981), 330, 359, n. 1, 367, n. 1.

[37]Fenton John Anthony Hort, *Notes Introductory to the Study of the Clementine Recognitions: A Course of Lectures* (London and New York: Macmillan, 1901), 115-19. It should be noted that the more explicit statement of Hort's intentions in the Table of Contents on p. x does not derive from Hort himself (see p. vi).

[38]Fenton John Anthony Hort, *Judaistic Christianity* (Cambridge, London, and New York: Macmillan, 1894), 152, 201. That these lectures were delivered later than the lectures on the *Pseudo-Clementines*, though they were published earlier, is apparent from pp. v-vi.
Lightfoot's position was adopted more wholeheartedly by William Patrick, *James the Lord's Brother* (Edinburgh: T & T. Clark, 1906), 231-32.

[39]H. U. Meyboom, *De Clemens-roman*, vol. 2, *Wetenschappelijke Behandeling* (Groningen: J. B. Wolters, 1904), 71, 73-74.

divided the passage into two parts: the book of the appearances of the true prophet (R 1.27-42) and the disputation of the apostles with the Jews concerning the true Christ (R 1.43, 53-71).[40] The first part was said to be merely an extract from a larger treatise on the true prophet that originally stood in the *Kerygmata Petrou*; Waitz stated in particular that R left out a section on Adam as prophet (H 3.17-28) that stood in B after chapter 27.[41] The purpose of these chapters was to prove that the true prophet had appeared throughout all time. Chapters 43 and 53-72, in contrast, defend the thesis that Jesus is the eternal Christ. Thus, the two sections have nothing to do with each other.[42] Chapters 43b-53a are isolated by Waitz as an insertion evidently by R, though they contain some material from the *Kerygmata Petrou*.[43] Particularly important is that Waitz offered an explanation of why at least part of R 1.27-71, namely, chapters 27-42, was not reproduced by H. H left these chapters out because he found similar material in Peter's speech in Tripolis (H 8.10-17 and its parallel R 4.9-13).[44]

The second part was said not to derive from the earlier source, the *Kerygmata Petrou*, in its original form. Waitz noted that the form of R 1.53-71 hardly suits a sermon of Peter and that Peter is even referred to in the third person in R 1.71.4. These chapters are neither Judaistic, for Jesus is placed above Moses in chapter 59.2-3, nor anti-Pauline, for Paul is presented as a defender of Judaism. Furthermore, there is nothing of the nomistic tendency of the *Kerygmata Petrou* in this passage, and John the Baptist is evaluated positively. Finally, since the *Kerygmata Petrou* was not concerned with the thesis that Jesus is the Christ, Waitz concluded that this section, and thus the "seventh book"

---

[40]Hans Waitz, *Die Pseudoklementinen, Homilien und Rekognitionen: Eine quellenkritische Untersuchung*, Texte und Untersuchungen zur Geschichte der altchristlichen Literatur, n.s., vol. 10, no. 4 (Leipzig: J. C. Hinrichs, 1904), 38.

[41]Ibid., 23, 38, 91.

[42]Ibid., 93.

[43]Ibid., 92-93, 38.

[44]Ibid., 22-23.

of R 3.75, was not originally a part of the *Kerygmata Petrou* but was rather added to it later, though not by the anti-Marcionite redactor.[45]

As concerns the source of this material, Waitz noted that the order of the apostles generally follows Matt. 10:2-4, except that the pairs Peter and Andrew and Thomas and Matthew have been separated. While the dissolution of the pair Peter and Andrew should be attributed to the redactor of the *Clementines* or of the *Kerygmata Petrou*, the division of Matthew and Thomas must be attributed to the author of the source. Since Thomas would be the last, R 1.54-65 must belong to an apocryphal writing that stood in some relationship to Thomas. R 1.66-71 forms a literary unit with chapters 54-65 and thus also cannot have anything to do with the *Anabathmoi Jakobou*. Furthermore, these chapters do not reveal the syncretistic Jewish Christian and anti-Pauline character of the writing described by Epiphanius.[46] In his supplementary notes Waitz then suggested that R 1.53-71 derives from conjectural *Acts of Thomas*.[47]

BOUSSET TO REHM

In the year prior to Waitz's study, the inaugural volume of the renowned German series "Forschungen zur Religion und Literatur des Alten und Neuen Testaments" was accompanied by the announcement that one of the subsequent volumes would be *Untersuchungen zu den pseudoclementinischen Schriften* by Wilhelm Bousset, extraordinary professor in Göttingen.[48] The appearance of Waitz's book evidently induced Bousset to redirect the results of his researches into an article, a detailed review of Waitz's work, and a book entitled *Hauptprobleme der Gnosis*.[49] In his review of Waitz's publication, Bousset expressed

---

[45]Ibid., 108-10, 167. See, however, below n. 53.

[46]Ibid., 167-69.

[47]Ibid., 386. See below n. 53 for Waitz's later variations from the position summarized above.

[48]This announcement is found on the back of the paperback cover of Hermann Gunkel, *Zum religionsgeschichtlichen Verständnis des Neuen Testaments*, Forschungen zur Religion und Literatur des Alten und Neuen Testaments, vol. 1 (Göttingen: Vandenhoeck & Ruprecht, 1903). I saw this announcement in the copy of the book in the Niedersächsische Staats- und Universitätsbibliothek in Göttingen.

[49]Wilhelm Bousset, "Die Wiedererkennungs-Fabel in den pseudoklementinischen

only one considerable reservation with respect to Waitz's delineation of
B: contra Waitz, R 1.27-71 cannot have stood in B. While R does
provide indications that the entire section lay before him, B would not
have allowed the chronological difficulties to remain, nor would he have
kept Paul so clearly distinct from Simon and have preserved the
statement that James fled to Jericho. R is rather responsible for
introducing this unified Jewish Christian section from the *Anabathmoi
Jakobou*.[50] R also added the chapters 44b-52 (from material of the
first book of the *Kerygmata Petrou*) along with the few scattered
references to the true prophet.[51] He then introduced an appropriate
title in the "table of contents" in R 3.75.[52]

In the next contribution--disproportionate to its size in both content
and influence--Alfred Schmidtke examined Epiphanius *Panarion*
30.16.6-9 in just over four pages of his study of the Jewish Christian
gospels and reached striking results with respect to R 1. Schmidtke
thought that Epiphanius concluded from B that the Ebionites used the
material that he summarizes in *Panarion* 30.16.7 and presents as an
example of the content of the Ebionite *Acts*, which Epiphanius (incorrectly) assumed to have existed. The *Anabathmoi Jakobou* thus is not
a distinct writing. *Panarion* 30.16.8 stands in reference to the
(supposed) Ebionite *Acts*, not to the *Anabathmoi*, and presents information that Epiphanius probably received from Origen's writings.

Schmidtke then used the report of Epiphanius to reconstruct the
section as it stood in B. He thus decided that there must have been a
long speech of James that R left out at chapters 68-69 and that dealt
with the temple, sacrifices, and the fire on the altar, particularly as is

---

Schriften, den Menächmen des Plautus und Shakespeares Komödie der Irrungen,"
Zeitschrift für die neutestamentliche Wissenschaft 5 (1904): 18-27; idem, review
of *Die Pseudoklementinen, Homilien und Rekognitionen: Eine quellenkritische
Untersuchung*, by Hans Waitz, in *Göttingische gelehrte Anzeigen* 167 (1905): 425-
47; idem, *Hauptprobleme der Gnosis*, Forschungen zur Religion und Literatur des
Alten und Neuen Testaments, vol. 10 (Göttingen: Vandenhoeck & Ruprecht, 1907).

[50]Bousset, review of *Die Pseudoklementinen*, by H. Waitz, 426-27.

[51]Ibid., 437-38. Here Bousset referred to the angel in R 1.32.4 and to the
minor role the prophet of truth plays in the story of Moses.

[52]Ibid., 436.

found in chapters 39 and 48. Indeed, all the material of chapters 43-52 originally stood in the disputations of James. Furthermore, the "redactor" (evidently R) first arranged the content of the seventh book of the *Kerygmata Petrou* into disputations not just of James but also of the twelve apostles (with the Jewish sects); he came upon this idea on the basis of Hegesippus, whose story of the martyrdom of James mentions the Jewish sects just before James's final speech.[53]

In the following period, R 1 was discussed briefly, for example, by Erlangen professor Theodor Zahn, who said the content of R 1.55-70, and probably also that of R 1.71-74 and R 2.7-13, was taken from the *Anabathmoi Jakobou*.[54]   M. R. James wrote in a similar vein with

---

[53]Alfred Schmidtke, *Neue Fragmente und Untersuchungen zu den judenchristlichen Evangelien: Ein Beitrag zur Literatur und Geschichte der Judenchristen*, Texte und Untersuchungen zur Geschichte der altchristlichen Literatur, vol. 37, no. 1 (Leipzig: J. C. Hinrichs, 1911), 181-85.

Hans Waitz was initially impressed with Schmidtke's study and adopted the view that the material in R 1.43-72 formed an original part of the *Kerygmata Petrou* (Hans Waitz, "Clementinen," in *Realencyclopädie für protestantische Theologie und Kirche*, ed. Albert Hauck, 3d ed., rev. and enl. [Leipzig: J. C. Hinrichs, 1913], 23:315).   A few years later, however, he returned to his initial position in this regard, though now he adopted Schmidtke's view that Epiphanius is responsible for calling this section of the *Pseudo-Clementines* the *Anabathmoi Jakobou* (Hans Waitz and Heinrich Veil, "Auszüge aus den Pseudo-Clementinen," in *Neutestamentliche Apokryphen*, ed. Edgar Hennecke, 2d ed., rev. and enl. [Tübingen: J. C. B. Mohr (Paul Siebeck), 1924], 161).   In "Die Pseudoklementinen und ihre Quellenschriften," *Zeitschrift für die neutestamentliche Wissenschaft und die Kunde der älteren Kirche* 28 (1929): 245, Waitz adjusted his position again and now attributed the insertion of "Book 7" into the *Kerygmata Petrou* to the anti-Marcionite redactor.

[54]Theodor Zahn, *Die Apostelgeschichte des Lucas*, 3d and 4th ed., Kommentar zum Neuen Testament, vol. 5, (Leipzig and Erlangen: A. Deichertsche Verlagsbuchhandlung Dr. Werner Scholl, 1922-27), 300-301, n. 57. Compare also his remark in idem, *Forschungen zur Geschichte des neutestamentlichen Kanons und der altkirchlichen Literatur*, pt. 6, *I. Apostel und Apostelschüler in der Provinz Asien, II. Brüder und Vettern Jesu* (Leipzig: A. Deichert'sche Verlagsbuchhandlung Nachf. [Georg Böhme], 1900), 279, that R 1.44, 55-71 (or 73) had reworked material from a writing with the title *Anabathmoi Jakobou*. Reinhold Seeberg, *Lehrbuch der Dogmengeschichte*, vol. 1, *Die Anfänge des Dogmas im nachapostolischen und altkatholischen Zeitalter*, 3d ed., enl. and rev., Sammlung theologischer Lehrbücher (Leipzig and Erlangen: A. Deichertsche Verlagsbuchhandlung Dr. Werner Scholl, 1920), 256, n. 2, similarly spoke of the *Anabathmoi Jakobou* as a source of B (preserved in R 1.27-74).

reference to Lightfoot's suggestions.[55] Carl Schmidt drew attention to the considerable parallels in Hegesippus's presentation of James's martyrdom and concluded that the author of this section, which had been incorporated as the seventh book of the *Kerygmata Petrou*, was dependent on Hegesippus.[56] Oscar Cullmann then argued in his dissertation that--contra Waitz--R 1.54-71 was indeed to be seen as representing the original seventh book of the *Kerygmata Petrou*, that Waitz had exaggerated the supposed differences from the rest of the *Kerygmata*, which furthermore cannot be precisely controlled owing to the lack of parallel material in H, and that this book contains some very archaic elements such as the indication that the disciples of John the Baptist considered him to be the Messiah.[57] Yale professor emeritus Benjamin W. Bacon, who was impressed by Schmidtke's concise arguments but perhaps misunderstood them,[58] thought that the *Anabathmoi Jakobou* and Hegesippus were both dependent on the *Gospel of the Hebrews*, which, though not necessarily containing all the material that Epiphanius found in the *Anabathmoi Jakobou*, was intended to counter Acts 1-15.[59] Bacon's case is far from being logically convincing, for the facts that Hegesippus used the *Gospel of the Hebrews* and that he shares material with the (supposed) *Anabathmoi Jakobou* by no means necessarily imply that the latter common

---

[55]Montague Rhodes James, trans., *The Apocryphal New Testament: Being the Apocryphal Gospels, Acts, Epistles, and Apocalypses with Other Narratives and Fragments*, corrected ed. (Oxford: Clarendon, 1953), 20-21.

[56]Carl Schmidt, *Studien zu den Pseudo-Clementinen nebst einem Anhange: Die älteste römische Bischofsliste und die Pseudo-Clementinen*, Texte und Untersuchungen zur Geschichte der altchristlichen Literatur, vol. 46, no. 1 (Leipzig: J. C. Hinrichs, 1929), 325, n. 2, 29-30, n. 4. According to pp. 22-23, the figure of the inimicable man is a fabrication of B.

[57]Oscar Cullmann, *Le problème littéraire et historique du roman pseudo-clémentin: Étude sur le rapport entre le gnosticisme et le Judéo-Christianisme*, Études d'histoire et de philosophie religieuses publiées par la faculté de théologie protestante de l'Université de Strasbourg, no. 23 (Paris: Librairie Félix Alcan, 1930), 90-91. In n. 3 to p. 82 Cullmann assigned R 1.27-42 to the first book of the *Kerygmata Petrou*.

[58]Benjamin W. Bacon, *Studies in Matthew* (London: Constable & Co., 1930), 489-90, for example, where he seems to have failed to realize that Schmidtke did not assume the existence of a writing with the name *Ascents of James*.

[59]Ibid., 489-90, 494.

material formed part of the *Gospel of the Hebrews*. Eduard Schwartz's comments on R 1 indicate that he considered R 1.55-71 to have been created by R on the basis of merely Acts 5 and 9.[60] Joseph Thomas noted Bousset's theory that R 1.27-72 derived from the *Anabathmoi Jakobou* and stated that the unique view of baptism in this passage (baptism replaces sacrifice) encourages the attribution of this section to a special source, which in terms of content is at least close to the *Anabathmoi*; the section's moderate Ebionism and absence of Elchasaite influence led Thomas to suggest a date of the end of the first century or the first half of the second.[61]

A more definitely positive attitude to the thesis of the *Anabathmoi Jakobou* as a source of R 1 was then taken by Herbert James Bardsley in a work that suffered virtually total neglect in further Pseudo-Clementine studies.[62] Through a series of speculative reconstructions Bardsley advanced beyond others to attempt to establish contours of the original *Anabathmoi Jakobou* that accommodated the information both from Epiphanius and from R 1, as well as from other sources.[63] He dated this writing to circa 100 C.E. and attributed it to Cerinthus.[64] It was employed in the anti-Marcionite revision of the early eight-book Ebionite romance of Clement, of which it formed the opening part, and was turned into a narrative of Peter by R.[65]

While Hugh J. Schonfield also broadly adopted the view that the *Anabathmoi Jakobou* were a source of the *Pseudo-Clementines*,[66] a

---

[60]Eduard Schwartz, "Unzeitgemäße Beobachtungen zu den Clementinen," *Zeitschrift für die neutestamentliche Wissenschaft und die Kunde der älteren Kirche* 31 (1932): 184; compare also p. 189, n. 2.

[61]Joseph Thomas, "Les ébionites baptistes," *Revue d'Histoire Ecclésiastique* 30 (1934): 290-91; idem, *Le mouvement baptiste en Palestine et Syrie (150 av. J.-C.-300 ap. J.-C.)*, Universitas Catholica Lovaniensis Dissertationes, 2d ser., vol. 28 (Gembloux: J. Duculot, 1935), 119-20.

[62]Herbert James Bardsley, *Reconstructions of Early Christian Documents*, vol. 1 (London: S.P.C.K., 1935).

[63]Ibid., 31-32.

[64]Ibid., 32.

[65]Ibid., 267-68.

[66]Hugh J. Schonfield, *The History of Jewish Christianity from the First to the Twentieth Century* (London: Duckworth, 1936), 92. See also Schonfield's

more detailed examination of the *Pseudo-Clementines* as a whole was offered by Bernhard Rehm in his qualifying research. Rehm attributed R 1.27-74 to R and considered the Old Testament and Acts to be the main sources and, following Carl Schmidt, Hegesippus to be probably a subsidiary source; a few elements could derive from B.[67] The late and secondary character of the entire section was said to be evidenced by a number of features, among which are the inconsistent chronological information and the designation of James as "archbishop" in R 1.68.2.[68] Rehm furthermore attributed R 1.69.6-8a to a Eunomian interpolator.[69]

H. J. SCHOEPS

As an emigrant to Sweden during A. Hitler's government of Germany, Hans Joachim Schoeps undertook an extensive study of Jewish Christianity and allocated over seventy pages--unfortunately at points disorderly or confused--to an excursus entitled "The Question of Ebionite Acta Apostolorum," which dealt primarily with the historical retrospect in R 1.[70]   Schoeps followed Schmidtke in the view that

---

According to the Hebrews (London: Duckworth, 1937), 114, 188-91; here it is stated, following Bacon, that the *Ascents of James* is a Jewish Christian work expanded from the Hebrew *Gospel of the Hebrews* also used by the *Toldoth Jeshu*.

[67]Bernhard Rehm, "Zur Entstehung der pseudoclementinischen Schriften," *Zeitschrift für die neutestamentliche Wissenschaft und die Kunde der älteren Kirche* 37 (1938): 162, 146.

[68]Ibid., 162, n. 243.

[69]Ibid., 96-97.

[70]Hans Joachim Schoeps, *Theologie und Geschichte des Judenchristentums* (Tübingen: J. C. B. Mohr [Paul Siebeck], 1949), 381-456.   A much more straightforward presentation is found in his *Jewish Christianity: Factional Disputes in the Early Church*, trans. Douglas R. A. Hare (Philadelphia: Fortress, 1969), 38-61, though the details of many of his arguments are not repeated there.   Schoeps also reviewed his position on R 1, and on the *Pseudo-Clementines* in general, in several other publications, some of which are cited in the following.   Unfortunately, these publications serve to clarify his thoughts only to a limited extent.   While he indicated at points that his position had shifted (for example, in *Jewish Christianity*, 16, he expressed skepticism about source criticism of the *Pseudo-Clementines*; see *Theologie und Geschichte des Judenchristentums*, 457, for perhaps the initial impulse behind this purported shift), he continually referred back to his previous publications for the details of his arguments, and he essentially continued to assume the validity of his positions presented in *Theologie und Geschichte des Judenchristentums*.   The result of this procedure is that the bases of his position

Epiphanius's remarks about the *Anabathmoi Jakobou* (which consisted of only *Panarion* 30.16.7) were intended simply to give an example of the content of the Ebionite *Acts*, though he differed from him in thinking that Epiphanius had actually seen a writing entitled *Anabathmoi Jakobou*.[71] Schoeps's thesis was that the report of the apostles' controversy with the Jewish sects, the disputation of James and Caiaphas, and the attacks on Paul in the *Pseudo-Clementines* all derive from the Ebionite *Acts* mentioned by Epiphanius.[72]

These Ebionite *Acts* perhaps contained a history of the congregation in Jerusalem from the time of Jesus' death to the flight to Pella. In any event, this supposedly Aramaic writing included the discussion of the apostles with the Jewish sects preserved in R 1.43-44a, 54-65, the speech of James and the attempted assassination as reflected in R 1.66-71, and a derogatory report about the conversion of Paul and his disputations with Peter, parts of which are found in H 17.13-20. It probably also included the vicious story about Paul's past in Epiphanius *Panarion* 30.16.8-9 and possibly an account of his death.[73] The author of B rearranged some of this material first used by the *Kerygmata Petrou*. He inserted chapters 44b-52,[74] and he drastically abbreviated the speech of James.[75] Chapters 68-69 were said to betray the original content of this speech. It thus contained three parts: (1) the dual *parousia* of Jesus, (2) the antecedent history of the messianic prophet in Israel, and (3) the institution of baptism. Material from this speech was transferred in part to Peter and may be found

---

become blurred, while his presentation becomes increasingly thetical, bolstered only by copious references to his previous publications.

[71] *Theologie und Geschichte des Judenchristentums*, 382, 454.

[72] Ibid., 383-84.

[73] Ibid., 440, 437, 451-53, 418. See however *Jewish Christianity*, 59, where Schoeps said that the fact that all twelve apostles speak in chapters 54-65 makes it obvious that the author of the novel (B) created this literary scene. One should note the essential similarity of the reconstruction by Schoeps to that by Lipsius, discussed above.

[74] *Theologie und Geschichte des Judenchristentums*, 437.

[75] Ibid., 408.

especially in chapters 36-42, 48, 55, 61-62, and 64 but also in chapters 27-35 and parts of chapters 44b-53.[76]

As regards the relationship of these Ebionite *Acts* to the *Anabathmoi Jakobou*, Schoeps considered it possible that in the *Acts* chapters 66-71 bore the title *Anabathmoi Jakobou*[77] and probable that the speech of James once circulated as an independent writing that Epiphanius knew as the *Anabathmoi Jakobou*.[78] Hegesippus was evidently dependent on the Ebionite *Acts*, though he displaced the speech of James by connecting the attempted assassination in the *Acts* with the actual death of James, which occurred some twenty-five years later.[79] While Schoeps thought that the Ebionite *Acts* should be dated in the first third of the second century,[80] he stated that he did not consider them to be a historical source that should be treated seriously, for they are a tendentious presentation composed long after the events discussed.[81] Nevertheless, Schoeps was apparently of two minds on

---

[76]Ibid., 408-9. This thesis is similar to Schmidtke's (discussed above), but the differences in the supporting logic are considerable and should not be lost from sight. Schmidtke, for example, argued from Epiphanius's knowledge of B that B had a longer speech of James. Schoeps cited Schmidtke for support of the view that James's speech was originally much longer, but this reference is not as legitimate as Schoeps seems to lead his reader to believe, for Schoeps's other remarks totally undercut Schmidtke's logic: the speech, according to Schoeps, had already been abbreviated by B. Schoeps's reason for assuming that James's speech was originally much longer--at least as far as the reader can see on p. 408-- is that the discussion of the sources to be consulted for the disputation occupies a third of the entire section (chapters 66-71). It is at points such as this one that one must bewail Schoeps's failure to develop and state his case in a logically thorough manner, particularly because so many of his detailed observations are of great value.

With respect to the material on primeval history (in chapters 27-33), see Schoeps's further comments in "Die Urgeschichte nach den Pseudoklementinen" in his volume of collected essays *Aus frühchristlicher Zeit: Religionsgeschichtliche Untersuchungen* (Tübingen: J. C. B. Mohr [Paul Siebeck], 1950), 1-37. Schoeps decided here, p. 28, that this material derives from an older, originally independent source. This material was evidently already part of the *Kerygmata Petrou*, and it may have been from a Jewish Christian *Book of Adam* (p. 37).

[77]*Theologie und Geschichte des Judenchristentums*, 437-38.

[78]Ibid., 454.

[79]Ibid., 415, 438.

[80]Ibid., 453.

[81]Ibid., 439.

this matter, for at places he suggested that the Ebionite *Acts* may well preserve memories of events in the 40s.[82]

G. STRECKER

What may be characterized as the currently most influential study with respect to R 1 is Georg Strecker's 1955 Bonn dissertation, which was published as a book in 1958. With arguments that will be discussed in detail at the beginning of chapter 4 Strecker identified chapter 33 as the starting point and chapter 71 as the end of a section containing peculiar material.[83] Parallels with other passages in the *Pseudo-Clementines* were said to reveal that this material formed part of B.[84] As did Waitz (compare also Bousset, Schmidtke, and Schoeps), Strecker considered chapters 44.3-53.4a to be secondary, though he differed from Waitz in attributing this addition to B. In B this discussion occurred during Simon's delay of the disputation for one day and followed instructions about the true prophet and spurious pericopes. It presented the path of the true prophet in the world from the creation to the congregation in Jerusalem.[85] R is said to have changed B only in minor ways (a few interpolations and perhaps some omissions). The larger insertion by B reveals that B found the remaining parts in a source.[86] This thesis is "simpler" than the view that the *Kerygmata Petrou* introduced this source.[87]

---

[82]For example, ibid., 417. Compare also point six on p. 435 with the statement regarding the use of the canonical Acts on p. 439. On pp. 440-45 he discussed the possibility that the speech of James reflected in the Ebionite *Acts* was used as a written source by Luke in the composition of the speech of Stephen. In his *Jewish Christianity* he was more definite about the historical value of R 1; on p. 46 he lists the "facts" yielded by the section with respect to the earliest period of the church.

For the critical reaction to Schoeps's work, see the reviews of his main study that he lists in his *Urgemeinde, Judenchristentum, Gnosis* (Tübingen: J. C. B. Mohr [Paul Siebeck], 1956), 2 with n. 2.

[83]Georg Strecker, *Das Judenchristentum in den Pseudoklementinen*, Texte und Untersuchungen zur Geschichte der altchristlichen Literatur, vol. 70, 2d ed., rev. (Berlin: Akademie, 1981), 221.

[84]Ibid., 41.

[85]Ibid., 41-42, 236.

[86]Ibid., 220-21.

[87]Ibid., 223.

As regards the relationship of this material to the *Anabathmoi Jakobou*, Strecker decided that all of Epiphanius *Panarion* 30.16.7-9 pertains to the *Anabathmoi Jakobou* as they lay before Epiphanius and that thus these two writings differ considerably. They do, however, share a portrayal of James speaking against the temple and sacrifice, reports of *anabathmoi*, and anti-Paulinism. Thus Strecker concluded that the writing mentioned by Epiphanius (AJ I) and the source of B (AJ II) derive from a common archetype (AJ), though the differences are such that AJ I cannot be used to reconstruct and interpret AJ II. AJ II contained a sketch of the history of salvation from Abraham to the Christian congregation in Jerusalem; its conclusion is lost. It was composed by a litterateur and thus has generally little historical value. The references to the tradition about Pella and affinities with the theology of Aristo of Pella led Strecker to locate the origin of the source in or near Pella. Confusion about the edict of Hadrian reveals that it was written not before the year 150.[88]

Strecker's other remarks consist of detailed observations on the text that will be considered at other points in this study. Worthy of special mention here, however, is his view that AJ II did not know the figure of the (true) prophet at all (compare Bousset).[89]

POST-STRECKER

A response to Strecker's study is found in Karlmann Beyschlag's investigation into the reports of James's martyrdom.[90] While Beyschlag basically accepted Strecker's thesis of the AJ II-source, he correctly pointed out that in contrast to earlier studies Strecker had not given sufficient attention to the parallels between this source and Hegesippus, particularly with regard to the martyrdom of James.[91] Beyschlag's own investigations led him to a position between Schoeps

---

[88]Ibid., 251-54.

[89]Ibid., 223.

[90]Karlmann Beyschlag, "Das Jakobusmartyrium und seine Verwandten in der frühchristlichen Literatur," *Zeitschrift für die neutestamentliche Wissenschaft und die Kunde der älteren Kirche* 56 (1965): 149-78.

[91]Beyschlag, "Jakobusmartyrium," 150-51. See Strecker, *Das Judenchristentum in den Pseudoklementinen*, 249-50, for the brief reply to Schoeps that only the fall of James is common to the two reports.

and Strecker: AJ II, which should be dated about 150 C.E.,[92] is dependent not on Acts itself, with which it was unacquainted,[93] but rather on pre-Lukan traditions.[94]

Strecker's position was subsequently briefly mentioned (apparently with approval) by M. Simon[95] and A. F. J. Klijn and G. J. Reinink.[96] It was subjected to a more extensive review by Scott Kent Brown in his 1972 Brown dissertation, which was supervised by William R. Schoedel.[97] While Brown's presentation unfortunately contains a number of inaccuracies and misconceptions,[98] there can be no doubt

---

[92]Beyschlag, "Jakobusmartyrium," 150.

[93]Ibid., 155-56.

[94]Ibid., 162-65.

[95]Marcel Simon, "La migration à Pella: Légende ou réalité?" *Recherches de Science Religieuse* 60 (1972): 49. See also James Julius Scott, Jr., *The Church of Jerusalem, A.D. 30-100: An Investigation of the Growth of Internal Factions and the Extension of Its Influence in the Larger Church* (Ann Arbor, Mich.: University Microfilms, 1969), 273, n. 1, who wrote that relics of the *Ascents* or *Steps of James* may be found in the latter parts of R 1. Compare Wayne A. Meeks, ed., *The Writings of St. Paul: Annotated Text, Criticism*, Norton Critical Editions (New York: W. W. Norton, 1972), 183, where Meeks, after translating passages from H that he describes (p. 178 in the note) as "from 'The Preachings of Peter' (*Kerygmata Petrou*)," writes in a note to R 1.69.8-71.6, "The Pseudo-Clementine novelist has here used a different source, stemming from the Jewish-Christian community that fled from Jerusalem to Pella at the time of the Jewish revolt in A.D. 68." Meeks, however, does not speak of any relationship between this writing and the *Anabathmoi Jakobou*, which he discusses on pp. 177-78.

[96]A. F. J. Klijn and G. J. Reinink, *Patristic Evidence for Jewish-Christian Sects*, Supplements to Novum Testamentum, vol. 36 (Leiden: E. J. Brill, 1973), 31.

[97]Scott Kent Brown, *James: A Religio-Historical Study of the Relations between Jewish, Gnostic, and Catholic Christianity in the Early Period through an Investigation of the Traditions about James the Lord's Brother* (Ann Arbor, Mich.: University Microfilms, 1972).

[98]Perhaps the most serious of these (in terms of his presentation) is the incorrect statement in ibid., 233, "Strecker has observed traces of anti-Paulinism in Gentile Christian sources from the second century." Strecker, *Das Judenchristentum in den Pseudoklementinen*, 253-54, to which Brown referred, contains nothing of the sort. Other inaccuracies are found particularly in the remarks on previous research. Incorrect and confused are, for example, the statements about Waitz and Schoeps on p. 199. Footnote 32 to p. 210 evidently mistakenly contains the reference in footnote 33 to p. 211. Brown also failed to use the Syriac *Pseudo-Clementines*, which is of some consequence for the validity of his results.

that his attempt to think through and extend previous scholarship, particularly Strecker's position, is a valuable contribution. Brown began with a discussion of the compass of the source. He noted Strecker's arguments and sorted out the more compelling, but he seems to have thought he could best determine the limits of the source through identification of common themes.[99] He failed to notice that his observations are insufficient criteria for precise delineation; they do not prove, for example, that new material begins precisely at chapter 33, as he would like to think. Nevertheless, these comments are of some value, though perhaps not always for the question of the exact compass of the source; on this issue Brown largely and ultimately simply accepted Strecker's position.[100] A key role in Brown's remarks is played by his assertion that R 1.43.2 is an addition deriving from the author of AJ II; it did not stand in his source, the *Anabathmoi Jakobou*.[101] This is Brown's first important step in profiling AJ II against its source. Next, AJ II, not the *Anabathmoi Jakobou*, is said to have been the one to draw on Acts.[102] Such observations are used finally to bolster Brown's main thesis with regard to AJ II, namely, that its author was a gentile Christian and that he was appealing to a Jewish audience around the year 150.[103] The chief element suggesting that the author was a gentile is the attitude toward the gentile mission.[104] Central for Brown's view that the author was appealing to a Jewish audience is his proposal that R 1.43.2 is an addition by this writer.[105] Brown placed emphasis on the contention that AJ II is not a book of acts but rather "a tract used for propaganda purposes which

---

[99]Brown, *James*, 192-99.

[100]See his result in ibid., 199, n. 13. His omission of R 1.43.2 here must be a mistake, for on p. 198 he asserted that the author of AJ II added this statement.

[101]Ibid., 197-98.

[102]Ibid., 229. See especially pp. 225-28 for a detailed refutation of Beyschlag's arguments that AJ II is independent of Acts.

[103]Ibid., 234.

[104]Ibid.

[105]Ibid., 232.

included combatting the Lucan interpretation of early Christian history."[106] As regards the question of the relationship of this source to Hegesippus, Brown took a stance close to Strecker: there is no clear evidence of a literary connection between the two.[107]

In contrast to Brown's study, a major divergence from Strecker's position was proposed in 1976 by the Catalonian New Testament and patristic scholar Josep Rius-Camps. In a lengthy article, Rius-Camps developed a new, comprehensive theory of the evolution of the *Pseudo-Clementines*. As regards R 1.27-71, he evidently did not see any need to speak of a source AJ II, for parallels with B are found throughout the passage.[108] Unfortunately, Rius-Camps did not list and discuss these parallels, the larger purpose of his article not allowing him to pause.[109] He did state that R is generally close to B in this section.[110] Rius-Camps thought that R also preserved the immediate context of this material in B; thus the delay for seven days and the motif of repetition, for example, are attributed to B. R did, however, leave out the early morning discussion, which preceded R 1.20 and dealt with the true prophet (H 2.1-14, 3.11-21).[111] The purpose of R 1.27-74 is to introduce the reader to the correct understanding of the law, contra Marcion's interpretation.[112]

---

[106]Ibid., 231.

[107]Ibid., 267-68. See also p. 220. Compare Strecker, *Das Judenchristentum in den Pseudoklementinen*, 249-50.

[108]Josep Rius-Camps, "Las Pseudoclementinas: Bases filológicas para una nueva interpretación," *Revista Catalana de Teologia* 1 (1976): 107. He was more definite about rejecting Strecker's thesis of an AJ II in idem, "Sucesión y ministerios en las Pseudoclementinas," in *La potestad de orden en los primeros siglos*, by Mons. Capmany et al., Teología del sacerdocio, vol. 9 (Burgos: Ediciones Aldecoa, 1977), 170. In n. 12 there he stated that it is very probable that B was inspired by Hegesippus in redacting R 1.43-44.3, 53-74. On p. 174 he suggested that the material might derive from dialogues of Bardaisan, but he considered it impossible to separate out this material.

[109]He did, however, announce a future study of the section ("Las Pseudoclementinas," 111).

[110]Ibid., 107.

[111]Ibid., 108, where Rius-Camps offers a chart of the contents of B for the first period of the stay in Caesarea.

[112]Ibid., 110.

A year later, J. Louis Martyn, professor at Union Theological Seminary, published a study of R 1.33-71 that is characterized by extremely close adherence to Strecker's views. The reader lacking knowledge of German will thus find here a rehearsal of some of Strecker's arguments and of most of his major conclusions. Martyn does, however, sometimes explicate elements of his position that are not found in such clarity in Strecker's study. Thus Martyn emphasized more strongly than Strecker that the community of the author is one that practiced circumcision.[113] Further, he explicitly defined the author's main intention: to point out the identity of his community in distinction to non-Christian Judaism and to "heretical" Pauline Christianity.[114] It is in the light of these two points of distinction that Martyn concluded that the material is clearly Jewish Christian.[115] The author had read Acts and intended to correct it radically, "perhaps even to replace it."[116]

Completely new in Martyn's study is his detailed investigation of the relationship of AJ II to the Gospel of John. He concluded that AJ II does not present a single quotation from John,[117] though certain motifs in R 1.62, 65, 67, 68 are shared with the first verses of John 16 and the latter parts of John 7 and 9 (most evident in AJ II's conflation of characteristics of Gamaliel and Nicodemus).[118] Since the Johannine material reflects the situation of a Jewish Christianity

---

[113]J. Louis Martyn, "Clementine Recognitions 1,33--71, Jewish Christianity, and the Fourth Gospel," in *God's Christ and His People: Studies in Honour of Nils Alstrup Dahl*, ed. Jacob Jervell and Wayne A. Meeks (Oslo, Bergen, and Tromsö: Universitetsforlaget, 1977), 271. Compare Strecker, *Das Judenchristentum in den Pseudoklementinen*, 251, where he spoke of "the positive evaluation of circumcision and ritual observance (R 1.33)."

[114]Martyn, "Clementine Recognitions," 270, 291.

[115]Ibid., 271.

[116]Ibid., 273. Useful are the synoptic presentations of material from AJ II and Acts on pp. 279-82, though here as elsewhere in his study (particularly pp. 273-74) Martyn relied too readily on Rufinus's Latin and neglected the Syriac (see his remark in n. 42 on p. 294, which reveals that he has used Rufinus's translation as the basic text).

[117]Ibid., 276.

[118]Ibid., 278-85, 289.

being heard or tried before a Jewish court, Martyn decided that it was quite possible that AJ II was dependent on one such unified tradition that was also used in the Gospel of John, though he did not exclude the possibility that AJ II is simply recalling some of the Johannine motifs by memory.[119]

While others continued to adopt Strecker's position with little or no change,[120] a second study devoted exclusively to this section of the *Pseudo-Clementines* was published by Arnold Stötzel in 1982.[121] Though there are grievous errors in this article,[122] which was originally delivered as part of the author's qualifying examination at Munich's Catholic theological faculty, Stötzel--consciously or unconsciously-- raised some issues worthy of further discussion. Thus, he followed Schoeps, and departed from Strecker's dominant position, in viewing the material of R 1.27-32 and H 17.13-19 as also part of the source, which he called the *Anabathmoi Jakobou*.[123] His most important contributions, however, relate to the self-understanding of the congregation that stands behind the source. The survey of salvational

---

[119]Ibid., 286-91.

[120]See, for example, Luigi Cirillo, *Évangile de Barnabé: Recherches sur la composition et l'origine*, Beauchesne religions (Paris: Éditions Beauchesne, 1977), 240 (less definite, however, in idem, "L'antipaolinismo nelle Pseudoclementine," *Richerche Storico Bibliche*, 1989, fasc. 2 [July-December], 137), Andreas Lindemann, *Paulus im ältesten Christentum: Das Bild des Apostels und die Rezeption der paulinischen Theologie in der frühchristlichen Literatur bis Marcion*, Beiträge zur historischen Theologie, vol. 58 (Tübingen: J. C. B. Mohr [Paul Siebeck], 1979), 108-9, and William H. Harter, *The Causes and the Course of the Jewish Revolt against Rome, 66-74 C. E., in Recent Scholarship* (Ann Arbor, Mich.: University Microfilms, 1984), 114-15 (this dissertation was apparently submitted to Union Theological Seminary in New York in 1982).

In contrast, F. F. Bruce, *Peter, Stephen, James, and John: Studies in Early Non-Pauline Christianity* (Grand Rapids, Mich.: William B. Eerdmans, 1979), 116-18, adopted the views of Schoeps.

[121]Arnold Stötzel, "Die Darstellung der ältesten Kirchengeschichte nach den Pseudo-Clementinen," *Vigiliae Christianae* 36 (1982): 24-37.

[122]I mention only the confusion of B and the *Kerygmata Petrou*, ibid., 26, and the incorrect statement in n. 21 on p. 34 concerning what Strecker designated AJ II. These mistakes are indicative of a general lack of penetration into the issues of Pseudo-Clementine studies.

[123]Ibid., 26, 29.

history demonstrates that this Jewish Christian congregation[124] views itself as the legitimate heir to the history of nations and revelation.[125] Worthy of special note is Stötzel's denial that the section contains references to the Pella-tradition. Stötzel emphasized that R 1.37, 39 actually support the view that this congregation was expecting to return to Jerusalem as its legitimate inhabitants. For this reason, Stötzel dated the source after the year 70 but before 135.[126]

In the following year, Gerd Lüdemann, professor of New Testament in Göttingen, presented an investigation of R 1 that was intended to test a "new approach" to Pseudo-Clementine studies, namely, an analysis primarily in terms of the history of traditions.[127] He thus began his study by examining the well-known group of traditions that run parallel to R 1.66-70. Similarities and differences between Hegesippus and R 1.66-70 led Lüdemann to the following conclusion: both are dependent on an older source in which James held a successful christological speech and then fatally fell from a high place at the temple. The *Second Apocalypse of James* is also dependent on this source.[128]

---

[124]Ibid., 27. There Stötzel cited R 1.32.1 and R 1.30.5 in support of this identity.

[125]Ibid., 29.

[126]Ibid., 31-32.

[127]Gerd Lüdemann, *Paulus, der Heidenapostel*, vol. 2, *Antipaulinismus im frühen Christentum*, Forschungen zur Religion und Literatur des Alten und Neuen Testaments, vol. 130 (Göttingen: Vandenhoeck & Ruprecht, 1983), 230 (*Opposition to Paul in Jewish Christianity*, trans. M. Eugene Boring [Minneapolis: Fortress, 1989], 170-71). This "new" approach is actually just how Schoeps said he intended to proceed after he became skeptical of his own source critical results (see above, n. 70). That Lüdemann was able to carry out this new approach in a more thorough manner than did Schoeps is perhaps owing to the fact that Lüdemann had not developed his own source critical theories to the *Pseudo-Clementines* in his previous publications but had rather simply adopted Strecker's. See, for example, his dissertation, *Untersuchungen zur simonianischen Gnosis*, Göttinger theologische Arbeiten, vol. 1 (Göttingen: Vandenhoeck & Ruprecht, 1975), 142, n. 55, and the bulk of pp. 93-98. Lüdemann made a cleaner transition to this new approach (history of traditions) than did Schoeps, though elements of the older approach still affected his argumentation. See the following.

[128]Lüdemann, *Antipaulinismus*, 234-37 (*Opposition to Paul*, 174-77). Notice that Lüdemann wrote in two manners about the end of the section in R 1 that he analyzed. He began by speaking of R 1.66-70 (*Antipaulinismus*, 234 [*Opposition*

After these deliberations on the history of traditions, Lüdemann proceeded to perform a literary analysis of R 1.33-71. This part of his study is marked, on the one hand--and despite his intention of avoiding a literary critical starting point--by unreflected adoption of elements of Strecker's position and, on the other hand, by bold theses about the literary history of the section (which seem tacitly biased to reveal R 1.66-70 or 71 as the oldest tradition and thus to confirm the initial analysis in terms of the history of traditions). Thus Lüdemann explicitly followed Strecker in viewing R 1.44.3-53.4a as a heterogeneous element[129] and did not even raise the question of where the relevant section begins. Reminiscent of Schmidtke, in contrast, is Lüdemann's thesis that chapters 55-65 should be attributed as a whole either to B or to R, who composed this part on the basis of the content of chapters 33-43. The reasoning for this radical thesis is as follows: the content of these chapters and chapters 33-43 is similar; this section joins "artificially" onto the list in chapter 54 and presents no more informa-tion about the sects than does this chapter; and, finally, the speeches of the twelve apostles all close with the same concluding phrase.[130] This thesis is then used as the basis for the proposal that chapters 66.2-71, a self-contained unit, especially reflect the tradition available to the redactor, who in chapters 33-54 presents material from the speech of James as a speech of Peter (compare Schmidtke and Schoeps). This proposal is said to be probable because both sections contain the same themes (doublets) and because a tradition is "partic-ularly visible" in chapters 66-71.[131]

---

to Paul, 174]). In *Antipaulinismus*, 237 (*Opposition to Paul*, 177), he changed to R 1.66-71. What has apparently occurred is that Lüdemann has adjusted the ending point to fit the literary analysis that follows in his presentation--a palpable indication of contaminated method.

[129]*Antipaulinismus*, 237, n. 35 (*Opposition to Paul*, 299, n. 35). See below, n. 131.

[130]*Antipaulinismus*, 239-40 (*Opposition to Paul*, 179).

[131]*Antipaulinismus*, 240-42 (*Opposition to Paul*, 180-81); citation from *Antipaulinismus*, 242 (my translation; *Opposition to Paul*, 181). The thematic parallels are listed in *Antipaulinismus*, 240 (*Opposition to Paul*, 180), but it should be noted that over half of the references are to passages either outside the section 33-54 or else in the section 44.3-53.4a, which, as was noted above, Lüdemann

Lüdemann next asked about the relationship to the *Anabathmoi Jakobou.* In view of the similarities and discrepancies in content, he decided that the *Anabathmoi Jakobou* is dependent on the set of traditions behind R 1.33-71 but completely drops the report of martyrdom. Lüdemann then inferred that the *Anabathmoi Jakobou* is not important for the pre-history of the traditions in R 1 (the R 1-source).[132] This conclusion (a variant form of Strecker's argument, above p. 21?) is disconcerting, for if the *Anabathmoi Jakobou* is dependent on the tradition that stands behind R 1.33-71, then its relevance seems to pertain precisely to the pre-history of (the traditions in) R 1, even if the *Anabathmoi Jakobou* is secondary in its (apparent) lack of reference to the martyrdom of James. It could provide, for example, some substantial evidence for the view (of Lüdemann) that the R 1-source contained a longer speech by James.

Lüdemann followed Strecker in dating and locating the R 1-source.[133] He also basically assumed that the source was from a Jewish Christian congregation, which, however, had evolved to reject legal observances (contra Martyn), criticize the law, and preach to the gentiles.[134] Similarly, the criticism of Paul as a defender of the law

---

dismissed at first as belonging to another layer of tradition--whatever this view, adopted from Strecker, is supposed to mean in the context of Lüdemann's study. This confusion muddles Lüdemann's argument. Furthermore, when Lüdemann spoke of chapter 71 as the end of the relevant section it is never clear if he actually meant 71.6. Did the R 1-source contain the reference to Damascus in 71.4? If it did, this would possibly have important implications for the nature of the anti-Paulinism (see Lüdemann's remark, *Antipaulinismus*, p. 246, n. 73 [*Opposition to Paul*, 302, n. 73]).

For further criticisms of Lüdemann's logic, see Robert E. Van Voorst, *The Ascents of James: History and Theology of a Jewish-Christian Community*, Society of Biblical Literature Dissertation Series, no. 112 (Atlanta: Scholars Press, 1989), 41-42.

[132]*Antipaulinismus*, 241-42 (*Opposition to Paul*, 180-81).

[133]*Antipaulinismus*, 242-43 (*Opposition to Paul*, 181-82).

[134]*Antipaulinismus*, 243-45 (*Opposition to Paul*, 182-83). The "reasons" for this assumption are evidently (1) that the proclamation of the gospel to the gentiles is said to follow the Jewish war, (2) that James is honored, and (3) that the tradition about the preservation of Christians from the war supposedly implies that the author's congregation claimed to be the heir of the primitive community (*Antipaulinismus*, 244 [*Opposition to Paul*, 182-83]).

is said to be based on older Jewish Christian anti-Paulinism rooted in the congregation.[135]

Lüdemann's analysis harvested criticism from Tübingen professor of New Testament Martin Hengel, who judged it "superficial" and stated that almost the only features common to R 1 and the *Anabathmoi Jakobou* are the anti-Paulinism and an interest in James.[136] While Hengel also expressed his basic skepticism about precisely isolating old Jewish Christian sources in the *Pseudo-Clementines*,[137] he nevertheless stated that the anti-Paulinism in the section derives from Ebionite acts of the apostles, mentioned Jewish Christian sources of the *Pseudo-Clementines*, and even quoted from the *Kerygmata Petrou*.[138]

Other scholars, in contrast, remained more single-hearted in their adoption of Strecker's views.[139] This statement applies generally to Wilhelm Pratscher's book on James, especially in his remarks on James in the AJ II-source. One finds here again largely a rehearsal of Strecker's observations; this review is instructive at times, but the neglect of the Syriac version is painfully evident almost through-out.[140] Pratscher did go beyond Strecker, however, in his detailed evaluation of the reports on the martyrdom of James.[141] In

---

[135]*Antipaulinismus*, 245-48 (*Opposition to Paul*, 183-85).

[136]Martin Hengel, "Jakobus der Herrenbruder--der erste 'Papst'?" in *Glaube und Eschatologie: Festschrift für Werner Georg Kümmel zum 80. Geburtstag*, ed. Erich Gräßer and Otto Merk (Tübingen: J. C. B. Mohr [Paul Siebeck], 1985), 75-76, n. 17, 77, n. 22.

[137]Ibid., 77, n. 22.

[138]Ibid., 77, 98, 90.

[139]See, for example, Martin I. Webber, *Ιάκῶβος ὁ Δίκαιος: Origins, Literary Expression and Development of Traditions about the Brother of the Lord in Early Christianity* (Ann Arbor, Mich.: University Microfilms, 1985), 237-43, Fabrizio Tosolini, "Paolo in *Atti* e nelle Pseudoclementine (*Recognitiones* I, 33-71)," *Augustinianum* 26 (1986): 369-400, and Oskar Skarsaune, *The Proof from Prophecy, A Study in Justin Martyr's Proof-Text Tradition: Text-Type, Provenance, Theological Profile*, Supplements to Novum Testamentum, vol. 56 (Leiden: E. J. Brill, 1987), 252-53 and elsewhere.

[140]Wilhelm Pratscher, *Der Herrenbruder Jakobus und die Jakobustradition*, Forschungen zur Religion und Literatur des Alten und Neuen Testaments, vol. 139 (Göttingen: Vandenhoeck & Ruprecht, 1987), 124-34. Pratscher mentions only one Syriac variant (p. 132, n. 38).

[141]Ibid., 229-55.

Pratscher's view, the original text of Hegesippus and AJ II derive from a common body of Jewish Christian tradition (not a "source"), and neither was influenced by Acts in the report of James's death.[142]

Strecker's position has also been reasserted by Robert E. Van Voorst in a longer study that was carried out virtually simultaneously with the present work.[143] Van Voorst is to be commended for undertaking both a history of research as well as a translation of parts of the Syriac of R 1.27-71. Both sections nevertheless contain an undue number of mistakes and omissions and cannot adequately serve as the basis for future study.[144]

---

[142]Ibid., 247-48, 252, 255.

[143]Van Voorst, *The Ascents of James*. For the following, compare also my review of this work in *Critical Review of Books in Religion*, 1991, 344-46.

[144]To mention only a few examples: In the history of research the names of Schmidtke, Schmidt, Bardsley, Hengel, and Pratscher are not to be found. The large, critical study by Rius-Camps is mentioned virtually by name alone in a footnote concerning an article by Wehnert (Van Voorst, *The Ascents of James*, 23, n. 108). The omission of these scholars has hindered Van Voorst from fathoming the possibilities for the interpretation of R 1.27-71 and has fostered his entanglement in the web of Strecker's hypotheses.

Furthermore, Waitz's position is misrepresented on pp. 14-15, and his later studies are neglected throughout. P. 16 misrepresents Meyboom by mistranslating the Dutch word meaning "impossible" as "unlikely." Finally, the assertion that "B. Rehm argued that source criticism behind *G* is fruitless" (p. 18) betrays a lack of penetration not only of the article by Rehm being cited (see Rehm, "Entstehung," 157: "The basic writing is an original work only to the smallest extent"; after mentioning several of B's sources Rehm writes again on the same page, "Closer treatment of the question of sources would demand an investigation in itself") but also of Rehm's later studies that dealt precisely with these sources.

In the Syriac translation there are noticeable omissions toward the end of R 1.34.6 and in R 1.70.1. Serious mistranslation is encountered in R 1.37.3, 38.5, 44.1, 55.1, 2, 3, 57.3 (often wild neglect of grammar and syntax). Furthermore, the Armenian fragments of the section are not employed and, indeed, are never mentioned. Moreover, even though Van Voorst translated some of the Syriac, he neglected to consider the Syriac of R in the parts he did not translate (quite apparent on pp. 33 and 37, n. 15). He also made misstatements about the Syriac he translated. For example, he wrote on p. 159 concerning R 1.71.5, "The S[yriac] MSS have a lacuna." To the contrary, there is only one Syriac manuscript of this passage, and it does not contain a lacuna.

The Latin translation is, in contrast, much more reliable, not least, one suspects, because of the existing modern versions. A dependence on these versions rather than on the most recent critical text by Rehm is reflected in the translation of R 1.70.3. The text underlying Smith's translation (Thomas Smith, trans., "Pseudo-Clementine Literature," in *The Ante-Nicene Fathers: Translations*

In the analytical sections, Van Voorst employed literary criteria to isolate R 1.33.3-44.3, 55-62, 64.1-69.1, 69.8-71 as based on material from a source.[145] He then proceeded, in a discussion of barely two pages, to identify the source: the similarities with Epiphanius's description of the *Anabathmoi Jakobou* "outweigh the dissimilarities," and therefore the source of R 1 can be identified with this writing.[146] This important decision in Van Voorst's study remains inadequately developed. The considerable dissimilarities between the material in R 1 and Epiphanius's *Anabathmoi Jakobou* as well as Strecker's distinctions between "AJ I" and "AJ II" go unexplained. There is furthermore no discussion of the relationship of this source to Hegesippus.

Van Voorst next provided a commentary to his parallel translations of the Latin and Syriac parts of R 1 isolated as a source.[147] Here, a few subsidiary points of interpretation are thought through to a greater extent than before, yet the larger discussion is not notably advanced on any major point. Together with the largely scattered remarks of previous scholars, these rather meager notes must serve until a commentary can be written on a grander scale.

Van Voorst's final picture is essentially, if not exactly, the same as J. L. Martyn's portrayal of a Jewish Christian church in Pella that observes the Jewish law. Martyn's picture was in turn, of course, largely based on Strecker. The weakness of this "tradition" in scholarship has become even more apparent in Van Voorst's work: just as the overview of previous research either cannot comprehend or else simply ignores those scholars who have diverged from the larger framework

---

of the Writings of the Fathers down to A.D. 325, ed. Alexander Roberts and James Donaldson, American reprint rev. A. Cleveland Coxe, vol. 8, *The Twelve Patriarchs, Excerpts and Epistles, the Clementina, Apocrypha, Decretals, Memoirs of Edessa and Syriac Documents, Remains of the First Ages* [reprint ed., Grand Rapids, Mich.: William B. Eerdmans, 1978], 95), which is evidently the basis of Van Voorst's rendering, is found in the older editions, though it is not listed in Rehm's apparatus. See also, for example, R 1.60.7, where Van Voorst has adopted Smith's "us" instead of the "you" in the text.

[145]Van Voorst, *The Ascents of James*, 30-41. On his Table 2 on pp. 39-40, see below, n. 66 to chapter 4.

[146]Ibid., 45.

[147]Ibid., 77-161.

of Strecker's literary critical analysis of the Pseudo-Clementine corpus as a whole, so the entire premise of Van Voorst's study remains an unexamined and unmentioned acceptance of Strecker's highly speculative literary hypotheses.[148] This explains why Van Voorst's monograph lacks any systematic treatment of the redactional work of B and R in R 1.

In contrast to Van Voorst, Simon Legasse (in a few concise remarks) has followed Lüdemann's proposal much more closely than Strecker's.[149] Legasse furthermore picked up some insights of F. Tosolini to understand the anti-Paulinism of the source as a gesture that would again open the door for conversion of Jews.[150]

In his brief comments relevant to R 1.27-71, Jürgen Wehnert combined the views of Schwartz and Rehm with those of Strecker. Like Strecker, he spoke of a Jewish Christian source contained in R 1.33-71, but like Schwartz and Rehm, he thought the insertion of this material was performed not by B but by R.[151] Details of this position are not provided.

Finally, Howard M. Teeple, in a section of his 1955 dissertation first published in 1993, briefly suggested that this section of R is based on two underlying sources: (1) a Discourse of the Twelve Apostles in R 1.26c-43 that in turn excerpted a Jewish document in R 1.27-35, 37-39, and (2) Disputes of the Twelve Apostles in the Temple in R 1.44a, 53c-62, 66-71. While these sections may have been two parts of the

---

[148]See, for example, unquestioning acceptance of details from Strecker's quite speculative construction of *Kerygmata Petrou* in ibid., 112, n. 43, and often elsewhere.

[149]"La polémique antipaulinienne dans le judéo-christianisme hétérodoxe," *Bulletin de Littérature Ecclésiastique* 90 (1989): 17-22.

[150]Ibid., 22.

[151]Jürgen Wehnert, "Die Auswanderung der Jerusalemer Christen nach Pella--historisches Faktum oder theologische Konstruktion? Kritische Bemerkungen zu einem neuen Buch," *Zeitschrift für Kirchengeschichte* 102 (1991): 242, n. 20, 249 with n. 35; idem, "Abriß der Entstehungsgeschichte des pseudoklementinischen Romans," *Apocrypha* 3 (1992): 228, 234. The approaches of Lüdemann and Wehnert have been combined by Knut Backhaus, *Die "Jüngerkreise" des Täufers Johannes: Eine Studie zu den religionsgeschichtlichen Ursprüngen des Christentums*, Paderborner theologische Studien, vol. 19 (Paderborn, Munich, Vienna, and Zurich: Ferdinand Schöningh, 1991), 275-98.

same document, the first is concerned with demonstrating that Jesus is the prophet foretold by Moses whereas the second argues that Jesus is the Christ.[152]

Conclusion

Though the historical review speaks for itself and each investigator will want to draw his or her own consequences, the following remarks will provide an indication of some corollaries that seem to impose themselves.

This history of the past 150 years of research has disclosed a broad consensus that at least part of R 1.27-71 is based on an older source. Great divergence exists, however, regarding the exact compass, nature, and identity of this source. Opinion has varied from a complete Ebionite acts of the apostles to the *Anabathmoi Jakobou* to Hegesippus to nothing other than the canonical Acts. The purpose of the present study will accordingly be less to determine *if* a source underlies this material than to specify precisely the *nature* of the source involved. The quality of this investigation and of all future investigations will depend on the degree to which all pertinent information can be mustered and integrated.

One main cause of the divergence of opinion in past research is the variegated, but extremely important, role played by Epiphanius *Panarion* 30.16.6-9. Schmidtke's thesis that Epiphanius was drawing on B for much of this section went perhaps the furthest in assigning significance to Epiphanius for the interpretation of the passage, but Epiphanius's (disputed) witness has ultimately been closely involved with the understanding of R 1.27-71 ever since Köstlin called attention to it.[153] Judgments concerning the meaning and relevance

---

[152]Howard M. Teeple, *The Prophet in the Clementines*, with an Introduction by F. Stanley Jones, Religion and Ethics Institute Occasional Papers 2 (Evanston, Ill.: Religion and Ethics Institute, 1993), 10-12.

[153]It is sobering to note, however, that the first person to postulate that R 1.27-71 was based on a source, Adolf Hilgenfeld, did not employ Epiphanius at all in this regard; rather, he found decisive support for his postulation in the references to earlier Kerygmas of Peter sent to James.

of Epiphanius have, however, differed from each other to the point of being diametrical.

This observation on the history of research should lead, I believe, to the general recognition that there are two completely different sets of evidence for the history of the material in R 1: (1) the witness of Epiphanius (and other external sources such as Hegesippus and the other reports on James's martyrdom) and (2) internal literary criteria. As in similar cases, there is a pressing need here to achieve clarity about how these different sets of data are being used, for unmethodical combination of the two will threaten (and in several cases reviewed above has already damaged) logical consistency. The following study will be performed without using Epiphanius's witness to support hypotheses regarding the supposed source. The reason for this procedure does indeed involve a judgment concerning Epiphanius's remarks. While this verdict can be presented in full detail only in chapter 4, it may summarily be stated here that though Epiphanius evidently did know an actual writing entitled *Anabathmoi Jakobou* (contra Schmidtke), there is no sufficient reason to bring this writing into an unusually close relationship with R 1.27-71. Consequently, in the following study Epiphanius's remarks on the *Anabathmoi Jakobou* will initially be left to one side and thus will not be allowed to interfere with other observations on the literary character of the section under consideration. For the sake of methodological consistency, the witness of Hegesippus and related traditions will also not be allowed to interfere with the literary criteria that will determine if a source is present. While an approach in terms of the history of traditions, which proceeds from an analysis of the known parallel traditions (particularly Hegesippus), is palpably tempting, it fails to enable an analysis of the entire passage. In the case of one proponent of such an approach, Lüdemann, the result was a contaminated method and, consequently, muddled results. For these reasons, this study will employ only purely literary criteria to argue that the section is based on a source; the relationships of this material with other writings will be discussed at the end of the investigation.

Next, it should be noted how the history of research discloses that Strecker's position gained dominance soon after its publication and has maintained this position till the present. While it is true that several scholars have varied in certain respects from Strecker, the major points of his view still stand unrefuted and, one feels, virtually unexamined. Only Rius-Camps has questioned the entire basis of Strecker's position. Since Rius-Camps has been the only scholar to formulate a broader thesis on the genesis of the *Pseudo-Clementines* as a whole, his divergence from Strecker's understanding of R 1.27-71 and the others' conformity perhaps reveal one reason why Strecker's view has been able to maintain its dominance: decisions about R 1.27-71 are ultimately closely intertwined with larger decisions about the genesis of the entire Pseudo-Clementine corpus, and thus the failure of most scholars to address these larger issues on their own perhaps provides at least one clue as to why Strecker's position has been so widely adopted with only minor changes.

This situation as well as the rest of the history of research make it evident that there is no shortcut available to avoid these larger questions. One will inevitably be involved with the problems of the identity and work of B, R, and H, whether one wants to face these issues or not (witness, for example, Lüdemann's "new" approach via the history of traditions).[154] The methods that must be employed in evaluating this section are the standard ones of comparison of ideas and motifs in this passage with those of other parts of the *Pseudo-Clementines*. Thus, the isolation of a set of distinctive or, especially, divergent ideas may be marshaled to justify, or at least support, the conclusion that a source is being employed. While literary seams may also provide clues as to the history of the material, it is a broader comparison of H and R that must finally form the basis for an overarching thesis regarding the literary genesis of the *Pseudo-Clementines* and the place of R 1.27-71 in this process. However, especially because previous research into the *Pseudo-Clementines* has been so

---

[154]In other words, as long as one remains within Strecker's framework regarding these larger questions, one will hardly achieve very divergent results regarding the section presently under consideration.

focused on the isolation of sources older than B, there has been insufficient discussion of the precise identity of B, H, and R. Since it is beyond the scope also of the present study to remedy this situation completely, the results obtained in this study must necessarily remain open to correction by subsequent investigations into these authors. Nevertheless, and inversely, careful investigation of R 1.27-71 at the current state of knowledge about these authors will doubtlessly be able not only to achieve useful and solid insights into this section but also to suggest implications about the identity of B, H, and R.[155]

One distinctive element in this section may be singled out here for comment: the divergent chronological framework. While this feature certainly provides a valuable clue to the literary history of the section, the survey of research reveals how variously such a clue may be evaluated. Some scholars have taken it as an indication that R added the section (e.g., Uhlhorn and Bousset), others as a sign that R could not have introduced the section (e.g., Lehmann). One may conclude that this element in itself is not sufficient as a basis for unequivocal judgments on the literary history.

These remarks point one toward another notable aspect in the history of research: the absolutist tone employed to pronounce even some of the most extremely hypothetical views. One may say that this tone has not helped research. Different degrees of probability should instead be carefully distinguished, and then weight should be explicitly given to what is most certain. One should thereby try to make it easier for subsequent research to correct shortcomings or modify views without being forced to reject virtually entire portions of previous research as inextricably entwined with untenable hypotheses (see especially Schoeps's later writings).

Even when this absolutist tone in much of previous research is exposed, it is still somewhat surprising to find such contradictory characterizations of R 1.27-71. To some, it is the most Jewish Christian section to be found anywhere in the *Pseudo-Clementines* (e.g., Hilgenfeld); to others, it is not Jewish Christian at all (e.g.,

---

[155]The above comments are thus intended to stir up more sensitivity to these larger problems during the investigations of R 1.27-71.

Waitz). While a mediating position has also been proposed (Lüdemann), one must wonder why such contradictory characterizations of the same material are possible. Part of the problem may lie in the various definitions of Jewish Christianity and in the lack of a clear history of this phenomenon. In view of the history of research, this study will want to employ the characterization "Jewish Christianity" with some care and explain why this designation is appropriate or inappropriate to the material under consideration.

With regard to the two extant versions of the text, it may be noted that attention has always focused on Rufinus's Latin. While certain critical scholars cited the Syriac after Lagarde published it (e.g., Lightfoot and Zahn), others have simply left it to one side. There is thus a pressing need to make the Syriac generally available in a reliable modern translation (chapter 3). The issue of how the Syriac and Latin should be evaluated also seems to call for an explicit treatment. This problem of the relative value of the two versions will now be taken up.

II

THE LATIN AND SYRIAC VERSIONS AND THE LOST GREEK *RECOGNITIONS*

The Problem

The problem of the text of R (including R 1.27-71) is posed above all by the fact that save only small fragments, the Greek R has been lost; larger portions of R are preserved only via two versions (Latin and Syriac). Modern research is fortunate in having generally reliable editions of these two versions,[1] but for the critical scholar the

---

[1]The lack of a critical edition of the Latin R was long bemoaned in Pseudo-Clementine studies. It was the outstanding American librarian and patristic scholar Ernest Cushing Richardson who first began collecting information on all extant Latin manuscripts. He labored at this task for at least thirty years and identified various families of witnesses, but the publication of his virtually complete edition was thwarted by the outbreak of World War I. Largely on the basis of Richardson's travails, Bernhard Rehm produced the current critical edition (Bernhard Rehm, ed., *Die Pseudoklementinen II: Rekognitionen in Rufins Übersetzung*, ed. Georg Strecker, 2d ed., rev., Die griechischen christlichen Schriftsteller der ersten Jahrhunderte, vol. 51 [Berlin: Akademie, 1994]; for the preceding information, see Rehm's foreword, VII-IX). Probes into the Latin manuscripts by members of the Pseudo-Clementine working group of the Association pour l'étude de la littérature

disagreements of the two translations raise the question ever anew of which, if either, accurately reflects the original. This rather fundamental issue has generally been neglected by past research, largely because most scholars who have dealt with the *Pseudo-Clementines* have been incompetent in Syriac. What nevertheless has been said by others should be briefly reviewed as a springboard for the investigations to be pursued here.

One man who was competent in Syriac, the formidable Paul de Lagarde, made this comment on Rufinus's version: "His translation of the *Recognitions* is by far not as bad as seems to be thought in various quarters."[2] Perhaps a somewhat perverse form of the position

---

apocryphe chrétienne (including myself) have revealed that Rehm's edition contains inaccuracies in its listings of the readings of the various groups of manuscripts. Questions about Rehm's stemma (and sub-stemmas) have also found justification. A new edition could doubtless achieve greater accuracy.

The Syriac has been edited twice: Paul Anton de Lagarde, ed., *Clementis Romani Recognitiones Syriace* (Leipzig: F. A. Brockhaus; London: Williams & Norgate, 1861), and Wilhelm Frankenberg, *Die syrischen Clementinen mit griechischem Paralleltext: Eine Vorarbeit zu dem literargeschichtlichen Problem der Sammlung*, Texte und Untersuchungen zur Geschichte der altchristlichen Literatur, vol. 48, no. 3 (Leipzig: J. C. Hinrichs, 1937). I am engaged in preparation of a new edition of the Syriac, which intends to be accompanied by a complete English translation (Corpus Christianorum, Series Apocryphorum).

For the following, compare my study, "Evaluating the Latin and Syriac Translations of the Pseudo-Clementine *Recognitions*," *Apocrypha* 3 (1992): 237-57, which contains additional discussion and more references.

[2]Paul de Lagarde, "Clementina herausgegeben von Paul de Lagarde, 1865," in *Mittheilungen* (Göttingen: Dieterichsche Sortimentsbuchhandlung [A. Hoyer], 1884), 53.

A neglected and noteworthy first attempt (before the publication of the Syriac) to evaluate Rufinus's translation using Rufinus's own statements, the preserved Greek fragments, and the statements of other ancient writers on the Greek *Recognitions* was undertaken by Adolph Schliemann, "Die clementinischen Recognitionen eine Ueberarbeitung der Clementinen," *Theologische Mitarbeiten* 4, no. 4 (1843): 5-12. He finds the evidence supports "the faithfulness of the translation" (p. 7). Gerhard Uhlhorn, *Homilien und Recognitionen*, 32-38, proceeded along similar lines and also took into account the passages of H that ran parallel to R. Uhlhorn similarly concluded that this evidence leads to the judgment that Rufinus's rendering is "generally a true translation" (p. 37), though he admits some cause for wariness (p. 38). It is unfortunate that these balanced arguments were overlooked by later scholarship.

countered by Lagarde is reflected in the remarks of Oxford scholar F. W. Bussell, who--apparently totally ignorant of the Syriac--attributed the entire form of R to Rufinus's "well-known power of excision and modification" unleashed on the text he was translating, B.[3] W. Frankenberg, who in contrast was well informed of the existence of the Syriac version, also spoke of "the complete unreliability of the Latin translation" and stated that the Syriac should be given decisive preference in reconstructing the original text.[4] This same opinion had already been promoted as an "untimely" remark by Eduard Schwartz, an autodidact in Syriac panoplied with the manuscript of Frankenberg's retroversion. Schwartz had nothing good to say about the Latin, "a slovenly unreliable concoction."[5]

Others found this position too one-sided. Thus B. Rehm characterized Frankenberg's judgment as "very hard,"[6] and W. Kutsch declared Frankenberg's assessment "not very cautious" because the part where the Greek, Latin, and Syriac have been preserved (the initial section of the *Pseudo-Clementines*) "by no means justifies such an unfavorable evaluation."[7] And though Hans Waitz similarly protested against the purely negative appraisal,[8] J. Rius-Camps has also recently spoken rather one-sidedly of overcoming "the deficiencies of Rufinus's

---

[3]F. W. Bussell, "The Purpose of the World-Process and the Problem of Evil as Explained in the Clementine and Lactantian Writings in a System of Subordinate Dualism," in *Studia Biblica et Ecclesiastica: Essays Chiefly in Biblical and Patristic Criticism*, by members of the University of Oxford (Oxford: Clarendon, 1896), 4:149, n. 1.

[4]Frankenberg, *Clementinen*, XI, IX.

[5]Schwartz, "Beobachtungen," 154. Compare with this excessive condemnation the more balanced paraphrase of Frankenberg's findings by Rudolf Abramowski, "Pseudoclemens: Zu W. Frankenbergs Clemensausgabe," review of *Die syrischen Clementinen mit griechischem Paralleltext: Eine Vorarbeit zu dem literargeschichtlichen Problem der Sammlung*, by Wilhelm Frankenberg, in *Theologische Blätter* 18 (1939): 149.

[6]Rehm, "Entstehung," 88, n. 37.

[7]Wilhelm Kutsch, review of *Die syrischen Clementinen mit griechischem Paralleltext: Eine Vorarbeit zu dem literargeschichtlichen Problem der Sammlung*, by Wilhelm Frankenberg, in *Orientalia*, n.s., 8 (1939): 185.

[8]Hans Waitz, "Die Lösung des pseudoclementinischen Problems?" *Zeitschrift für Kirchengeschichte* 59 (1940): 305.

translation" by comparing the Syriac.[9]   Other scholars have simply
refrained from judgment and have said that because of the loss of the
Greek there is no way to evaluate Rufinus's translation of R.[10]

The problem will be approached here by first briefly discussing
Rufinus as a translator and examining his specific remarks on his
rendering of the *Pseudo-Clementines* into Latin. Then, other criteria will
be sought that enable a decision on the relative values of the Syriac
and Latin versions.

Rufinus the Translator and His Comments on His Version of the Pseudo-Clementines

Condemnation of Rufinus as a translator has a long history that
reaches back to internecine squabbles with his quondam friend Jerome.
Rufinus found defenders then as he has now, and though it is still
customary to inquire into his capabilities by posing the question of
whether Rufinus or Jerome was the better translator, the ultimate
answer to this continuing debate will be only of indirect relevance to
the present problem: the precise nature of Rufinus's translation of the
Pseudo-Clementines.

There exists no doubt that Rufinus sometimes translated very freely.
Perhaps the most renowned such example is his rendition of Origen's
De Principiis.[11]   Here, as also in some other cases, Rufinus
consciously rearranged the text and added explicative remarks. Yet it
is important to remember that Rufinus never intended to conceal this
fact. Indeed, in his prefaces he states explicitly when he had rendered

---

[9]Rius-Camps, "Las Pseudoclementinas," 108-9; citation from p. 109.

[10]Heinrich Hoppe, "Rufin als Uebersetzer," in *Studi dedicati alla memoria di
Paolo Ubaldi*, Pubblicazioni della Università Cattolica del Sacro Cuore, 5th ser., vol.
16 (Milan: Società editrice "Vita e pensiero," 1937), 141 with n. 2, Friedhelm
Winkelmann, "Einige Bemerkungen zu den Aussagen des Rufinus von Aquileia und
des Hieronymus über ihre Übersetzungstheorie und -methode," in *Kyriakon:
Festschrift Johannes Quasten*, ed. Patrick Granfield and Josef A. Jungmann
(Munster: Aschendorff, 1970), 535, and similarly Schmidt, *Studien*, 29, n. 2.

[11]See, for example, the remarks on the circumstances and nature of this
translation by Francis X. Murphy, *Rufinus of Aquileia (345-411): His Life and
Works*, The Catholic University of America Studies in Mediaeval History, n.s., vol.
6 (Washington, D.C.: Catholic University of America Press, 1945), 82-110.

in such a free manner. Rufinus was quite aware of the distinction between this "ornate" mode of rendition and "simple" translation.[12] Moreover, these were recognized categories in the translation theory of his day.[13]

As concerns the *Pseudo-Clementines*, it should also be kept in mind that this translation was undertaken after his free renderings of Origen and thus after these and other works had been publicly criticized.[14] Rufinus himself made the following statement concerning his translation of Pseudo-Clement: "To the extent that we were able, we applied ourselves to diverge not only not from the meaning but also not even from the wording and the modes of expression. Though this procedure renders the style of the narrative less ornate, it makes it more

---

[12]See, for example, Rufinus's remarks in *Epilogus in Explanationem Origenis super Epistulam Pauli ad Romanos*, especially p. 276, lines 16-24 (Simonetti). One encounters a failure to note this distinction in Rufinus's work, for example, in Craig Koester, "The Origin and Significance of the Flight to Pella Tradition," *Catholic Biblical Quarterly* 51 (1989): 102-3, in Torben Christensen, "Rufinus of Aquileia and the *Historia Ecclesiastica, lib. VIII-IX*, of Eusebius," *Studia Theologica* 34 (1980): 129-52, and in idem, *Rufinus of Aquileia and the* Historia Ecclesiastica, *Lib. VIII-IX, of Eusebius*, Det Kongelige Danske Videnskabernes Selskab, historisk-filosofiske Meddelelser, vol. 58 (Copenhagen: Munksgaard, 1989). Much of the other literature on Rufinus's translations, which need not all be listed here, similarly engages in generalizing statements that lump all of the renderings together. An awareness of the distinction, in contrast, is displayed by M. Monica Wagner, *Rufinus, the Translator: A Study of His Theory and His Practice as Illustrated in His Version of the* Apologetica *of St. Gregory Nazianzen*, The Catholic University of America Patristic Studies, vol. 73 (Washington, D.C.: The Catholic University of America Press, 1945), 8-9.

[13]On this distinction in the work of Rufinus and in the ancient world of his time, see Heinrich Marti, *Übersetzer der Augustin-Zeit: Interpretation von Selbstzeugnissen*, Studia et Testimonia Antiqua, vol. 14 (Munich: Wilhelm Fink, 1974), 64-81, 86-93.

[14]Caroline P. Hammond, "The Last Ten Years of Rufinus' Life and the Date of His Move South from Aquileia," *Journal of Theological Studies*, n.s., 28 (1977): 428, has suggested 407 as the date of the translation. Murphy, *Rufinus*, 235, assigns it to the year 406. Schwartz, "Beobachtungen," 166, in contrast, wanted to place it before the rendition of Eusebius's *Historia Ecclesiastica* ("402 or shortly thereafter"). Hammond has shown anew that this view, which would not seriously affect the statement above in the text, is very unlikely. Lüdemann's statement that Rufinus translated R "before the end of the fourth century" (*Antipaulinismus*, 228, n. 3) seems to be just a mistake (corrected in *Opposition to Paul*, 296, n. 3).

faithful."[15]   In other words, Rufinus intended his version to be a simple one,[16] while at the same time he admitted that he had left out "some things said about the Ingenerate God and the Generate and about a few other subjects."[17]

Is there reason to doubt Rufinus's statement that he had undertaken a generally faithful translation? To answer this question, we shall now search for criteria that enable evaluation of the two versions. Since the present inquiry is focused on R 1.27-71, it is appropriate that the following discussion be led primarily by the question of the quality of the two translations in this particular section.

---

[15]*Prologus in Clementis Recognitiones* 11 (Rehm). The English translation is my own.

[16]It should be noted that Rufinus apparently changed in his approach to this undertaking.   When he wrote his *Epilogus in Explanationem Origenis super Epistulam Pauli ad Romanos* he thought that he would have to do a great deal of editing as he translated, and he intended to place his own name in the title (p. 277, lines 41-49 [Simonetti]; cf. Winkelmann, "Bemerkungen," 538; for the reasons that stood behind this initial position, see his *De Adulteratione Librorum Origenis* 3).   In other words, Rufinus was planning an ornate translation (this is evident from the contrast between the statement that in translating Clement he knew *quod laborem labor multiplicata sorte suscipiet* and his description of his rendering of Origen's homilies on Joshua, Judges, and three Psalms with the words *simpliciter ut inuenimus, et non multo cum labore transtulimus* [*Epilogus in Explanationem Origenis super Epistulam Pauli ad Romanos*, p. 277, line 46, p. 276, lines 19-20 (Simonetti); see also p. 276, lines 8-10, for Rufinus's explanation of what he means by the word *labor*]).   Rufinus evidently soon changed his mind and decided to adopt the literal mode of translation.   One proposal as to the background of this shift is as follows.   Rufinus probably originally planned to translate H, for he had been told (or discovered on his own) that H, in contrast to R, preserved the ending of the novel (see *Prologus in Clementis Recognitiones* 9 [Rehm]) and that R had been corrupted by Eunomians (see *De Adulteratione Librorum Origenis* 3; whether the *Epistula Clementis*, which Rufinus translated earlier, formed a part of his copy of R, of H, or of both versions cannot be determined with absolute certainty; I suspect he found it in his copy of H).   He then realized that he would have to do a great deal of doctrinal editing of H, and consequently he announced that the final work would carry his own name in the title.   Later he examined R more carefully and realized that this version was much less dangerous doctrinally, that the unorthodox passages were few enough to be simply eliminated or quickly reworded, and that the ending in H could easily be transferred to R (see Rehm, "Entstehung," 80-86, for the demonstration that Rufinus added R 10.52.2-65.5 from H).   Thus he decided to translate R (with the ending of H) instead of H.   This decision made his task both easier and less susceptible to the criticisms of his "ornate" renderings, for now he could employ the literal mode.

[17]*Prologus in Clementis Recognitiones* 10-11 (Rehm).

Evaluation of the Two Versions

THE ARMENIAN FRAGMENTS AS A CRITERION FOR EVALUATION

There has been virtually no previous discussion of the methodological principles that allow one to decide between the Syriac and the Latin where they differ. This situation perhaps explains why the recent discovery of Armenian fragments from the first three books of R was not seen to have immediate bearing on this problem.

In 1978 Charles Renoux published five fragments of R (1.7.2-3, 21.7-8, 34.3-35.1, 45.3-5, 3.29.2-3) from an Armenian manuscript of approximately the fourteenth century.[18] Renoux stated that the introductory phrases of the fragments, which are part of a christological florilegium, seem to indicate that the selections were taken from a preexisting Armenian version.[19] He provided a Latin translation of the fragments and placed this alongside Rufinus's version. While he noted the divergences and explained some as redaction in accommodation to their context in the florilegium, he also mentioned that in some cases the Armenian agrees with the Syriac.[20]

May these fragments be used as a criterion to evaluate the two versions? The divergences from both the Syriac and the Latin, as well as the sporadic agreements with each, make it clear that the Armenian was not translated from either of these two versions; the Armenian thus evidently presents another independent translation from the original Greek. These fragments therefore do provide a valid criterion for the evaluation of the Syriac and the Latin (as well as for establishment of the underlying Greek): whenever they agree with one version against the other, one may rest assured that that version has best preserved the original text. The only limitation of this criterion lies in the fact that only fragments of the Armenian have been preserved (or, in any event, published).

---

[18]Charles Renoux, "Fragments arméniens des Recognitiones du Pseudo-Clément," *Oriens Christianus* 62 (1978): 104.

[19]Ibid., 105.

[20]Ibid., 105-6.

What do these fragments reveal about the reliability of the Syriac and the Latin? Collation of the texts[21] discloses a virtually equal amount of specific agreements with each of the versions against the other. Thus in the first fragment from R 1.27-71 (R 1.34.3-35.1) the main specific positive agreements[22] with the Latin are (1) the statement that the true *prophet appeared to Moses*, (2) the statement that the sea was constricted *as ice,* and (3) the mention of the *people* in 35.1. Specific agreements with the Syriac are (1) the qualification of the Egyptians as *oppressing*, (2) the qualification of the people as *beloved* by God, (3) *the prophet* as the subject dividing the sea, (4) the repetition of the reference to the *division* of the sea and to the *Egyptians who had been in pursuit* in R 1.34.7, and (5) the qualification of the people in R 1.35.1 as a *great multitude*. The other fragments yield similar results, and on the basis of these collations one can only conclude that the two versions are of virtually the same value, though the Syriac possibly deserves (very) slight preference.[23]

---

[21]Compare the notes ibid., 106-13. See now also Valentina Calzolari, "La tradition arménienne des *Pseudo-Clémentines*: État de la question," *Apocrypha* 4 (1993): 278-84. A synoptic translation of the versions may be found below in chapter 3.

[22]Owing to the nature of the case (comparison of three translations), the textual decisions are complicated. Thus in the following only the major and clear agreements are listed; the places where specific additional material in the Syriac or Latin is not confirmed by the Armenian are not listed.

[23]Particularly the last Armenian fragment (R 3.29.2-3) reveals greater agreement with the Syriac. In a recent tabulation of the agreements between the versions in all five Armenian fragments, Calzolari, "La tradition arménienne des *Pseudo-Clémentines*," 284, states that there are thirty specific agreements between the Armenian and the Syriac while the distinctive readings the Latin shares with the Armenian number only twelve.
Even before the discovery of the Armenian fragments there was material that could have been employed for an absolute evaluation of the Syriac and Latin translations. Nilus of Ancyra excerpted the original Greek of R 2.20.4-21.4, and Rehm printed this passage in his edition of R. Comparison of this Greek fragment with the Latin and Syriac again shows that neither version deserves absolute priority. Each is more accurate than the other in specific instances, though here again the Syriac proves itself somewhat more reliable. A similar result is yielded by the Greek fragment of R 3.26.4-5 (in Rehm, *Rekognitionen*, 116) from John Damascene, *Sacra Parallela*, where one should read τὸν instead of εἰς in the last line; a more complete form of this excerpt is found in the *Florilegium Achridense*; this text was published by Marcel Richard, "Quelques nouveaux fragments des

While this result is based on an objective criterion, the existence of only a few small Armenian (and other) fragments is not enough to rule out the possibility absolutely that these snippets could yield a biased picture. Since the Armenian fragments have been somewhat arbitrarily preserved, however, this possibility seems very unlikely, and thus the achieved result may in any event serve as a broader framework for the text-critical decisions in this study. Nevertheless, each decision between the Latin and Syriac versions must finally be undertaken on a case by case basis. Since the Armenian is not available in most passages, in these cases other criteria are necessary if one wants to determine whether the Syriac or the Latin deserves priority. Are there other criteria that could confirm or correct the witness of the Armenian fragments and that may be applied more broadly?

OTHER CRITERIA

The first chapters in R 1.27-71 consist largely of a retelling of the · Old Testament biblical narrative. The science of evaluating translations undertaken by ecclesiastical writers knows of a criterion that may be applied in such cases: has the translator adjusted his text to conform with the version of the Bible current in his mother tongue? In terms of the section of the *Pseudo-Clementines* currently under consideration, this criterion asks whether variants in the Latin and the Syriac can be accounted for on the basis of accommodation to the Vetus Latina or the Peshitta. This standard means that the version that is farthest from this biblical account is most likely to be original. In particular, whenever the Latin or the Syriac agrees literally with the Vetus Latina or the Peshitta, these words are immediately open to suspicion, for the translator might have neglected some original aspect of the text in preference for the biblical account with which he was most familiar.

What does this criterion reveal about the reliability of the Syriac and the Latin? Examination again discloses virtually an equal amount of evidence for and against each version. As an illustrative example, the results of the examination of R 1.27, which is particularly close to Genesis 1, may be presented.

---

pères anténicéens et nicéens," in idem, *Opera Minora*, vol. 1, no. 5 (Turnhout: Brepols; Leuven: University Press, 1976), 83.

A simple case of the effectiveness of this criterion is met immediately in R 1.27.1-2 where the Latin must use a plural for "darkness" (as in the Vetus Latina and Vulgate) whereas the Syriac had available a singular corresponding to the Greek. Rufinus has appropriately changed the related verbs to the plural.

In R 1.27.2 one may see, on the one hand, that Rufinus has changed the order of light and day and darkness and night to accord with the biblical account. The Syriac, on the other hand, is probably culpable of having introduced the verb "call."

In R 1.27.3 the Syriac is perhaps responsible for introducing the active subject "he" (God) as well as for leaving out the statement "in the middle of that first heaven and earth," which fits the context. Similarly, in R 1.27.6 the Syriac probably added the verb "gather," and in R 1.27.7 it probably again introduced the verb "call." The Latin, conversely, has probably adopted from Genesis the reference to "species" of plants in R 1.27.8.

This sample reveals that both the Syriac and the Latin have accommodated to the biblical narrative and that they have done this to approximately the same degree. Since other passages disclose a similar state of affairs,[24] it may be stated that this second criterion for the evaluation of the Syriac and Latin versions essentially confirms the result obtained by the first criterion: the two versions are of virtually the same value. Both translations seem to have been conscientious undertakings, though neither seems to have aimed at extreme literalness.

Other criteria for the evaluation of the two versions arise in the identification of proclivities on the side of each translator. It was noted above that Rufinus explicitly stated his difficulty with certain theological and christological passages in the *Pseudo-Clementines*. Is there evidence in R 1.27-71 of changes or omissions in this regard? One such passage that immediately catches the eye is R 1.69.6-7, which, as noted in the history of research, Rehm attributed to a Eunomian

---

[24]From the New Testament material, see for example the accommodation to Matt. 5:5-6 by both versions in R 1.61.2.

interpolator. There can be little doubt that Rufinus has modified the passage, whereas the Syriac has remained closer to the original.

A proclivity of the Syriac translator probably reveals itself in R 1.40.2, where the Syriac alone has a very negative statement about the Jewish people. It is hard to imagine why Rufinus would have left this sentence out, whereas one might assume that a Syriac environment, where Jews and Christians had continued in their debates and conflicts, might have easily occasioned such an addition, which in its utter negativity is out of suit with the rest of the section.

Result

The result of these observations on the two versions may be stated simply: the two versions are of approximately the same value, and neither deserves absolute priority. Both the Armenian fragments and the other criteria for evaluation disclosed that each translation was made fairly conscientiously, but that each has varied from absolute literalness in not a few cases. The resulting differences between the two renditions constitute a considerable portion of the text. This state of affairs means that for scholarly purposes neither version should be read by itself if the intention is to gain a conception of the original R.[25]

---

[25]Where only the Latin of R has been preserved (R 4-10 in essence), there is most often no way of controlling absolutely when one is at the whims of the translator. There is certainly at least some legitimacy in Frankenberg's statement that wherever only the Latin exists, it should be used with the greatest caution (Frankenberg, *Clementinen*, X). Nevertheless, the insights into Rufinus's work gained above should not be forgotten.

III

TRANSLATION OF *RECOGNITIONS* 1.27-71
(SYRIAC, LATIN, AND ARMENIAN)

Introduction

The preceding chapter has made it apparent that when one is concerned with the original text of R 1.27-71, absolute reliance cannot be placed on either the Syriac or the Latin version. Since Latin is more accessible to most students of early Christianity and since the Latin *Pseudo-Clementines* have already been rendered into English,[1] the Syriac version has tended to be neglected. The present chapter intends to redress this problem by making the entire Syriac text available for the first time in a modern language.[2] To ease comparison with the Latin, an English rendering that draws on the most recent edition of this

---

[1]Most recently by Smith, "Pseudo-Clementine Literature."

[2]While Frankenberg did render the Syriac into Greek, his reconstruction cannot always be assumed to echo what the Syriac says; it reflects rather what Frankenberg thought the Syriac translator had before him in Greek. Any additions, clarifications, or even sometimes omissions attributable supposedly to the Syriac

version is provided in a parallel column.[3] An English translation of the Armenian fragments is also included.[4]

Translation

Syriac	Latin
(1.27.1) "In the beginning, when God made heaven and earth like one house, the shadow that came from the bodies of the world darkened those that were within it.	(1.27.1) "In the beginning, when God had made heaven and earth just as one house, the shadow that was given off from the bodies of the world cast from itself darkness onto those things that had been enclosed within.
(2) This [shadow] was swallowed up as nothing by the light that shone forth according to the will of God. Then, when the darkness was reckoned to be night, the light was called day.	(2) But when the will of God had introduced light, the darkness that had been made out of the shadow of the bodies was immediately swallowed up. Then, light being considered day, darkness was considered night.
(3) "In the midst of the waters	(3) Now, however, the water that

---

translator are thus not represented in Frankenberg's Greek.   See Frankenberg, *Clementinen*, XII-XIII.

The present translation has been made on the basis of the manuscripts in consultation with the editions by Lagarde and Frankenberg.   On Van Voorst's translation, see supra chapter 1, nn. 2, 144.

[3]The translation is based on a comparison of the editions and apparatuses of J. B. Cotelier, E. G. Gersdorf, and Rehm, *Rekognitionen* (see here pp. CVII-CVIII for bibliographical references and text-critical explanations), along with my own collations of select Latin manuscripts; see chapter 2, n. 1, on the status of Rehm's edited text.

[4]My English rendering derives from a comparison of the notes and Latin translation in Renoux, "Fragments arméniens des Recognitiones," 109-12, with the notes and French translation of Calzolari, "La tradition arménienne des *Pseudo-Clémentines*," 263-84. It also employed a preliminary version of the last mentioned article that performed a linguistic analysis of the Armenian fragments (presented at the meeting of the Pseudo-Clementine working group of the Association pour l'étude de la littérature apocryphe chrétienne outside Geneva in March 1989).

that were inside, he stretched out the firmament, solid waters, made something like a partition,

and called it heaven. So, through the oldest name he conferred honor on them.

(4) Thus, at that moment, he divided this entire stretched out globe, which had been one house, into two regions.

(5) This was the reason for its division: in order that the upper region might be an abode for the angels and the lower might be apportioned to humans.

(6) "Then, through the will of the director, the waters that had remained below were left for the chasms of the earth and were gathered together.

Thus, dry land became visible.

(7) The assembly of the waters was called the seas.

(8) The earth that became visible brought forth plants,

and it made manifest springs and the course of the rivers on the mountains in their boundaries

was within the world was distended, hardened similar to ice and solid as crystal, in the middle space between that first heaven and earth, and in this manner through a firmament the middle spaces of heaven and earth are, as it were, separated. And the maker called this firmament heaven, it being named with the designation of the older one.

(4) Thus, he divided the structure of the whole world, which was one house, into two regions.

(5) Now this was the cause of the division: that the upper region might provide a realm for the angels while the lower one for the humans.

(6) After these things, the place of the sea and the created underworld received what remained of the waters in the lower areas, through the command of the eternal will. As they flowed to the sunken and hollow areas, dry land became visible.

(7) But the seas were made by the collecting of the waters.

(8) After these things, the earth that appeared produced diverse kinds of plants and shrubbery, and it also brought forth springs and rivers not only in the plains but also in the mountains.

(9) so that there might be a suitable dwelling place for humans, who were about to come. In this way each of them would be able to pass through there and desire what should be, I mean, either the good or the bad.

(1.28.1) "After these things, he adorned the heaven with stars. He made the sun and the moon that they might give forth light, the one during the night and the other during the day, and also [that they might] point out the things that are, the things that are to come, those things that are temporal, and the things that are eternal.

(2) Then, for this reason they also served as signs for both times and seasons. They are seen by all, but they are comprehended by the diligent.

(3) Then he commanded that living things issue forth from the earth and the water, and he made the paradise that he called 'the place of delicacies.'

(4) "After these things, he made the human, the one on account of whom he had previously prepared all these things, whose form is older, and on account of whom everything received the grace to be, which things came

(9) Now all things were thus prepared in order that the humans who would inhabit it would have the faculty to use all these things at will, that is, to will either the good or else even the bad.

(1.28.1) "After these things he adorned this visible heaven with stars. He placed also the sun and the moon in it in order that the day might use the light of one of them and the night that of the other and, similarly, in order that they might be an indication of things past, present, and future.

(2) For they were made as signs of times and of days, which are in fact seen by all but are understood by the learned and intelligent alone.

(3) Later, when he had ordered living creatures to be produced from the earth and the waters, he made paradise, which he also called 'place of delicacies.'

(4) "Now after all these things, he made the human, for whom he had prepared everything,

whose internal species is older, and on account of whom all things that are were made, being submitted for his service and

into existence and were assigned for his service and his habitation.

(1.29.1) "When therefore everything that is in the heavens, the earth, and the waters was complete, humans also increased. And the eighth generation arose. Righteous men who had been living in the likeness of angels rejected their previous manner of life owing to the beauty of women and indiscriminately had intercourse. They were practiced so that they did everything senselessly.

(2) Those who received their existence in the succession received also this: that they would increasingly do evil.

These also enticed all humans, partly through fear and partly through persuasion, to sin against the maker of all.

(3) "From them, those who were of old called the giants were begotten in the ninth generation. They were not snake-footed, as the myths of the Greeks relate, but were rather huge people who resembled great mountains in the size of their bodies. Their bones have been placed in various localities as a warning against unfaithfulness, about which places I told you at another time.

being given for the usages of his habitation.

(1.29.1) "When therefore everything that is in heaven and earth and also the waters was complete and the race of humans had also increased, in the eighth generation just men who had lived the life of angels were allured by the beauty of women and descended to promiscuous and illicit sexual intercourse.

(2) And from this time, doing everything indiscriminately and against the order, they transformed the state of human affairs and the divinely given order of life, so that they forced all humans, either through persuasion or through power, to sin against their creator God.

(3) Next, in the ninth generation, those giants were born who are mentioned of old, not snake-footed as the myths of the Greeks relate,

but produced with immense bodies, whose bones of immense size are still shown in a number of places as a portent.

(4) The righteous providence of God brought the flood on these [people], and the world was purified by the flood. Everything became like chaos, and the multitude of the wicked perished.

(5) "However, one righteous person, who was found at that time and whose name was Noah, was delivered in the ark with his three sons and their wives. After the withdrawal of the waters, he entered in with the living creatures that were with him, and he proceeded forth with the young offspring and dwelt in the world.

(1.30.1) "In the twelfth generation, they began to increase by the blessing with which God had blessed them, and they received the first commandment, that they should not eat blood, for the flood had taken place precisely because of this.

(2) "In the thirteenth generation, the middle son of Noah first abused his father, and his offspring was accursed to slavery.

(3) While his elder brother received as a lot the middle portion of the earth, which contains the region Judaea, and the third received the eastern portion, the

(4) But against these the just providence of God issued a flood to the world, so that the world might be washed of their pollution while every place might be turned into sea for the sake of the death of the impious.

(5) However, one just man was found then, by the name of Noah, who, having been saved in the ark with three sons and their wives, became the inhabiter of the world after the ebbing of the waters together with the animals that he had enclosed with him as well as the seeds.

(1.30.1) "In the twelfth generation, after God had blessed the human beings and they began to be multiplied, they received the precept that they should not taste blood. For precisely because of this the flood was brought about.

(2) In the thirteenth generation, when the middle of Noah's three sons did injustice to his father, with a curse he inflicted the condition of slavery on his posterity.

(3) In the meanwhile, his older brother received the lot for habitation that is in the middle of the earth, in which is located the land of Judaea; the younger received the region of the east, while he

western part fell to him [sc. the middle son].

(4) "In the fourteenth generation, a person from the cursed seed was the first to build an altar for the purpose of magic and in order to give the honor of blood to demons.

(5) "In the fifteenth generation, men first worshipped fire and constructed idols. Now, until that time one language had prevailed, the language pleasing to God: Hebrew.

(6) "In the sixteenth generation, people arose from the east and came to the places of the portions of their fathers. They named the places after their [sc. their fathers'(?)] names.

(7) "In the seventeenth generation, Nimrod the first acceded to the throne in Babylon and built a city. From there he migrated to Persia and taught them to worship fire.

(1.31.1) "In the eighteenth generation, walled cities were built. People arranged for armies, weapons, judges, and law, just as they wished; they built temples, and they bowed down to their rulers as if to gods.

(2) "In the nineteenth generation, the grandsons of the one

[sc. the middle son] took the region of the west.

(4) In the fourteenth generation, a certain one from the accursed lineage first built an altar for the sake of magical art and offered the honor of blood to demons.

(5) In the fifteenth generation, humans first set up an idol and worshipped it. Until that time the language of the Hebrews, which had been divinely given to the human race, held sole dominance.

(6) In the sixteenth generation, the sons of men moved from the east and came to the lands of their fathers. Each one called the place of his lot after his own name.

(7) In the seventeenth generation, Nimrod the first reigned in Babylon, built a city, migrated from there to the Persians, and taught them to worship fire.

(1.31.1) "In the eighteenth generation, walled cities were built, troops and weapons were arranged, judges and laws were set up, temples were constructed, and the heads of the nations were worshipped as gods.

(2) In the nineteenth generation, the descendants of the one who

who was cursed after the flood left the boundary of their land (for they had received as an allotted portion the western part) and drove those to whom the middle portion had fallen to the east, into Persia. They then dwelt in the places of those who had been expelled.

(3) "In the twentieth generation, a son first died the death of his soul before his father, due to impious intercourse.

(1.32.1) "In the twenty-first generation, there was a wise man from the race of those who were expelled, whose descent was from the first-born of Noah. His name was Abraham, from whom our race, the Hebrews, who are also called the Jews, multiplied. (2) Now when the whole world was in error and, owing to ungodliness, was on the verge of being destroyed not by water but by fire, and when the scourge had begun in Sodom in order to pass through all the world, he, by his knowledge of God and his love for him, by means of which he had especially pleased him, saved the whole world from being destroyed.
(3) Though in the very beginning everyone was in error, he

was cursed after the flood left their proper boundaries, which they had received by lot in the western regions, expelled those who had received the middle part of the earth into the lands of the east, and drove them to Persia, while they themselves took the places of the expelled in an unjust way.

(3) In the twentieth generation, a son first died naturally before his father because of the sin of incest.

(1.32.1) "In the twenty-first generation, there arose a certain wise man from the lineage of those who had been expelled, from the seed of the first-born of Noah's sons, named Abraham, from whom the race of us Hebrews is descended.
(2) When the whole world was again subject to various errors and on account of the enormity of the iniquities a speedy destruction was prepared for it not again by water but by fire, and when the plague, which had started at Sodom, was threatening the entire earth, he snatched the world from perishing at once by the friendship with which he had an intimacy with God, whom he had highly pleased. (3) From the beginning, however, when everyone else

recognized, through the art of the Chaldeans and from the pattern of the stars, the one who arranged them. In the providence of God, whom he had recognized,

(4) the angel approached him and

testified to him concerning his election and the land which was incumbent upon his race. It was not that he would give, but he promised him that he would requite and return.

(1.33.1) "Now when Abraham was in anxiety and was desiring to know the things that are, just as they are, the prophet of truth, the one who alone has known the will of every person, appeared to him. (2) In one day he revealed everything to him and assured

him also regarding God, the origin of the world, its dissolution, the immortal soul, and the ways that are pleasing to him; also that the dead will rise, that there will be a judgment, and that those who are found in virtue will receive for eternity hidden good things while those who are evil will suffer the punishment of the eternal fire. As I should say generally, he

was in error, since he was a skilled astrologer, he was able to recognize the maker from the pattern and order of the stars, and he understood that everything is governed by his providence. (4) Hence, an angel also came to him in a vision and instructed him more fully concerning the things he had begun to perceive. And he also showed him what was due to his race and posterity, and he promised that these places not so much are to be given to them as they are to be returned.

(1.33.1) "When, therefore, Abraham desired to know the causes of things and contemplated it with an intent mind, the true prophet, who alone knows the hearts and disposition of humans, appeared to him (2) and revealed to him everything he was desiring. He taught the knowledge of the deity, similarly disclosed the beginning and end of the world, and exhibited the immortality of the soul and the habits of life by which God is pleased. He also declared that the dead will rise, the future judgment, the reward of the good, and the punishment of the evil, all regulated by just authority. And when everything had been properly and adequately

revealed everything to him. Then he resumed his incomprehensible place. (3) Therefore, while Abraham was yet in ignorance of greatness, just as the trustworthy story relates and the prophet of truth testifies and again as I related the reasoning of these things to you at another time, he had two sons. One of them was henceforth called Ishmael, and the other, Eliezer, from whom [pl.] the tribes of the Arabs and the Persians descended.

(4) Some of them also mixed with the Brahmins who were their neighbors. Some of the descendants of the one who dwelt in Arabia were dispersed to Egypt, to which they were near. (5) Hence, some Indians and Egyptians are circumcised, and they purify themselves additionally through other purifications. But as regards some of them, the length of time changed the goodness of their purification to evil.

(1.34.1) "This person, however, who in the time of his ignorance had two sons, when he came into knowledge of the truth from God prayed that, because he was righteous, there might be

taught, he returned to his invisible place.
(3) But while Abraham was involved in ignorance up to this point, as we also already told you,

two sons were born to him, of whom one was called Ishmael and the other Eliezer. From the one the barbarian nations descend, while from the other the peoples of the Persians descend. (4) Of these some have imitated the life of the Brahmins and related customs, while others took up residence in Arabia, some descendants of whom were even dispersed into Egypt. (5) Hence, then, certain of both the Indians and the Egyptians learned to be circumcised and to be of a purer observance than the others, though with the passing of time most of them have changed the symbol and indication of purity unto impiety.

(1.34.1) "Since, however, he had received these two sons during the time in which he had lived in ignorance of things, when he had received the knowledge of God, he asked him, since he was just, that he might have offspring a son to Sarah, who was his lawful wife from youth but who was barren. (2) And the one whom he called Isaac was given to her. Isaac begot Jacob, and Jacob the twelve, and the twelve the seventy-two.

from Sarah, who was his legitimate wife, though she was sterile. (2) And he received the one whom he called Isaac, of whom Jacob was born, and from Jacob the twelve patriarchs, and from them the seventy-two.

Syriac	Armenian	Latin
(3) "Now when a famine arose, their whole family went to Egypt. For four hundred years they multiplied in the blessing and promise of God. They were being afflicted in wickedness by the Egyptians, (4) but as they were being mistreated, the prophet of truth, Moses, came to them. He punished the oppressing Egyptians, who did not let the people of the Hebrews go so that it might go forth and journey to the land of its fathers. He scourged them with ten plagues from heaven, and thus he sent forth	(3) When four hundred years had passed and through the blessing of God and through the centuries they had been multiplied, the Egyptians began to afflict them. (4) The true prophet saw their afflictions, appeared to Moses, and visited the oppressing Egyptians, who were hindering the Hebrews from leaving to go to the country of their home, with ten celestial [illegible word], beat the rod, and led the people who were	(3) When a famine arose, these came to Egypt with their whole house, and having multiplied through the blessing and promise of God for four hundred years, they were afflicted by the Egyptians. (4) While they were being afflicted, the true prophet appeared to Moses. He also visited the Egyptians, who were preventing the people of the Hebrews from going out from among them and returning to their fatherland, with ten heavenly plagues, while he led the people

from Egypt the people who were beloved by God. (5) Because of this, the Egyptians who remained with their king so that they might become his accomplices in wickedness went out,
(6) overtook the Hebrews, and beleaguered them in a place that was on the shore of the sea. They wanted to destroy them all with swords. And because they were desiring to approach them, the prophet divided the sea through his prayer to God. He formed it into two parts so that it was divided, and in this manner the people crossed through. The entire company of Egyptians, in its presumption, entered after them and perished.
(7) For as the last of the Hebrews was going up [out of the

beloved by God from the land of Egypt.

(6) The prophet immediately came to that place because of the prayers that they had offered. He commanded the sea to divide itself into two parts and he made the people of Israel to cross. And the Egyptians, who dared to hurry all together, plunged in and drowned.
(7) For as the last of the Hebrews was

of God out of Egypt.

(5) But those who were left over from the Egyptians, having conspired in the impetuosity of their king, followed the Hebrews.
(6) When they had found them on the shore of the sea and

intended both to kill and eradicate all,

Moses divided the sea into two parts through a prayer poured out to God so that the water on the right and the left was held solid as if ice and the people of God might transverse as it were a dry road. But when the Egyptians who were following them had rashly entered, they were killed.
(7) For when the last of the people of Hebrews ascended, the

sea], the last of the Egyptians was going down [into the sea]. Then the sea, which was firmly fixed through the

command of the one who had divided it, rushed forth back to its previous state,

and, by it, the Egyptians who had been in pursuit received punishment.

(1.35.1) "Then Moses, at the command of God who knows all things, led the many myriads of Hebrews to the desert.

ascending, the whole multitude of Egyptians was entering. Then the sea, held here and there like ice, was released and became one through the command of the one who commanded it to divide itself.

And the Egyptians who were following went under in it and died.

(1.35.1) Then Moses through the command of the omniscient God led the numerous people of the myriads of Hebrews and conducted it out in the desert.

last of the Egyptians descended into the sea, and when the waters of the sea, which had been held constricted as if ice, were released by the command of the one who had done the constraining, they immediately received the freedom of their nature and punished the throng of the impious.

(1.35.1) "After these things Moses led the people of Hebrews in the desert by the command of the God who foreknows all things.

Syriac

He left to one side the short road that leads from Egypt to Judaea and led them to the wide desert, so that by a journey of forty years, since they were following the vices that had been added to them in Egypt through the strong habit of the length of time, another time, with the legislation, would come and temper and

Latin

And, leaving the shortest road that leads from Egypt to Judaea, he led the populace through the long circuits of the desert so that by exercises for forty years a renewal by changed custom might destroy the evils that had grown into them from the customs of the Egyptians by usage for a long time.

might be able to change them.

(2) "Finally they arrived at Mount Sinai. Through heavenly voices they heard the law of God

in all ten commandments, first among which is this: that when they observe the law they not create for themselves any other cultic image.

(3) "But as Moses went to the mountain for forty days,

those multitudes who had seen Egypt punished through ten plagues, had crossed through the divided sea on foot, had received heavenly manna for food, from the stone that was following them had drunk water, the taste of which was transformed by the power of God however they wished, (4) and again were travelling under the belt of fire and the pillar of cloud in the day because the parching heat was on them-- but in the night, because of the darkness, the pillar of fire enlightened them--

(5) while Moses tarried, those [multitudes] made a golden image of the idol that is in Egypt and that is called Apis. They worshipped it--those who, after all these tokens had accustomed

(2) In the meantime they arrived at Mount Sinai, and from there the law was given to them through heavenly visions and voices, written in ten commands, the first and greatest of which was that they should worship God himself alone and should not erect for themselves any other figure or form for worship. (3) But when Moses ascended to the mountain and remained there forty days, the people who had seen Egypt stricken with ten plagues, the sea split, the entry on foot, manna then given to them from heaven for bread, drink supplied from the following rock, which sort was changed for them by the power of God into the taste that anyone desired, (4) who were shaded by a cloud during the day when they were under the parching expanse of heaven, lest they be scorched by the heat, while at night they were given light through a column of fire lest the horror of darkness should be added to the vastness of the desert--(5) when, then, Moses tarried they made a golden head of a calf according to the type of Apis whom they saw worshipped in Egypt and worshipped it. They were unable to

them, were not able to cast this evil from their heart and put it away.

(6) Because of this, Moses, when he descended from the mountain at the command of God, left, as I said previously, the short road that leads from Egypt to Judaea and led them into the wide desert, just as I previously related, for a period of forty years. Evils had been added to them from the strong habits from the extended period in Egypt. Another period, which would come with the legislation, would both temper and be able to change them. (1.36.1) Because of this, even Moses, as he came down from Mount Sinai and saw the crime, understood, as a good and faithful steward, that it was not possible for the people easily to cease and stop all of the desire of the love of idolatry, in which thing, which had been added to it [sc. the people] from the evil upbringing with the Egyptians, there had been the great length of time. Therefore, he allowed them to sacrifice. But he told them to do this in the name of God so that it might be possible for one half of this desire to be cut down and rendered void.

eliminate and remove from themselves the impurities of old habit even after the many and great miracles that they had seen.
(6) Because of this Moses left the

short road that leads from Egypt to Judaea and led them by the great circuit of the desert so that he might be able, as we said above, to dispel the evils of the old habit by the substitution of a new custom.

(1.36.1) "In the meantime, when the faithful and wise steward Moses perceived that the vice of sacrificing to idols had become deeply ingrained in the people owing to the association with the Egyptians and that it was not possible for the root of this evil to be taken from them,

he allowed them to sacrifice, but he permitted this to be done to God alone, in order that he might eliminate, so to speak, half of the deeply ingrained vice.

"Now concerning the correction of this other half in another time and through the hand of another as would be meet in providence, he spoke in this manner: (2) 'The Lord your God will raise up for you a prophet like me. Listen to him in all matters. Everyone who is not obedient to him will die in death.' This shows that he will give up his soul to destruction.

(1.37.1) Along with these things he separated out for them a place where alone it would be lawful for them to perform sacrifices. (2) All this was laid out for them so that when the appropriate one [or: time] should come they would be able through him to understand that God desires kindness, not sacrifices. At that time, the prophet who is to say these things to them will be sent out. Those who believe in him will be led, through the wisdom of God, to a fortified place of the land, as if to life, and preserved because of the battle that will afterwards come to destroy those who have not been persuaded because of their doubt.

(3) Now, this war will not arise hastily and suddenly. But even before the coming of the prophet

But he reserved the other half to be emended by another person and at another time, namely, by the one of whom he himself said, (2) 'The Lord your God will raise up for you a prophet like me; hear him with respect to all that he might say to you. For whoever should not hear that prophet--his soul will be banished from his people.'

(1.37.1) "Furthermore, he appointed a place in which alone it would be legal for them to sacrifice to God. (2) He did all this with the prospect that when an opportune time came

and they learned by the prophet that God desires mercy and not sacrifice they might see the one who would teach them that

the chosen place of God is his wisdom, in which it is appropriate for offerings to be made to God. This place, however, which seemed for a while to be chosen, though it was often ravaged by attacks of enemies and military destructions, they would also finally hear to be destined to thorough destruction. (3) To verify this matter, even before the arrival of the true prophet, who

who was prepared to come to abolish sacrifices, this war came many times upon them by the providence of God. (4) They have been in captivity and have been taken away to a different nation so that they no longer had the place where the lawgiver had allowed them to sacrifice. Whenever they observed the law without sacrifices, they were restored and ransomed. This happened to them many times in order that they might understand that they were ransomed whenever they observed the law without sacrifices and that, when they returned to their place and offered sacrifices, they were thrust out and were cast forth from it, so that they might cease sacrificing forever.

(5) They, however, were slow to recognize this, though a few did benefit from it. Now even the understanding of these few was darkened by the multitudes of those who held the contrary opinion, those who were not able to penetrate all of this. For not to distinguish and understand is proper to the multitudes, and to understand through the intellect is proper to the few.

would reject sacrifices together with the place, it was often ravaged by enemies and burned with fire.

(4) The nation was led away into foreign nations unto captivity.

When it fled to the mercy of God it was called back from there so that by these things it might be taught that when it offers sacrifices it is expelled and given over into the hands of enemies, but when it effects mercy and justice without sacrifices it is freed from captivity and restored to the fatherland.

(5) Yet it happened that only a few understood this. For though many were able to perceive and heed these things, they were nevertheless constrained by the common irrational opinion.

For proper thought with freedom belongs to the few.

(1.38.1) "After Moses had managed and arranged these things, he also established for them a commander, called Joshua, the one who would lead them by the quickening word of God to the land of their fathers. Then he [sc. Moses] went up and died before all. (2) The death was such that up to now not a single person has been able to find his grave. (3) The multitudes went up to the land of their fathers and, by the providence of God, in the very moment when they were simply seen, put the evil nations to flight. They took possession of it in their tribal portions as the land of their fathers. (4) During the time of judges and when they did not have kings, they steadfastly remained in their places. (5) When they made for themselves [rulers who were] tyrants rather than kings, they abolished the place that had been predestined for them as a house of prayer, in preference for a temple. As if at the initiative of the kingdom they were perforce driven to find that they would do what was against their will. So it was that by the occasional bad kings who ruled over them they were led into greater impiety.

(1.39.1) "Then, as there was

(1.38.1) "After then Moses had arranged these things, he placed over the people someone named Auses, who would bring them back to the fatherland, and he himself ascended to a certain mountain at the command of the living God and died there.

(2) The death of this one was such that until this day no one has found his grave. (3) When then the people only reached its patrimony, at their first advance the inhabitants from the iniquitous nations were immediately put to flight by the providence of God, and they received their paternal inheritance by appointed lot.

(4) Then, for a certain amount of time as they were governed by judges and not by kings, they remained in a quite stable state. (5) But when they sought for themselves [rulers] more tyrants than kings, they built for the royal ambition a temple precisely in the place that had been predestined for them for prayer,

and thus as impious kings orderly succeeded each other, the people turned to even greater impieties.

(1.39.1) "But when the time

this need for the required reformation, the time came when it was fitting for the prophet to appear who was proclaimed earlier by Moses. At his coming, by the mercy of God, he would admonish [or: instruct] them first to stop and cease with their sacrificing. (2) In order that they not think that they were being deprived of the forgiveness of sins that accrued through sacrifices and in order that this might not be a hindrance with the result that they would not believe, baptism through water for the forgiveness of sins was instituted. What in truth gives forgiveness of sins was manifested to them. It is able to preserve in eternal life those who are perfect so that they will not die.

(3) Thus, everyone who has pleased God in his unspeakable wisdom will be delivered from the war that, on account of those who have not believed, is ready to come to destroy them. As they did not want to do what was in their free will, this very thing, when they have left their country and when this place that has been uprooted from them is no longer there for them, even though against their will, they will

began to approach when what we said was lacking in the institutions of Moses would be completed, the prophet, whom he had predicted would appear and who first of all would admonish them by the mercy of God to cease with sacrifices, (2) lest they think that with the ceasing of the sacrifices remission of sins could not be effected for them,

instituted for them baptism by water, in which they might be absolved from all sins through the invocation of his name, and henceforth following a perfect life they might remain in immortality, purified not through the blood of animals but through the purification of God's wisdom. (3) Indeed, a sign of this great mystery is established showing that everyone who believes in this prophet who was predicted by Moses and is baptized in his name will be preserved unharmed from the destruction of the war that is impending on the unbelieving nation and the place itself. But the nonbelievers will be exiled from the place and the kingdom so that perhaps against their will

endure, as is pleasing to God, so that they might be sober.

(1.40.1) "As therefore these things were thus decreed, the good prophet appeared and performed signs.

(2) Even so the ancient people did not believe, although it was prepared beforehand to believe.

For they are people who are more wretched than any, who are willing to believe neither good nor bad for the sake of virtue. But on top of this, the nonbelievers did not hesitate to abuse with pretexts that they made up, and they even called them gluttonous and demoniacs.

(3) All this enabled evil to achieve victory over the wicked. The situation was such that if the wisdom of God had not helped the ones who love the truth, perhaps even these would have erred. (4) But to us he made his declaration, he who, when he came, first of all appointed us twelve so that we might be apostles and then the seventy-two selected disciples, so that the multitudes might understand even thus through a type that this one was the prophet to come who

they might understand and be obedient to the will of God.

(1.40.1) "These things having thus been arranged beforehand, the one who had been expected arrived providing his proofs, by which he should be made manifest, signs, and wonders. (2) But not even so did the people believe, who had been educated to believe these things for so long.

And not only did they not believe, but they added blasphemy to disbelief by calling the one who had come for their salvation an insatiable person, a slave of the stomach, and led by the demon. (3) So much does depravity prevail through the workings of evils that if the wisdom of God had not been with those who loved the truth, the impious error would have almost immediately captured all.

(4) Therefore he chose us first twelve who believed him, whom he called apostles, and later seventy-two other most faithful disciples so that the multitude might believe through the recognition of the image of Moses that

had been previously announced by Moses.

(1.41.1) "But perchance a number is easy for anyone to form. But one is not able to perform the signs and wonders that he did in his advent, for Moses performed signs in Egypt,

(2) and the prophet like him who arose performed signs among the people, banished every sickness,

and proclaimed eternal life. Owing to the evil transgression of the wicked they brought upon him the punishment of the cross. He, however, transformed even this, through his power, into the good and beautiful. (3) For this whole world suffered with him in his passion. For even the sun darkened, the stars were in uproar, the sea was shaken, mountains were shattered, graves were opened, and the veil of the temple was rent in twain as if it were mourning in sorrow for the destruction of the place that was ready to come. (4) Because of these things, therefore, the whole nation was disturbed, and it was compelled into inquiry about the affair. But the intellect of some, when the whole world was

he is the one whom Moses predicted as the coming prophet.

(1.41.1) "Yet one might perhaps say that it is possible for anyone to imitate a number. And what will he say about the signs and wonders that he performed? For Moses performed miracles and healings in Egypt. (2) The one likewise whom he predicted would arise as a prophet like himself, though he cured every sickness and every infirmity in the people, did innumerable miracles, and preached eternal life, was brought to the cross by the impious.

This deed, however, was changed to good by his power. (3) Indeed, as he was suffering, the whole world suffered with him, for both the sun was darkened and the stars were in uproar, the sea was disturbed, the mountains were burst, graves were opened, and the curtain of the temple was torn as if lamenting the imminent destruction of the place.
(4) And though the whole world was disturbed,

not even now were they moved

disturbed, was not moved into inquiry concerning this.

(1.42.1) Therefore, since it was meet, because they were not persuaded, for people from the gentiles to be called for the completion of the number that was shown to Abraham, this confusion arose.

(2) It troubled the whole nation, hastily obscured the perverting power that is opposed to free people, and prepared them for the fire from the majesty.

Thus it is that those who wish to be drawn near to the word of salvation will be stronger than the power that hinders them and will easily attain through their will the victory that is in salvation.

(3) "Now, as he suffered, there was darkness from the sixth hour until the ninth.

When the sun appeared and restored things again to their nature, the evil ones of the people turned back to their habits.

(4) For some said that the one who suffered and was not found, though he was being guarded, was a magician, and they were

at all to inquiry about such great things.

(1.42.1) "But since it was necessary for the nations to be called in the place of those who remained unbelievers so that the number that was shown to Abraham might be filled, the saving proclamation of the kingdom of God was sent out into the whole world. (2) Because of this, disturbance broke out among the worldly spirits who always obstruct those seeking freedom and look for means of errors for the destruction of God's edifice, while those who strive for the glory of salvation and freedom, having become stronger by resisting and exerting no little effort against them, come to the crown of salvation not without the palm of victory.

(3) Meanwhile, although he suffered and darkness weighed upon the world from the sixth hour to the ninth, when the sun had been brought back and things were restored to order, the depraved people yet again abandoned their fear and returned to themselves and to their practices.

(4) Moreover, certain of them who guarded the place with all watchfulness said that the rising one whom they were unable to

not afraid to be rash and act deceitfully.

(1.43.1) Nevertheless, the justice of the truth was conquering. For they acted deceitfully with us because we were few, but things did not turn out for them. For again increasingly, as if by the jealousy of God at all times,

we grew even more numerous than they, so that even their priests were afraid lest by the providence of God and to their shame, the whole nation should come to our faith. They were frequently sending and asking us to speak with them about Jesus, whether he is the prophet who was foretold by Moses, that is, the eternal Christ. (2) For concerning this alone is there a difference between us who believe in Jesus and those among our people who do not believe. (3) Now, while they were frequently beseeching us and while we were looking for a convenient time, one week of years passed from the time of the passion of Jesus. The church in Jerusalem, which was established by our Lord, was growing while it was led uprightly and straightforwardly by James,

detain was a magician; others alleged that he was stolen. (1.43.1) Nevertheless, the truth was conquering everywhere.

For as a sign that these things were being done by divine virtue, we, who were very few, in the passing of days and at the stipulation of God were being made much more than those. Thus the priests eventually became afraid lest to their confusion by the providence of God the entire people should come to our faith. They frequently sent to us asking that we speak to them about Jesus whether he is the prophet whom Moses predicted, who is the eternal Christ. (2) For only in this regard does there seem to be a difference between us who believe in Jesus and the unbelieving Jews. (3) Now while they were frequently asking us about this and we were seeking an opportune moment, a week of years passed from the passion of the Lord, and the church of God established in Jerusalem was growing, having multiplied abundantly and being governed through most correct stewardship by James, whom our Lord appointed bishop.

(1.44.1) "Therefore, as we twelve apostles were gathered in the days of the Passover with the greater part of the community at Jerusalem, we assembled together with the brethren in the day of the festival. Each of us was beseeching James to tell us the summaries of the things that had happened among the people, and he told us in a few words. (2) Caiaphas the high priest sent priests to us who were apostles and asked us to come to him so that either we might persuade him that Jesus is the eternal Christ or that he might persuade us that he is not, so that all the people might take up that faith.

He besought us to do this many times, (3) but we declined no fewer times. We entreated, because we were looking for a suitable time."

(4) And I, Clement, responded to him, "I think that what they were inquiring about, namely, whether he is the Christ, is very beneficial to the discussion about the fear of God. For, as you said, even the high priest, along with the rest, was frequently sending and inquiring so that he might

who was ordained by the Lord as bishop there.

(1.44.1) "But when we twelve apostles assembled for the day of the Passover with a great multitude
and each of our brethren had entered the church,

James asked what things had been done by us in the various localities, and we briefly explained while the people listened. (2) Meanwhile, priests had been sent to us and Caiaphas the high priest was asking us to go to him so that either we might teach him by reason that Jesus is the eternal Christ or he might teach us that he is not in order that the entire people might come together in one of the two faiths. He frequently prevailed upon us to do this, (3) but we often delayed, always looking for a more opportune time."

(4) And I Clement responded to these things, "I believe that also the matter being questioned, whether he is Christ, is very helpful for the justification of faith,

otherwise the high priest

would not have frequently asked

either learn or teach the matters concerning him."

(5) Peter responded to me, "You have spoken rightly, O my dear Clement, and you have thoroughly understood. For just as it is impossible to see without the eye, to hear without the sense of hearing, to smell without the nostrils, to speak without the tongue, and to feel without the hands, so it is impossible to know the things that are pleasing to God without the prophet of truth. For in this way, because of foreknowledge, he is the prophet of the fear of God alone."

(6) After this I responded to him and said, "I know that he is the prophet of truth because you have taught us, but I want to know what the Christ is and why he is called thus, so that knowledge about him might not be unstable in me."

(1.45.1) Now Peter began to speak as follows: "God, who made the world and who is lord of everything, appointed chiefs over everything, even over plants and rocks, springs and rivers,

and every creature. For there are many that I might enumerate like them. (2) Thus, he appointed as chiefs an angel over the angels, a

either to learn or to teach about Christ."

(5) Peter said, "You have responded correctly, Clement.

For just as no one can see without eyes, hear without ears, smell without nostrils, taste without a tongue, or touch something without hands, so it is impossible to know which things please God apart from the true prophet."

(6) And I responded, "I have already learned through your teaching that he is the true prophet. But I wish to learn what 'Christ' is or why he is called thus so that knowledge of such a matter might not be vague and uncertain for me."

(1.45.1) Then Peter began to teach me in this manner: "When God made the world, as the lord of all he established chiefs for all the creatures, even for trees, mountains, springs, and rivers and, as we said, for everything that he made. For it would be excessive to go through everything individually. (2) Well then, he established an angel as the spirit over the spirits, a star over the stars, a bird over the birds, a beast over the beasts, an insect over the insects, a fish over the fish, and over humans, a human, who is the Christ.

chief for the angels, a spirit for the spirits, a star for the stars, a demon for the demons, a bird for the birds, a beast for the beasts, a serpent for the serpents, a fish for the fish, and for the humans a human, who is Christ Jesus.

Syriac	Armenian	Latin
(3) Now, he is called Christ especially through the ritual of the fear of God. For with all chiefs there is a shared name and a distinctive name. Now the appellation 'king' is shared, but what is particular to the Parthians is 'Arsac', to the Romans, 'Caesar'. Thus also 'Christ' is [particular] to the Jews.	(3) But he is named Christ particularly because of a rite of piety. For to all powers there is one name that is common and one that is distinctive. A common name as king for the Parthians is Arsac, for the Romans it is Caesar, and thus for the Jews it is Christ.	(3) He is called Christ by virtue of a special rite of piety. For just as there are common names of kings, such as Arsaces among the Persians, Caesar among the Romans, and Pharaoh among the Egyptians, thus among the Jews the king is called by the common name of Christ.
(4) The reason that he might be called Christ is that he was the Son of God and became human. And because he was the first chief, his Father anointed him in the beginning with the oil	(4) But this is the reason for giving him the name Christ: though he was the Son of God, he came, became a human, and the one [who was] in the beginning became the beginning. In the beginning the Father	(4) Now this is the reason for this appellation: precisely because though he was the Son of God and the beginning of all, he became a human, him the Father first anointed with oil that had been taken from

that comes from the tree of life.

(5) Thus, in the same way, according to the

predestination of his Father for the righteous, when they have come there, just as they have traveled a difficult road because of their toil, thus also for their rest he too will anoint with the same oil those who are like him. Thus, they will shine forth as light, receive the Holy Spirit, and be immortal in life everlasting.

anointed him. Just as he was anointed from the tree of life,

(5) he himself will anoint from it with oil, according to the predestination of the Father, the pious similar to him when they have arrived there after having passed through difficult paths, according to the hardship of labors unto their rest.

Thus, shining as light and receiving the Holy Spirit, they will become immortal.

the tree of life. On the basis of that ointment, therefore, he is called Christ.

(5) Hence then even he, according to the

predestination of the Father, will anoint every one of the pious with similar oil for the refreshment from labor when they have attained to his kingdom as ones who have prevailed over a difficult road.

Thus both their light will shine and, filled with the Holy Spirit, they will be granted immortality.

Syriac

(6) "But I know that I told you about the nature of the tree of life at another time.

(1.46.1) Now, however, I should like to tell you also about its imitation.

(2) In this present age, the first high priest, Aaron, was anointed with fabricated anointing oil, which was in the likeness of the

Latin

(6) But I remember that I sufficiently explained to you the entire nature of this tree, from which that ointment was taken.

(1.46.1) "But now, too, I shall briefly recall you to remembrance of an example of all these things.

(2) In the present life when the first high priest Aaron was anointed with a chrism of a mixture made after the likeness of the

true oil.

He reigned over the people. Now, for this reason, as if he were a king, he received first-fruits and poll-tax similar to tribute and issued commands. As a judge of the things here below he was entrusted with the [task of] distinguishing between the things that are clean and the things that are unclean. He also was a prophet to Moses, as if to one greater than he, for his assistance was not of his own will. (3) Now, everyone who was anointed with the fabricated oil, as if he was made a partaker of the rule that is his [sc. Aaron's]--he, too, was deemed worthy of rulership, the office of prophet, or the high priesthood. (4) Now this gift of the device of the oil was temporal. Therefore, know how powerful that cherished and pure ointment is that is from God and that is about to be given, when he knew that also this [temporal] one that is from him would give the gift of temporal rule. (5) For what is there in the present world that is greater than the expectation of the office of prophet, high priesthood, or kingship?"

(1.47.1) I, Clement, answered him, "I recall that you, Peter, told me concerning the first man who

spiritual ointment that we mentioned above, he became the leader of the people and as a king he accepted first-fruits and tribute individually from the people.

Also, having accepted the lot of judging the people he adjudicated with regard to clean and unclean things.

(3) Now also if someone else was anointed with that oil, in the same way having received power from it he became either a king, a prophet, or a high priest.

(4) If this temporal grace composed by humans was this powerful, then understand how great that ointment is that was taken by God from the tree of life,

for the one that was made by humans confers such exceptional dignities among humans. (5) For what in the present age is more glorious than a prophet, more celebrated than a high priest, more sublime than a king?"

(1.47.1) I responded to these things, "I recall, Peter, that you said regarding the first human came into being that he was a prophet. But you did not tell me that he was anointed. (2) Now, if no one is a prophet without the unction, how was the first man a prophet though he was not anointed?"

(3) Peter laughed and answered me, "If the first man prophesied, it is also clear that he was anointed. Therefore, because the high priest who recorded the law was silent about his [sc. the first man's] anointing, this matter is revealed to us. (4) For example, if he had shown that he was anointed, then we would know that the one who was anointed is a prophet because of the unction, even if it were not so written. Because he showed that he was a prophet, it is clear to us that he was also anointed. For without the unction, he would not have been a prophet. (5) Now, it would have been appropriate for you to say, 'If the unction was fabricated by Aaron through a craft involving spices, how was the first man anointed with the craftsman's ointment

when the crafts did not exist?'"

(6) I answered him, "Do not turn me aside, Peter, for I am not

that he was a prophet, but you did not say that he was anointed. (2) Therefore, if no one is a prophet without the ointment, how was the first human a prophet, though he was not anointed?"

(3) Smiling, Peter responded, "If the first human prophesied, it is certain that he was anointed. For it is clear that the one who recorded the law in pages was silent about his anointing, yet he evidently left it for us to understand these things. (4) For just as if he had said that he had been anointed, then there could have been no doubt that he was also a prophet, even if it had not been written in the law, thus, since it is certain that he was a prophet, it is similarly certain that he was also anointed, because he would have not been able to prophesy without the anointing. (5) Yet it was more proper for you to have said, 'If the chrism was compounded with the science of perfumers by Aaron, how was the first human able to have been anointed with ointment from a developed science, when the sciences had not yet been discovered?'"

(6) And I responded, "Do not lead me astray, Peter, for I am not

talking about that temporal, fabricated ointment but about the pure uncompounded [ointment] that is eternal and with God and in the likeness of which, you say, this [ointment] was fabricated."

(1.48.1) Peter was angry, I think, and he said, "Why are you, Clement, supposing that everyone is able to know everything ahead of time? (2) But now, in order that we not abandon the issue that lies before us, I shall speak to you also about this plainly at another time when you have more experience. (3) But the high priest was anointed with the fabricated ointment and was esteemed worthy of the office of prophet. He kindled the altar fire, raised up fire, and showed it to the whole world. (4) Now after Aaron the high priest, the one who sprang forth from water also arose. I am speaking not about Moses, but rather about the one who was called the Son, Christ, through baptism. (5) He was also called Jesus. He extinguished the altar that was burning there for sins, (6) for when he appeared, the unction of the high priesthood, prophecy, and kingship ceased.

talking about the composite ointment and the temporal oil but about the one that is simple and eternal that you taught to have been made by God and in the image of which you say this one was compounded by humans."

(1.48.1) Peter responded seemingly indignant at these things, "Do you suppose that we are all able to know everything ahead of time? (2) But that we not now draw back from the proposed issue, we will clearly explain to you other matters in this regard when your progress becomes more apparent. (3) Now when the high priest or the prophet had been anointed with the composite oil and lit the altar of God, he was renowned in the entire world.
(4) But after Aaron, who was high priest, another is enlisted from the water. I am speaking not of Moses but of the one who was called Son by God in the baptismal water.
(5) For Jesus is the one who by the grace of baptism extinguished the fire that the high priest had lit for sins. (6) For when he appeared, the chrism ceased through which the office of high priest, prophet, or king was conferred.

(1.49.1) "Now his public coming was previously announced by the prophet Moses, who recorded the law of God for humans, and also by another before him, just as I told you at another time, (2) who predicted that he would come in his first humble advent and also in his second glorious advent. This is what he brought to pass. (3) For he completed the first advent when he came and taught and when the judge himself was condemned and put to death. (4) But in the second advent he will come to judge and condemn the wicked and to cause the righteous to rejoice.

(5) Now his second advent is believed on the basis of the first, for the same prophets who spoke about him with respect to the first one also spoke with respect to the second. Now, the two prophets are Jacob and Moses. (6) Now, the greatness of prophecy is that it was not prophesied in a fitting manner and according to the order that those should love him who were prepared to do so, lest someone might think that it was a likely occurrence and that prophecy does not exist.

(1.50.1) "What I am saying is that when Christ came, it was

(1.49.1) "So Moses, who transmitted the law to humans, foretold him to be coming, as also did another one before him, just as I also related to you previously.

(2) This one indicated that he would come humble in the first appearance, but glorious in the second.

(3) The first was already completed when he came and taught and was judged, though the judge of all, and killed.

(4) But in the second coming he will come to judge. He will condemn the impious, but he will receive the pious into the fellowship of the kingdom and into partnership. (5) Belief in his second coming is based on his first. For the prophets, particularly Jacob and Moses, spoke of the first, yet a few also of the second.

(6) But the greatness of prophecy is particularly borne out in that they said nothing about the future that accorded with the logical order of things.

Otherwise they might seem to be only wise men who determined what the logical order of things had indicated.

(1.50.1) "Now what I am saying is that it was logical for Christ

fitting and right for the Jews to believe him, for it was delivered to them to await him for redemption, just as the fathers, who knew everything well, delivered to them. It was not fitting for those who were from the peoples in error, who had heard neither of his name nor of his coming.

(2) But the prophet revealed beforehand incredible things, and he proclaimed what came to pass and said, 'He will be a hope for the nations.' That is, the nations will hope in him and not the Jews who received and heard, (3) which thing thus happened. For when he came, those who were awaiting him on the basis of tradition did not recognize him, but those who had not previously heard a single thing recognized him when he came, and because he has gone, they are expecting him. (4) Thus all these things of the prophecy that was not believed were exactly fulfilled, and he became the hope of the nations. (5) Therefore, the Jews erred with respect to the first coming of our Lord, and the strife that they have with us concerns Jesus alone. (6) For that the Christ is coming they also know, for they are awaiting him. But

to be accepted by the Jews to whom he came and to be believed as the one who was expected according to the tradition of the fathers for the salvation of the people but for the gentiles, to whom nothing about him had been promised or announced but rather to whom he had not ever become known even by name, to be hostile to him. (2) Yet the prophets said contrary to order and the logic of things that he would be the hope of the gentiles and not of the Jews.

(3) Accordingly, then, it also happened. For when he came he was not at all recognized by those who seemed to await him on the basis of the tradition of the ancestors. But those who had not heard anything whatsoever about him both believe that he has come and watch for him coming in the future. (4) Thus in all these matters that prophecy has proved faithful that said that he would be a hope of the nations. (5) Therefore the Jews have erred about the first coming of the Lord. Between them and us there is discord about this matter alone. (6) For even they know and expect that Christ is coming. But they do not know

they have not recognized that he who was called Jesus came in humiliation. (7) Thus it especially certifies and verifies that he is the one when they all do not believe in him. Our quarrel with them is this: whether this one who is coming and has come or another who has not yet come is the one prophet, just as I delivered to you at another time in the discussion about prophecy.

(1.51.1) "Now, God appointed him at the end of the world, for it was not possible for the evils of humans to be purified and expiated through anyone else and for this creation to be saved and to live. But I am speaking about the ways that are in the freedom of mind that is master of itself, while these [ways] were being preserved (2) --in order that he might reign with the righteous to whom he will come and those who, because they pleased him in secret, were translated in order to remain alive, when the heavenly Jerusalem has received the righteous, whose light is brighter than the light of the sun. (3) And then justice will be done to those who have done evil just as they deserve. Just as they considered a small matter even the life that had been given to them, they also

that he has already come in humility, namely, the one called Jesus. (7) And his coming is especially confirmed in the fact that not all believe in him.

(1.51.1) "God then appointed him near the end of the world, for it was impossible for the evils of mortals to be purged by anyone else, at least if the created nature of the human race was to remain intact, that is, with the freedom of the will unharmed.

(2) While this condition was preserved intact, he came to invite to the kingdom every just person and those devoted to pleasing him, for whom he had prepared unspeakable good things and the heavenly city Jerusalem, which will shine greater than the brightness of the sun in the habitation of the holy. (3) But the unjust and impious and those who have disregarded God

and have changed the life given

transformed [it] to evil, and they did not refrain from making the doing of justice into an occasion for evil. (4) It is not possible for the other things that will be there to be explained, neither for the angels nor for humans, but only that they know that God will be seated before the good because of good deeds and for boundless eternity he will please those who have kept and done the law."

(1.52.1) And as he said these things, I said to him, "If the righteous ones whom he finds will participate and delight in the kingdom of Christ, then those who have died beforehand have missed out on his kingdom."

(2) Peter answered and said, "You want me to reveal one of the hidden matters, Clement. Now, it is not irksome for me to tell you, as far as I am permitted to reveal. (3) From the beginning Christ has been in all generations, and he was secretly with those who wanted to be in the fear of God and who were awaiting him as one who was far off.

(4) For the advantage of those in

them to various shameful acts and the time for just action to an exercise of evil he will hand over to suitable retribution merited by them. (4) It is not, however, allowed for either angels or humans to disclose and reveal the other things that will be effected then. Yet it is alone sufficient for us to know that God will award the good with the eternal possession of good things."

(1.52.1) After these things had been said by him, I responded, "If the ones whom he finds just at his coming will enjoy Christ's kingdom, then will those who have died before his coming be completely deprived of the kingdom?"

(2) Thereupon Peter said, "Clement, you are forcing me to reveal parts of the ineffable. Yet it is not irksome to do as far as is allowed to be revealed.
(3) Christ, who was from the beginning and always, was always with the pious through the various generations, though secretly, and especially with those by whom he was awaited and to whom he had frequently appeared. (4) But it was not the time for there to be a resurrection of the dissolved bodies. Rather, the reward considered worthy by

whose time he appears is that they will rise not when their body has been dissolved but rather they will remain just as they are, if they be found righteous.

(5) For all those, whenever they have pleased him--as in the example of the first man who, because he had pleased him, was translated--similarly are in paradise and are being preserved for the kingdom of the good one. But as concerns those who have not fulfilled the measure of their righteousness, as with the remainder of the evil things that was in their bodies, their bodies will be dissolved and their souls will be preserved in a good place in honor. Thus, in the resurrection of the dead their souls will put on their body that was purified in its dissolution, and because of the effect of their good deeds they will inherit eternal life.

(6) For this reason, blessed are those who attain and receive the kingdom of Christ, who will also escape the punishment of hell, be delivered, and remain incorruptible, just as they have ardently desired to escape from the fearfulness of judgment.

God was that the person who was found righteous should remain longer in the body or in any event, as is clearly related in the writings of the law concerning a certain righteous person, that God translated him.

(5) For in a similar manner the rest were treated who fulfilled his will, so that being translated unto paradise they would be preserved for the kingdom.

As to those who were not able completely to meet the norm of justice but had certain remnants of evil in their flesh, while their bodies were dissolved their souls were kept in good and pleasurable regions.

Thus, in the resurrection of the dead, when they will receive their same bodies freed from impurities through the dissolution, they will take possession of an eternal inheritance as a reward for the things they did well. (6) For that reason, blessed are all who will have attained the kingdom of Christ, for they not only will escape the punishments of hell but also will remain incorruptible,

Again, they will be the first to see the Father, and they will be placed among the first who are before God.

(1.53.1) "Hence because there was not a little debate about Christ, those from the Jews who did not believe were excessively gnashing their teeth over us, as they were undecided, lest the one against whom they had previously sinned and offended truly be [the Christ]. (2) And again, fear was growing in them and becoming great, for as soon as he was nailed to the cross, everything suffered with him, and again because though his body was guarded, it was not found. And many were continually coming to the faith of the word concerning him. (3) Therefore, various ones who had not believed, with Caiaphas their priest, were troubled so that they were coming for a discussion about the one who suffered.

(4) "Because of this, as I said before, they sent to us many times and besought us in order that they might either learn or teach as to whether Jesus is the Christ. We drew up a plan to go to the temple, to testify concerning Christ before the entire people, and simultaneously also

will see God the Father first, and will achieve among the first the order of honor with God.

(1.53.1) "Because of this there is not a little debate about Christ, and all the unbelievers of the Jews are stirred up against us with immense rage, fearing lest he should be he, against whom they sinned. (2) The fear grows greater because they know that the moment they nailed him to the cross the whole world suffered with him, that his body could nowhere be found, though it had been kept by them under diligent custody, and that innumerable multitudes are coming to the faith of his name. (3) Hence, together with Caiaphas the high priest, they were also compelled often to send to us so that the truth of his name might be investigated.

(4) And since they were frequently requesting that they might either learn or teach regarding whether Jesus is the Christ, it seemed to us right to go up to the temple and to testify publicly about him before the entire people and simultaneously to criticize the Jews with regard to the many

to put many of them to shame with regard to the great crime. (5) For the people were divided into many beliefs that began in the days of John the Baptist.

(1.54.1) "For as Christ was ready to be revealed for the abolition of sacrifices and in order to reveal and show forth baptism, the slanderer who was opposed recognized from predestination the point in time and created sects and divisions, so that if the former sin should receive renunciation and correction, a second vice would be able to obstruct redemption.

(2) "The first of these then are the ones called Sadducees, who arose in the days of John when they separated from the people as righteous ones and renounced the resurrection of the dead. They put forward their unbelieving doctrine speciously when they said, namely, 'It is not right to worship and fear God in prospect of a reward for goodness.'
(3) In this doctrine, as I have said, Dositheus began and, after Dositheus, Simon, who also started to create differences of opinions as he wished in the likeness of the former.

(4) "Others again are called

things that are absurdly practiced by them. (5) For indeed the people were being divided into many parties having started from John the Baptist.

(1.54.1) "For when the coming of Christ was near, on the one hand to check sacrifices and on the other hand to impart the favor of baptism, the enemy understood from what had been predicted that the time was at hand and effected various schisms among the people so that, if the previous sin might possibly be abolished, the following offence would not be able to be corrected.

(2) The first was the schism of those who were called Sadducees, starting practically in the times of John. These began to separate themselves from the assembly of the people as more righteous than the others; they denied the resurrection of the dead and asserted this by an argument of unbelief saying that it is not appropriate for God to be worshipped as if for promised pay. (3) The initiator of this opinion was first Dositheus and, second, Simon.

(4) Another is the schism of the

Samaritans. They also renounce the resurrection of the dead and adore Mount Gerizim instead of the holy city Jerusalem.

(5) Now they do correctly await the one prophet who is to come to erect and establish unknown things just as Moses predicted. These fell into schisms through the cunning of Dositheus, and they were thus brought to nought so that they should not be restored by Jesus.

(6) "But both the scribes and the Pharisees,

(7) who were baptized by John, were thus instructed that the word of truth is like the key to the kingdom of heaven, which they received from Moses in order to hide it.

(8) "Now the pure disciples of John separated themselves greatly from the people and spoke to their teacher as if he was concealed [or: said that their teacher was, as it were, concealed]. (9) Hence, owing to all these schisms that had arisen among the people, the baptism of Christ was hindered from being believed.

(1.55.1) "Since then the high priest with the rest of the priests had often bidden us either to teach or to learn the things regarding Jesus,

Samaritans. Now while they, too, deny the resurrection of the dead, they assert that God should be worshipped not in Jerusalem but at Mount Gerizim. (5) Though they do, however, properly await the one true prophet on the basis of Moses' predictions, they have been hindered by the wickedness of Dositheus from believing that the one they awaited is Jesus.

(6) Both the scribes and the Pharisees are drawn away into another schism. (7) They were baptized by John, and holding on to the word of truth received from Moses' tradition as being the key to the kingdom of heaven, they hid it from the ears of the people. (8) Some of the disciples of John who imagined they were great separated themselves from the people and proclaimed their master as the Christ.

(9) Now all these schisms were arranged beforehand so that both the faith of Christ and baptism might be hindered by them.

(1.55.1) "Nevertheless, as we began to say, since the high priest, through the priests, was often asking us that we might hold a discussion with each other our whole company went up to the temple at the counsel of the whole church, (2) and we stood on the stairs with our whole company of believers. When everyone was silent, when there was great stillness, the high priest first began to soothe the people as if he was humbly willing, in love for truth, to inquire, while he was selecting them as witnesses and judges in order that the disputation that was prepared might take place.

(3) "Nevertheless, he wanted very much to praise them for they seemed to be speaking in favor of forgiveness of sins. He found fault, however, in our baptism, which was given by Jesus.

(4) "He spoke about this, and Matthew refuted him: 'One who is not baptized

not only is rejected from the kingdom of heaven but also is in danger at the resurrection of the dead and, even though he is good in his manner of life and righteous in his mind, will fall short of eternal life.' Now he spoke these things as if at ease, testified to related matters, and then was silent.

(1.56.1) "Then, the Sadducees,

about Jesus, when it seemed appropriate and pleased the entire church, we went up to the temple. (2) When we were standing on the stairs together with our faithful brethren and when absolute silence of the people had been achieved, first the high priest began to exhort the people that they should listen patiently and peacefully and that they should also be witnesses and judges of the things that were to be spoken.

(3) Then, exalting with many praises the rite of sacrifices that had been divinely granted to the human race for the remission of sins, he objected to the baptism of our Jesus as having been recently introduced against these. (4) But Matthew countered his declarations and clearly showed that if someone does not acquire the baptism of Jesus he not only will be deprived of the kingdom of heavens but also will not be without danger in the resurrection of the dead even though he be protected with the prerogative of a good life and a right mind.

Having pursued these and similar things Matthew was silent.

(1.56.1) "But the party of the

who do not believe in the resurrection of the dead, became furious when they heard. One of them cried out from the middle of the assembly and said, 'It is an error for us to believe that the dead will ever rise.'

(2) "Andrew, my brother, spoke against him and explained, 'It is not the case that it is an error for us to believe that the dead will rise,

for the prophet who was foretold by Moses as coming, who is Jesus, already demonstrated for this reason that the dead will rise. (3) But if it is not believed that this one is the prophet who was foretold by Moses to be coming, it is meet for us to inquire first whether this one be he. But when we have recognized that he is, it is proper for us to learn readily about everything in his teaching.' Now he spoke these things, testified to related matters, and then was silent.

(1.57.1) "But a Samaritan, who was devising and plotting what is opposed to the people and to God, said, 'The dead do not rise, and instead of the holy place that is in Jerusalem, Mount Gerizim is the house of worship.' As an adversary of Jesus, he said that he [sc. Jesus] was not the

Sadducees, which denies that there is a resurrection of the dead, was aggrieved so that one of them exclaimed from the midst of the people saying that those who believe that the dead will ever rise err greatly.

(2) My brother Andrew responded against this person and taught that it is not an error but rather a most certain belief that the dead will rise, according to what the one taught whom Moses predicted as the prophet to come.

(3) But if it should not seem to them that he is the one whom Moses predicted, "This matter," he said, "should first be inquired into so that when it has clearly been demonstrated that he is the one there may be no further argument about the things he taught." Having proclaimed these things and many things similar to them, Andrew was silent.

(1.57.1) "But a certain Samaritan, saying things detrimental to the people and God and asserting that neither will the dead rise and nor should the cult of God in Jerusalem be maintained but rather that Mount Gerizim should be venerated, added against us even [the claim] that our Jesus is prophet to come who was previously proclaimed by Moses.

(2) "James and John, the sons of Zebedee, spoke wisely against this one and one who assisted him.
(3) Now because they had received a command that they should not enter into their city, they devised a way by which they would neither speak with these with whom they refused to speak nor be silent, appear to have been conquered, and [thus] damage the good faith of the many. Wisely then they spoke with them by means of silence.
(4) For since it was dear to them to believe that the dead will rise and for the holy place, Jerusalem, to be honored, James found fault with those who were thinking wickedly, those who did not believe that the dead will rise. His brother declared that they were being offensive in a matter that was too grievous for him. 'For they praise Mount Gerizim and dishonor the holy place, Jerusalem.' He alleged immediately after this that if they had recognized Jesus, they would also, on the basis of his teaching, have consequently believed in the resurrection of the dead and would have honored the place,

not the one whom Moses predicted to be the coming prophet.
(2) The sons of Zebedee, James and John, vigorously resisted him and another person who pursued with him the same points. (3) Even though they were under a command not to enter their cities nor to convey to them the word of proclamation, nevertheless lest their speech

injure the faith of others if it was not refuted they responded so wisely and energetically that they put them to silence forever.
(4) For James argued with the favor of the entire people concerning the resurrection of the dead,

and John showed that if they would give up the error of Mount Gerizim they would consequently acknowledge that Jesus is the one who was expected to come according to Moses' prophecy,

Jerusalem. (5) Because of this, he said, 'It is pressing above all things for one to know if this one who performed signs and wonders as did Moses is the one who was foretold by Moses as the prophet to come.' Now they spoke these things, witnessed to related matters, and then were silent.

(1.58.1) "Then one of the scribes called out from the middle of the crowd and said, 'Your Jesus performed signs and wonders as a magician and not as a prophet.'

(2) "Philip spoke against him and said, 'By this statement you are also accusing Moses,

(3) for he performed signs and wonders in Egypt in the manner that Jesus performed them here.' He said these things so that he might understand that what he said against Jesus might also be said against Moses. Now he spoke these things, witnessed to related matters, and then was silent.

(1.59.1) "Then one of the Pharisees, as he heard these things, found fault with Philip when he said that Jesus was equal to Moses.

(2) "Bartholomew spoke against

(5) because as Moses performed signs and prodigies so did Jesus, and there is no doubt that the similarity of the signs testifies that he is the one of whom he [sc. Moses] said that he would come like himself. When they had borne witness to these matters and many others similar to them, they were silent.

(1.58.1) "And behold one of the scribes cried out from the middle of the people and said, 'The signs and wonders that your Jesus did--he did [them] as a magician and not as a prophet.'

(2) Philip strongly countered him by showing that by this reasoning he would be accusing even Moses.

(3) For since Moses performed signs and wonders in Egypt, while Jesus [performed] similar ones in Judaea, it cannot be doubted that what is said of Jesus is apparently also said of Moses. After Philip had borne witness to these matters and many similar ones, he was silent.

(1.59.1) "But when a certain Pharisee heard these things, he found fault with Philip because he would say that Moses is equal to Jesus.

(2) In response to him Bartholomew

him and declared, 'The fact is that we assert not that he is equal to Moses but rather that he is greater than Moses. (3) For what Moses was, a prophet, Jesus is, too; but what Jesus is, the Christ, Moses is not. Thus, what Moses is, Jesus is, too; but what Jesus is, Moses was not.' Now he spoke these things, witnessed to related matters, and then was silent.

(4) "After him, James the son of Alphaeus spoke and instructed, 'One should not believe in Jesus depending on whether the previous prophets spoke concerning him, but rather [one should believe] that the prophets are prophets depending on whether the one who is the Christ witnesses concerning them.

(6) For it is not right for one to receive faith in the greater and more excellent one through the witness of lesser ones. Rather, through the witness of the greater and more excellent one, one will know the lesser ones.' Now he spoke these things, also witnessed to related matters, and then was silent.

(7) "After him, Lebbaeus found

resolutely taught that we do not say that Jesus is equal to Moses, but rather greater. (3) For Moses was indeed a prophet, as Jesus was, too. But what Jesus was, namely, the Christ, Moses was not. Therefore the one who is both a prophet and the Christ is doubtless greater than the one who is only a prophet. When he had borne witness to these and many similar matters, he was silent.

(4) After him, James of Alphaeus addressed the people to show that one should not believe Jesus because the prophets spoke previously about him, but rather one should believe that the prophets are truly prophets because Christ gives testimony to them.

(5) To be sure, the presence and coming of Christ show that they were truly prophets. (6) For it was proper for testimony of faith to be given not by the inferior to the superior but rather by the superior to the inferior. Having pursued these matters and many similar to them, James, too, was silent.

(7) After him, Lebbaeus began

fault with the people in many ways, for they had not believed in Jesus who had helped them in every way through his exhortation, his healing, and his consolatory discourses. Moreover, they killed him and hated the very one who in every way had been their helper and their benefactor. Now he spoke these things, witnessed to related matters, and then was silent.

(1.60.1) "One of the disciples of John approached and boasted regarding John, 'He is the Christ, and not Jesus, just as Jesus himself spoke concerning him, namely, that he is greater than any prophet who had ever been. (2) If he is thus greater than Moses, it is clear that he is also greater than Jesus for Jesus arose just as did Moses. Therefore, it is right that John, who is greater than these, is the Christ.'

(3) "Simon the Canaanite argued against this one, 'John was greater than the prophets who were begotten of women but not greater than the Son of Man.

(4) Hence, Jesus, in addition, is the Christ, while he was only a prophet. The matters of Jesus are as far removed when

strongly to convict the people for why they would not believe Jesus, who had been so helpful to them by teaching the matters of God, by comforting the afflicted, by healing the sick, and by consoling the poor, but rather, for all these good things, they had paid him back with hate and death. When he had witnessed to the people regarding these matters and many similar to them, he was silent.

(1.60.1) "And behold, one of John's disciples asserted that John was Christ, and not Jesus. 'This is so much the case,' he said, 'that even Jesus himself proclaimed that John is greater than all humans and prophets. (2) If therefore,' he said, 'he is greater than all, he should doubtless be considered greater than both Moses and Jesus himself. Now if he is greater than all, he is Christ.'

(3) "Responding to these things, Simon the Canaanite asserted that while John was greater than all the prophets and all who are sons of women, he is not however greater than the Son of Man. (4) Therefore, Jesus is also the Christ, while John is only a prophet. The difference between him and Jesus is as large as that

compared with the matters of John as is the one who is sent out and proceeds ahead from the one who sends him to run out before him and as is the one who performs the service of the law from the one who institutes the law.' Now he spoke these things, witnessed to related matters, and then was silent.

(5) "After this one, Barabbas, who had become an apostle in the stead of Judas the traitor, exhorted the people not to hate and dishonor Jesus, (6) 'For it is better for the one who does not know Jesus to be the Christ not to hate him, since God has appointed a reward for love and not for hate.

(7) Further, since he took a body from the Jews and became a Jew, the destruction that God will bring on the one who hates him will not be a small one.' Now he spoke these things, witnessed to related matters, and then was silent.

(1.61.1) "Now after the advice of Barabbas, Caiaphas found fault with Jesus' teaching for this reason: 'He spoke vacant things when he came, (2) for he called the poor blessed and promised earthly rewards so that they, the

between the precursor and the one who is forerun and between the lawgiver and the one who serves the law.'

Having pursued these and similar matters, the Canaanite, too, was silent.

(5) "After him, Barnabas, also called Mathias, who was elected apostle in the place of Judas, began to warn the people not to hate Jesus or blaspheme him. (6) 'For it is much more proper even for the one who does not know Jesus or is in doubt about him to love him rather than to hate [him], for God has established a reward for love, but a punishment for hate. (7) 'For,' he said, 'why has not the fact that he took a Jewish body and was born among the Jews produced incentives for all of you to love him?' When he had said these and similar things, he stopped talking.

(1.61.1) "Then Caiaphas tried to find fault with Jesus' teaching by saying that he spoke vain things.
(2) 'He said the poor were blessed; he promised that there would be earthly rewards; he

virtuous, would inherit the earth

and would be filled with foods and drink and things similar to these.'

(3) "Thomas spoke against him and showed that he was unjustly furious over Jesus. He pointed out that the previous prophets, whom he had believed, themselves said similar things, but they did not explain how it will happen that humans will receive these things, while he also showed and revealed how they will receive them. Now he said this, testified to similar matters, and then was silent.

(1.62.1) "After him, Caiaphas gave heed to me, sometimes as if exhorting me and sometimes as if finding fault with me. He said, 'Be silent and do not proclaim about Jesus that he is the Christ, for you are bringing destruction on yourself since you have gone astray after him and are leading others astray.' (2) Again, he found fault with me as with someone rash, 'For while you were untaught and a fisher by trade you became a teacher by chance.'

(3) "Now when he said these things and things similar to these,

placed the highest reward in earthly inheritance; and he promised that those who observed righteousness would be filled with food and drink. He is caught teaching many such things.'

(3) "Thomas argued in response to him that he was objecting without avail. He pointed out that the prophets, whom even he believed, taught more of these things, though they did not show how these things would be or how they would be acquired. Jesus, however, had shown how these things should be received. When he had said these things and many similar ones, Thomas too was silent.

(1.62.1) "Then, Caiaphas again looked at me, in one moment as if warning and in another as if accusing, and said that I should henceforth cease from the proclamation of Christ Jesus, lest I do this to my destruction and, myself deceived in error, also lead others astray through my error.

(2) Then he further accused me of audacity because though I was an unlearned fisher and a boor, I was so bold as to assume the office of a teacher.

(3) "When he had said these things and many others similar to

I, too, spoke to him words similar to these: 'It is a small danger for me if, as you say, this one is not the Christ, for I have received him as a teacher of the law. But the danger for you is great and not small if, namely, he should be the Christ, what he in truth is. (4) For I believed in the one who appeared and was revealed, but you are professing that you are preserving your faith for another who is unknown. (5) Now if it is as you say, that I am simple, ignorant, and a fisher, and I am professing to know more than the wise elders,' I said to him, 'then this is what should especially frighten you. (6) If we had passed through instruction and had refuted you, the wise, then this would be a result of time and diligence that would be attributed to nature and not to the power of God.

(7) But because we are unlearned men and are overcoming you, the wise, in our refutation, who is there who possesses a mind to whom it is not clear that our concern is not human in origin but rather that this is the will of God, for whom all things are possible?' Now I said these and related matters to him.

them, I, too, responded with these words, 'For me it is less of a danger if, as he said, this person is not the Christ, because I would have received a teacher of the law. But for him it is a great danger if this person is the Christ, as indeed he certainly is. (4) For I believe the one who appeared. But for which other person, who has not at all appeared, does he believe to reserve his faith? (5) Now if even as a simpleton, as you say, an ignoramus, a fisher, and a boor I understand more than the wise elders, this,' I said, 'should cause you greater fear.

(6) For if arguing on the basis of some erudition I should conquer you, the wise and learned, then this would certainly seem to have come to me through training over an extended period and not through the favor of divine power. (7) But now, as I said, when we the ignorant overcome and surpass you, the wise, to whom with a faculty of understanding is it not apparent that this is the work not of human sophistry but rather of the divine will and favor?'

(1.63.1) "As we thus pursued

(1.63.1) "Thus we the ignorant and fishers testified against the priests concerning God who alone is in the heavens; against the Sadducees concerning the resurrection of the dead; in truth against the Samaritans concerning Jerusalem, though we did not enter into their city but rather spoke publicly outside; against the scribes and the Pharisees concerning the kingdom of heavens; against the disciples of John in order that they not be tripped up by him. Against all we said that Jesus is the eternal Christ.

(2) "Finally I counseled them that before we should go to the nations to preach the knowledge of the God who is above all, they should reconcile their people to God by receiving Jesus. (3) I said to them, 'For thus, when you have known Jesus, you will be able to receive the holy spirit, which is truth, through baptism of the name of the glorious Trinity.

(4) You will make confession, you will believe only in God regarding the things that he has taught, and thus you will receive redemption and eternal life. Otherwise this is not possible, even if you should

these and other matters in this strain, we the ignorant and fishers appropriately taught and bore witness to the priests concerning the one sole God of heaven; the Sadducees concerning the resurrection of the dead; the Samaritans concerning the sanctity of Jerusalem, though we did not enter their city but rather disputed publicly; the scribes and the Pharisees regarding the kingdom of heaven; the disciples of John, lest they stumble over John; and the whole people that Jesus is the eternal Christ.

(2) At the end I warned them that before we should go to the nations to preach to them the knowledge of God the Father, they should be reconciled to God by accepting his Son. (3) For I demonstrated that otherwise it is not at all possible for them to be saved, unless by the favor of the Holy Spirit they should hasten to be washed in the baptism of the trine invocation and should receive the eucharist of Christ the Lord. (4) Him alone they should believe in regard to what he taught so that they might have the right to obtain eternal salvation. Else, it is entirely impossible for them to be reconciled with

offer myriads of sacrifices.

(1.64.1) For we know that he [sc. God] is even more angered about your sacrificing after the end of the time for sacrifices.

(2) Precisely because of this the temple will be destroyed, and they will erect the abomination of desolation in the holy place. Then, the gospel will be made known to the nations as a witness for the healing of the schisms that have arisen so that also your separation will occur. (3) For throughout the ages the whole world was infested by an evil will either openly or obscurely. Nevertheless, the doctor was there for it as often as he was summoned for a visitation for its recovery. (4) Lo, we have witnessed to every one of you regarding the thing that is deficient in you. It is now yours to examine this matter that is beneficial to you and to do it.'

(1.65.1) "When I said these things, the whole assembly of

God, even if they should kindle for him a thousand altars and a thousand places for burnt offerings.

(1.64.1) "'For we ascertain as certain,' I said, 'that God is even more irritated with regard to the sacrifices you are offering, because at any rate the time of sacrifices has already expired. (2) And since you do not want to recognize that the time of offering sacrificial victims has already come to an end, for this reason even the temple will be destroyed and the abomination of desolation will be set up in the holy place. Then the gospel will be proclaimed to the nations as a testimony of you, so that your unbelief might be judged on the basis of their belief.

(3) For the entire world suffers at various times various diseases of evil, either all generally or else each one individually. Therefore, it needs a doctor to visit it for deliverance. (4) We, therefore, witness to you, and we announce what escaped each one of you. It is up to you to consider what is expedient for you.'

(1.65.1) "When I had said these things, the whole multitude

priests wailed out over the fact that I publicly spoke about the destruction of the temple. (2) But Gamaliel, who was the head of the nation and who was, because it was advantageous, secretly our brother in the matter regarding faith, perceived that they were intensely gnashing their teeth in the great anger towards us with which they were filled. He said these things: (3) 'Cease and keep your peace, O people, the children of Israel, for we do not know the nature of this trial that has come upon us. Therefore, leave these men alone, for if this matter is of human origin, it will come to nought, but if it is of God, why then are you transgressing in vain, as you are not able to do a thing? For it befits the will of God to be continually victorious over all things. (4) Now, since this day is passing away,

I wish to speak with them here before you all tomorrow so that I may confute their word of error.'

(5) Now those who were gnashing their teeth and were filled with fury and hate kept silent, thinking that we would be shown to be in error before all of them tomorrow. Now he promised

of priests wailed because I had prophesied to them about the destruction of the temple. (2) But when Gamaliel the head of the people (who was secretly our brother in faith but who by our counsel was among them) perceived that they were vehemently raging and were affected with great fury against us, rising he said,
(3) 'Be quiet for a little while, O Israelite men, for you do not perceive the trial that impends upon us. Therefore, leave these men alone. And if what they do is of human contrivance, it will quickly come to an end, but if it is from God, why do you sin without reason and accomplish nothing? For who is able to outstrip the will of God?

(4) Now therefore because the day is already turning into evening, while you listen in this same place tomorrow, I myself will dispute with these so that I might publicly reveal and plainly confute every error.'
(5) When these things had been said, their fury was somewhat repressed, especially through hope, because they expected that on the next day we would be publicly censured for error. And

them this and dismissed the assembly in peace.

(1.66.1) "We came and related to James what had been said. As we spoke to him, we ate, and we all lodged with him

and were praying all night

that on the following day, in the coming discussion, our word of truth might prevail and be victorious.

(2) "On the next day, James the bishop also ascended to the temple with our entire congregation. There, too, we found a great gathering waiting for us.

(3) All of us took the places of the preceding day in order that we might be visible to the entire people because we were in high places. (4) When there was a great stillness, Gamaliel, who as I said previously was our brother who was hidden from them because it was advantageous (for they especially accepted the advice of those who were thus, as if fellows of their way of thinking-- thus, he kept himself in hiding so that when something was plotted against us we should be able to know the various things and to

so he dismissed the people with peace.

(1.66.1) "But as we came to our James, expounding everything that had been said and done, we stayed with him after the food had been eaten, while we were making supplications to the omnipotent God throughout the entire night that the discourse of the future disputation might reveal the indubitable truth of our faith.

(2) "Therefore, on the following day James the bishop, both with us and with the entire church, ascended to the temple, where we found a vast multitude awaiting us since the middle of the night.

(3) Therefore we stood in the places where we were earlier, so that standing fairly eminently we would be seen by the entire people. (4) And when the utmost silence had been achieved, Gamaliel, who as we said above was of our faith but through an arrangement remained among them so that if at any time they should attempt anything hostile or wicked against us he might either curb them prudently through apt advice or counsel us so that we might be able either to take care or to turn [it] aside--

repel them from us, and he might be able to change peacefully those who are opposed to us through persuasion with appropriate advice) (5) spoke first wisely as if he were our enemy. Through his argument he attempted to persuade the people to listen in the love of truth to the words being spoken. He looked towards James the bishop and began with his discourse as follows.

(1.67.1) "'I am Gamaliel, who is an elder and who is praised among the teachers as regards the truth. I am not ashamed to learn from the young and ignorant something that is agreeable and helpful to my life. For it is the mark of people of the mind that there is nothing for them more precious than their soul.'

(2) He then explained, 'Neither kings nor friends nor members of a race nor fathers nor anything else is more excellent than the truth. (3) So as to excite and entice us,' he said, 'if you know something, do not be reluctant to tell our people also, for they are your brothers in respect to the

(5) this one then, acting as if he were against us,

first of all looking toward the bishop James, spoke in this manner:

(1.67.1) 'If I, Gamaliel, consider it a reproach neither of my erudition nor of my old age to learn something from the young and the inexperienced, if something perhaps that pertains to benefit or salvation may be acquired (for he who lives rationally knows that there is nothing more precious than the soul), why is it not amiable to all and greatly desired by all that one should learn what one does not know, that one should teach what one has learned?

(2) For it is most certain that neither friendship nor proximity of descent nor sublimity of rule should be more precious to a human than truth. (3) And you, brothers, if you know something further, may it not be displeasing to offer it to the people of God, that is, your brothers, while the

fear of God. (4/5) Let us therefore commit ourselves, O brothers, in faith to the love of genuine
hearing

in order that God may complete,
by the means that he chooses,
what is lacking either in us or in
you. (6) But if perchance you are
afraid owing to the fear of the
guile of those among us who
have been indiscriminately preju-
diced and you do not wish to say
something which is helpful to us,
I openly take up your cause and
swear to you by the living God

that I shall not permit anyone to
lay hands on you. (7) As there
are for you these crowds that are
near and are standing as witnesses and mediators and as this oath
has been given to you as a
pledge, let each one of you say
without hesitation what he has
learned while we listen in the love
of truth.'

(1.68.1) "Now when Gamaliel
said these things, he did not

whole people listens willingly and
with all repose to what you say.
(4) For why should the people not
do this, since it sees even me
along with itself equally wishing
to learn from you, if perchance
God has revealed something further to you? (5) But if you are
lacking in anything, then may it
similarly not be displeasing for
you to be instructed by us in
order that God might therefore
complete either side, if something
is lacking.
(6) But if some fear should perhaps disturb you because of several of ours who have minds prej-
udiced against you, and fearing
their snare you do not dare to say
what you plainly think, I therefore
wish to free you from the occasion for this anxiety. I swear to
you by the omnipotent and eter-
nally living God that I will not
permit anyone to lay hands on
you. (7) Therefore, since you
have this whole people as a witness to this my oath and as you
have the covenant as a fitting
pledge of our obligation, let each
of you without any delay express
what he has learned. And let us,
brothers, listen attentively and in
silence."

(1.68.1) "As Gamaliel was
saying these things, he was not

please Caiaphas. Just as I was thinking, he had thought something in his mind about him, and he took it upon himself to ask and inquire. (2) Now the high priest quietly sought, as if he were ridiculing Gamaliel and James the archbishop, that they make an inquiry and debate on the basis of scripture concerning Christ so that he might know whether Jesus truly is the one who was anointed or not.

(3) "James said, 'First, let us inquire as to the place where it is proper for us suitably to inquire.'

(4) "After being pressed for a long time, as was appropriate, he was constrained and concluded that we should make inquiry from the law.

(1.69.1) "Then James spoke in his discourse also concerning those who were prophets. He showed that they received from the law everything that they had said and that they truly spoke things that are in agreement with it.

(2) Then he spoke also concerning the Books of Kingdoms with respect to how, when, and by whom they were written, and with respect to how it is proper

greatly pleasing Caiaphas. He seemed to be suspicious of him, and he began subtly to interject himself more in the discussions. (2) For smiling at what Gamaliel had said, the chief of priests requested from James the chief of the bishops that the discussion regarding Christ be made on the basis of no other source than the scriptures, 'so that we might know,' he said, 'whether Jesus himself is the Christ or not.'

(3) "Then James said, 'First of all, let us ask on which scriptures it is particularly appropriate for the discussion to be based.'

(4) "After much time and difficulty, he was overcome by reason itself and responded that it should be based on the law, and after that he added a mention also of the prophets.

(1.69.1) "Our James began to show him that even what the prophets say, they took from the law

and spoke in harmony with the law.

(2) He also discussed certain matters about the Books of Kings, how, when, and by whom they were written, and how one should use them.

for us to employ them. (3) Then he spoke again concerning the law and the matters in it, so that through his discourse he clarified and demonstrated how matters are. Finally, he spoke concerning Christ. He made innumerable great demonstrations from everywhere that Jesus is the Christ: 'In him all things were fulfilled through his humble coming. (4) For he has two comings. One is of humiliation, in which he has come. But the second, in which he is coming, is of glory, and he will reign over those who have believed in him so as to do everything that he commanded.'

(5) Then he instructed the people, demonstrating that unless one wash in the name of the glorious Trinity in the waters whose flow is living, just as the prophet of truth showed, there will be no forgiveness of sins for him and he will also not enter into the kingdom of God. He showed that all these things were the predestination of the unoriginated God in the hiddenness of his being. (6) After these things he said, 'Do not then think concerning us that we are saying that there are two unoriginated ones, or one that was divided, or that he became a

(3) When he had discussed the law very fully and by a most lucid exposition brought to light the specific matters relating to Christ,

he showed through very many proofs that Jesus is the Christ and that everything that had been predicted regarding his humble coming is fulfilled in him. (4) For he taught that two comings of him had been predicted, one of humility, which he had fulfilled, and another of glory, which is expected to be fulfilled when he will come to give the kingdom to those who believe in him and who obey everything he enjoined. (5) When he had plainly instructed the people concerning all these things, he added also that unless one has been baptized in water under the name of the trine beatitude, just as the true prophet taught, one can neither receive forgiveness of sins nor enter into the kingdoms of heavens. And he confirmed that this is the design of the ingenerate God.

(6) To these remarks he also added the following, 'Do not think that we say there are two ingenerate gods or that the one has been divided into two or, as

feminine vessel for himself, as the impious say, "[God is] androgynous."' (7) But he spoke also concerning the Son the matter of how, and from whom, and that it is not that he is without beginning, and that therefore the matter of when [he was begotten] is not said concerning him. However, he would declare in secret what it is. (8) He also spoke much concerning the Paraclete and baptism. In seven full days he persuaded all the people together with the high priest so that they should immediately make haste to proceed to baptism.

(1.70.1) "Then a certain man who was the enemy entered the temple near the altar with a few others. He cried out and said,

(2) 'What are you doing, O men, the children of Israel? How have you been carried off so quickly by wretched men who have strayed after a magician?'

(3) "He said things such as these, and he listened to counter-arguments, and, when he was overcome by James the bishop, he began to create a great commotion so that the matters that were rightly being said in calmness would neither be put to the

the impious say, that the one was made for himself masculine and feminine. (7) Rather, we say that the Son is the only begotten of God, not from another source, but ineffably born of him.

(8) We speak similarly also of the Paraclete.' When he had said a number of things also about baptism, he persuaded the whole people and the chief priest during seven succeeding days to hasten immediately to acquire baptism.

(1.70.1) "When the matter had reached the point that they should come and be baptized, a certain hostile person entered the temple with only a few others and began to shout and say, (2) 'What are you doing O Israelite men? Why are you so easily duped? Why are you led headlong by the most miserable persons who have been deceived by a magician?' (3) When he had said these things, listened to responses, and was overcome by James the bishop, he began to stir up the people and to instigate disturbances so that the populace would not be able to hear the things that were being said.

test nor be understood and be-lieved.

(4) For this purpose, he let forth an outcry over the foolishness and feebleness of the priests and reproached them.

(5) He said, 'Why are you delay-ing? Why are you not immediately seizing all those who are with him?'

(6) When he had said these things, he rose first, seized a firebrand from the altar, and began to smite with it. (7) Then, also the rest of the priests, when they saw him, followed his exam-ple. (8) Then, in the great flight that ensued, some fell upon others and others were smitten. There were not a few who died so that much blood poured forth from those who had been killed. Now the enemy threw James from the top of the stairs. Since he fell and was as if dead, he did not smite him a second time.

(1.71.1) "But when they saw that this had happened to James, they approached and took him. Now they were more numerous

(4) He thus began to stir up ev-erything with outcries, to under-mine what had been arranged with great labor, and simulta-neously to reproach the priests, to aggravate with both abuse and rebukes, and like a maniac to incite each person to murder, saying, (5) 'What are you doing? Why are you dallying? O slack and sluggish, why don't we seize all these [people] with our hands and tear them to shreds?' (6) When he had said these things, he grabbed a brand from the altar and first initiated the massacre. (7) When the others saw him, they, too, were carried away with similar madness. (8) There was a clamor of all, of the smiting as well as of the smitten. Very much blood was shed. A con-fused flight ensued. When in the meantime that hostile person had made his way to James, he pushed him from the highest flight of stairs. Since he believed him to be dead, he made no effort to mishandle him further.

(1.71.1) "But our people as-sembled to raise him up.

For they were both more than the

than the others, but out of fear of God, they endured to be killed rather than to kill. While they were much stronger than the others, they seemed to be less, owing to the fear of God.

(2) "When evening arrived, the priests closed the temple, and we came to James's house and prayed there.
Before the dawn, we went down to Jericho. We numbered about five thousand men.

(3) "After three days, one of the brothers came and told us what had happened since the time that we were in the temple. For the priests were asking him to be with them as a priest in all their reckonings. They did not know that he was a member of our faith. Then, he told us how the enemy, before the priests, promised Caiaphas the high priest that he would massacre all those who believe in Jesus. (4) He departed for Damascus to go as one carrying letters from them so that when he went there, the nonbelievers might help him and might destroy those who believe. He wanted to go there first because he thought that Peter had gone there.

(5) "Now after thirty days he came upon us there in Jericho.

others in number and greater in strength, but because of reverence for God they endured to be killed by the minority rather than to kill others.

(2) Now when evening came, the priests also closed the temple. We withdrew to James's house and spent the night there in prayer. Before light we went down to Jericho, approximately five thousand men.

(3) After three days one of the brethren came to us from Gamaliel, whom we mentioned above, and brought us secret messages:

that hostile person had received a commission from Caiaphas the high priest to persecute all who believed in Jesus, (4) and to go to Damascus with his letters so that even there, when he had gained the help of the nonbelievers, he might bring destruction on the believers; but he was hastening particularly to Damascus because he believed that Peter had fled there.

(5) After about thirty days he passed through Jericho on his

We buried two brothers in that place at night. Each year their graves are suddenly white.

(6) They quenched the fury of many because they knew that they are members of our faith and that they were worthy of divine remembrance."

way to Damascus, at which time we had gone out to the graves of two of the brethren which would be whitened of themselves each year. (6) By this miracle the anger of many against us has been suppressed, for they see that our people are held in remembrance with God."

IV

ISOLATION OF THE SOURCE MATERIAL

Preliminary Redaction Criticism and Delimitation of the Source

LOCATION IN R

As it is situated in R, R 1.27-71 is part of Peter's initial instruction of Clement: After having met Barnabas in Rome, Clement sails to Caesarea, where Barnabas introduces him to Peter (R 1.12). Peter then invites Clement to accompany him on his way to Rome (R 1.13). Clement next requests some basic instruction (R 1.14), which Peter supplies by relating of the true prophet (R 1.15.1-17.1). Clement then compiles this material in a book and sends it to James (R 1.17.2-3). As the discussion continues, Peter announces that he will dispute with Simon the next day and then retires for the night (R 1.19.2-3). The next morning, however, Zachaeus informs Peter that Simon has delayed the disputation for seven days. Zachaeus then offers suggestions on how they might fill the intervening time by rehearsing arguments (R 1.20). Though Clement is sad because of the delay, Peter states that

111

it is for the best and that he will thus be able to expound the faith to Clement according to the tradition of the true prophet from the beginning to the end and without distraction during the seven days (R 1.21). In particular, Peter plans to explain the things that were spoken plainly but were written so obscurely that when they are read "in the synagogue" they are impossible to understand without a teacher (R 1.21.8, as may be reconstructed from the Syriac, Latin, and Armenian). Peter then explains, evidently for six days, matters (of the chapters of the law that were in question)[1] from the creation of the world to the moment when Clement arrived in Caesarea (R 1.22.1). Peter promises to supplement this "brief" exposition later with detailed explanations of the various points, and he states his intention to summarize what he has said, since they still have this one day before the disputation with Simon (R 1.22.3-4). Clement then assures Peter that he has remembered well and begins to recount some of the points Peter had made, which elicits Peter's joy (R 1.22.6-26.1).

Clement's statements give the reader a glimpse of the things that Peter had discussed. In particular, there is mention of Peter's account of the "infinite age" (R 1.22.5), of "the definition" (R 1.23.2-3, 8, 24.1-2), and of "predestination"[2] (R 1.23.3). All of this material seems to have been part of the "plain and simple account" (R 1.25.9) of matters from the beginning of the world to the present day. It is a recapitulation of this brief account that is offered in chapters 27-44.3, 53.1-74.2.

The Syriac seems to have preserved the original text in the statement that this account presents the tradition as the prophet of truth entrusted it to his disciples (R 1.26.3, 5; compare R 1.21.7 in both versions, R 1.74.4, H 10.3.3, and its parallel in R 5.2.1). The purpose of this teaching is to lead one to knowledge of God and thus to conduct in accord with the will of God (R 1.26.3-4).

---

[1]Only the Latin has the words in parentheses. In view of R 1.21.8, which speaks of things written obscurely, these words are probably original. Rehm, "Entstehung," 162, n. 243, incorrectly stated that in R the entire discussion in R 1.21-74 occurs on the same day.

[2]See Rius-Camps, "Las Pseudoclementinas," 109 with n. 42, and compare R 1.24.4, 45.5, 54.1, 69.5, 3.52.5, where the same Syriac expression is found.

R'S REDACTION IN THE CONTEXT

The question may now be raised of whether redaction by R in this context can be isolated.

One section that immediately strikes the reader as strange and dislocated is R 1.20.4-11. Here, Zachaeus makes a quite lengthy suggestion as to how he thinks the group should fill the intervening seven days. At the end he asks for Peter's opinion of his proposal. Peter responds by bluntly telling Zachaeus to go and say to Simon to take as much time as he likes. This awkward section was attributed by Rehm to a Eunomian interpolator;[3] Strecker saw in R 1.20.3-11 the hand of R and assigned only R 1.20.6-11a to the Eunomian.[4] However, the arguments for the attribution of any of this material to a Eunomian interpolator are insufficient.[5] It thus seems most likely that R is responsible for the entire section.[6]

The notion of a delay of the disputation for *seven* days has been attributed by most scholars to R,[7] though others have claimed that R has preserved the more original view here.[8] A decision on this point is often determinative for the appraisal of the whole of chapters 22-26. Strecker wrote, "In R 1.22-26 the hand of the Recognitionist is

---

[3]Rehm, "Entstehung," 97.

[4]Strecker, *Das Judenchristentum in den Pseudoklementinen*, 40.

[5]Rehm himself essentially admitted this; he nevertheless cited the use of the word *immaculatum* in R 1.20.7 to support his case. Rehm suspected that the original Greek word was ἄφθαρτος, "a word much used by Eunomius" that reappears in R 3.11.6 (Rehm, "Entstehung," 97 with n. 70). The Syriac and Latin, however, concur in the rendering "faultless," not "incorruptible." In R 3.11.6 the usage is completely different (the adjective modifies the image of the unbegotten power).

[6]Rius-Camps, "Las Pseudoclementinas," 106, in contrast, attributes the material to B.

[7]So Uhlhorn, *Homilien und Recognitionen*, 317, Lehmann, *Die clementinischen Schriften*, 463-64, Langen, *Die Klemensromane*, 128, J. Quarry, "Notes, Chiefly Critical, on the Clementine Homilies and the Epistles Prefixed to Them," *Hermathena* 7 (1890): 261, Meyboom, *De Clemens-roman*, 2:54, and Strecker, *Das Judenchristentum in den Pseudoklementinen*, 40.

[8]Hilgenfeld, *Recognitionen und Homilien*, 47-52, and Rius-Camps, "Las Pseudo-clementinas," 107.

unmistakable."[9] Rius-Camps advocated, to the contrary, assignment of the entire section to B.[10] Neither view, however, is nuanced enough. Thus, on the one hand, Strecker himself admitted that some of the doctrines mentioned in this section belong to B and that R 1.25.4-6, with its parallel in H 2.12.3, reflects the original story;[11] on the other hand, Rius-Camps emphasized the parallels in B to the extent of neglecting the question of R's redaction.

Of the singular material in these chapters, the "definition" in R 1.24.1-2 is particularly striking. This definition corresponds with Zachaeus's request in that both deal with the primal evolution from the original monad. The Platonic emphasis that time came into being with the world and the statement that a Second Will came from the First Will point in an Arian direction and lead to the supposition that this definition should be attributed to R.[12] From this perspective one is now able to perceive an Arian concern in R 1.20.7-11, where Zachaeus suggests that the discussion should proceed from a consideration of the "first, faultless cause of all" (R 1.20.7).[13] The Arian proclivity of the redactor is particularly evident in R 1.69.5b-8a, especially as preserved in the Syriac. Rehm again attributed R 1.69.6-8a to his Eunomian redactor, and he has been followed with little alteration by Strecker and his adherents.[14] But it must be objected that there is nothing

---

[9]Strecker, *Das Judenchristentum in den Pseudoklementinen*, 40.

[10]Rius-Camps, "Las Pseudoclementinas," 106-10.

[11]Strecker, *Das Judenchristentum in den Pseudoklementinen*, 40-41.

[12]Arius said of the Son, θελήματι καὶ βουλῇ ὑπέστη πρὸ χρόνων καὶ πρὸ αἰώνων (Hans-Georg Opitz, ed. *Athanasius: Werke*, vol. 3, pt. 1, *Urkunden zur Geschichte des arianischen Streites 318-328*, [Berlin and Leipzig: Walter de Gruyter, 1934-35], document 1.4 [p. 3, lines 1-2]). See also document 6.2 (p. 12, lines 8-9), 3 (p. 13, line 4).

[13]For a statement by Arius that God is the "cause of all," see Opitz, *Urkunden*, document 6.4 (p. 13, line 8).

[14]See Rehm, "Entstehung," 96-97, Strecker, *Das Judenchristentum in den Pseudoklementinen*, 43, 249, where he identifies the interpolation as 69.5b-8a, Martyn, "Clementine Recognitions," 270, 274-76, who speaks of an orthodox redactor, Lüdemann, *Antipaulinismus*, 237, n. 35 (*Opposition to Paul*, 299, n. 35), who describes the section as merely a secondary element, and Van Voorst, *The Ascents of James*, 38, who evidently agrees with the characterization as Eunomian. The passage was isolated as an addition to the present context already

specifically Eunomian in this passage. For support of his view Rehm could refer only to the rejection of the notion of two unoriginated ones and to the repetition of the view that God is androgynous in R 3.9.7 (i.e., in the midst of what Rehm considered to be the main Eunomian interpolation, R 3.2-11). This last term is also found, however, in R 10.17.3, 30.4 as well as in H 6.5.4, 12.1, 12.26.6. Furthermore, the view that James would not publicly proclaim the matter of "when" the Son was begotten but that he would do so in secret (R 1.69.7 Syriac) speaks against the proposed attribution to a neo-Arian.[15] Rehm himself states that a Eunomian would have been interested in eliminating the trinitarian baptismal statement,[16] but he did not explain why his supposed Eunomian interpolator[17] left it standing in R 1.69.5.

The net result of these observations is that R is an "Arian"[18] and that in the introduction to R 1.27-71 he has inserted the notion that

---

by Hilgenfeld, *Recognitionen und Homilien*, 91. Meyboom, *De Clemens-roman*, 2:255, cites Schliemann's suspicion, but I have not located the passage in Schliemann.

[15]Compare Thomas A. Kopecek, *A History of Neo-Arianism*, Patristic Monograph Series, no. 8 (Cambridge, Mass.: Philadelphia Patristic Foundation, 1979), 68-69, n. 2, for the neo-Arian rejection of such dissimulation.

[16]Rehm, "Entstehung," 97. See below, chap. 5, n. 15.

[17]R 3.2-11, the basis for Rehm's theory of a Eunomian interpolator, needs to be subjected to a thorough examination, for many elements in Rehm's position are not satisfactory. The parallels that he collected from the writings of Eunomius and his opponents require critical evaluation. The same statements are very often also witnessed for early Arianism. While Rehm sometimes admitted this (e.g., Rehm, "Entstehung," 91), the fact that he did not cite these parallels is indicative of the one-sided and uncritical nature of his collection. What is *specifically* Eunomian in this section? The more recent study by Michel Tardieu, "Une diatribe antignostique dans l'interpolation eunomienne des *Recognitiones*," in *ΑΛΕΞΑΝΔΡΙΝΑ: Hellénisme, judaïsme et christianisme à Alexandrie: Mélanges offerts au P. Claude Mondésert*, (Paris: Les Éditions du Cerf, 1987), 325-37, though helpful in other respects, similarly does not answer this question. Furthermore, as Uhlhorn, *Homilien und Recognitionen*, 40, partially saw, R 3.2.3 and 3.8.10 refer back to R 2.49.1, and this makes it likely that there was originally a theological and christological discussion in R at this point (R 3.48.1 also seems to point back to the christological discussion). That this discussion was then later modified is likely in view of the many substantial divergences of the Syriac and the Latin. These divergences deserve detailed investigation.

[18]This word is used here and throughout in a descriptive sense indicating not necessarily a conscious follower of Arius but merely someone who felt uneasy with "homoousios" and thus tended toward the theological direction commonly

Peter first taught Clement the doctrine of the evolution of the monad. The following passages thus derive from R: 1.20.5-11, 22.5-23.4, 23.8-24.4a, 69.5b-8a. Parallels with B, particularly in R 1.24.4b-6, 25.4, lead to the supposition that the complex introductory section, along with its notion of a delay of the debate for seven days, should be attributed to B. H left it out because it was too complicated.[19]

Strecker thought that R left out two large sections preceding R 1.27-74. The first dealt with the true prophet and is reflected in H 2.4-12, 3.11ff.; the second presented the doctrine of spurious pericopes and is found in H 2.38-52, 3.2-58. He stated that hints of these sections are found in R 1.21.7-9.[20] Rius-Camps also placed the discourse on the prophet here, but he denied that the doctrine of false pericopes was in B.[21] He is certainly right that R 1.21.8 does not contain any clear hint of the doctrine of spurious pericopes. This passage rather refers back to R 1.15 and H 1.18 and states only that the tradition of the prophet is necessary for the correct understanding of scripture. It must also be doubted that R has suppressed the discussion on the true prophet as found in H 2.4-12 and 3.11ff. Contra Strecker, there is nothing in R 1.21 that "hints" at this discussion. H seems rather to have extrapolated H 2.4-12 from the more

---

associated with Arius's name. For some efforts to develop more precise historical circumscriptions and terminology, see Rowan Williams, *Arius: Heresy and Tradition* (London: Darton, Longman and Todd, 1987), R. P. C. Hanson, *The Search for the Christian Doctrine of God: The Arian Controversy 318-381* (Edinburgh: T. & T. Clark, 1988), and Michel R. Barnes and Daniel H. Williams, eds., *Arianism after Arius: Essays on the Development of the Fourth Century Trinitarian Conflicts* (Edinburgh: T. & T. Clark, 1993). It is tempting to use the term "non-Nicene" instead of "Arian," but difficulties arise when speaking of the earliest stages of the debate.

[19]Rius-Camps, "Las Pseudoclementinas," 105, correctly pointed out that the motif of "remembering" is a common device in the *Pseudo-Clementines*. The same applies to the motif of repetition. Strecker's supposition, *Das Judenchristentum in den Pseudoklementinen*, 40, that R has here introduced the motif of repetition to cover up what he left out is thus not convincing.

[20]Strecker, *Das Judenchristentum in den Pseudoklementinen*, 40; compare Waitz, "Lösung," 322.

[21]Rius-Camps, "Las Pseudoclementinas," 108, 111.

confused presentation in B's introduction as reflected in R. It should be remembered that Clement had actually *recorded* the discourse on the prophet on the preceding day (R 1.17.2 and H 1.20.2). The contradictory and clumsy statement in H 2.4 about Barnabas having instructed Clement respecting prophecy in Alexandria is thus a clear sign of H's redaction.[22] Indeed, H 2.4-12 reveals several elements taken up from the section in B that he omitted. For example, the statement in H 2.10.1 that the true prophet should know how the world was made points to the exposition of the prophet's tradition on this point in R 1.27-32. Furthermore, H 2.6.1 stands parallel to R 1.21.7. H 2.11.1 is an exposition of what Andrew says in R 1.56.3. Similarly, the doctrine in H 2.12.3 is probably taken from the context as reflected in R 1.25.4; it is changed from Peter's summary of his own teaching to the doctrine and proclamation of the true prophet.

It may consequently be seen that R has not eliminated any longer discussions immediately prior to R 1.27-71. While Strecker cited R 1.74.3-4 in support of his reconstructed presentation,[23] the wording of the passage actually speaks against his construction. The mention of teaching concerning the true prophet in 1.74.3 clearly points back to R 1.16-17, Peter's teaching immediately after Clement's arrival. R 1.74.4 is referring not to two separate presentations--as Strecker forces the text to say--but rather to the one long exposition that is described in similar terms in R 1.21.8-22.1 and R 1.25.9-10 and that is summarized in R 1.27-74.[24]

---

[22]H is probably responsible for adding all of the references to Alexandria (H 1.8.3, 2.4.1, 22.3). The notion that B contained a discussion of the prophet at this point goes back to Waitz, *Die Pseudoklementinen, Homilien und Rekognitionen*, 21-22. There he incorrectly wrote that R 1.17.1 had "announced" this discourse. R 1.17.1 clearly refers, however, to the discourse on the prophet that Clement heard and recorded on the day of his arrival in Caesarea (R 1.17.2).

[23]Strecker, *Das Judenchristentum in den Pseudoklementinen*, 43.

[24]The case for attributing all of R 1.63 to R (so Strecker, *Das Judenchristentum in den Pseudoklementinen*, 42-43) is not necessarily convincing, despite the approval granted by Brown, *James*, 199, and Van Voorst, *The Ascents of James*, 37-38 (though the last two proponents do not explicitly assign the material to R). Those so concerned with defending Strecker's position might be interested in knowing that Strecker later explicitly refers precisely to an element of this chapter in his discussion of the distinctive views of AJ II; see Georg Strecker, "Das Land

ORIGIN OF THE MATERIAL IN R OR IN B?

The preceding section has already provided evidence that the passage R 1.27-74 was part of B. It was seen there that R added the notion that Peter first taught Clement regarding the evolution of the monad. Assignment of this element to R's redaction makes it likely that the section R 1.27-74 lay before him in B and that there it was introduced by a section similar to R 1.21-26 (minus R's redaction). However, it was seen in the history of research that a number of scholars assigned R 1.27-74 to R (originally Uhlhorn, Bousset, Schwartz, and Rehm). It thus seems appropriate to raise the question anew of whether R 1.27-74 formed a part of B or was created by R.

The observation that the chronology of our section contradicts the opening section of the *Pseudo-Clementines* has been used as an argument both for and against attribution to R (originally Uhlhorn, Bousset, and Rehm, on the one hand, and Lehmann, on the other hand). Only R 9.29.1 again mentions "seven years" that had elapsed. While this last passage numbers the years since the advent of Christ, R 1.43.3 enumerates them from the passion. As already stated in the conclusion to chapter 1, these data on the chronology in the *Pseudo-Clementines* fail to provide clear evidence for or against attribution of our section to B or R.

Another way of approaching the question is to ask why H would have omitted the section if he found it in B. The history of research revealed that Waitz offered one explanation: H left the section out because he found similar material in Peter's speech in Tripolis (H 8.10-17 and its parallel R 4.9-13). This is a possible explanation, but one cannot say it carries positive power to convince that R 1.27-71 was part of B. The same must be said of John Chapman's proposal that H

Israel in frühchristlicher Zeit," in *Das Land Israel in biblischer Zeit: Jerusalem-Symposium 1981 der Hebräischen Universität und der Georg-August-Universität*, ed. Georg Strecker, Göttinger theologische Arbeiten, vol. 25 (Göttingen: Vandenhoeck & Ruprecht, 1983), 198. Notice should also be taken of the comments by Schoeps, *Theologie und Geschichte des Judenchristentums*, 403-4, who saw instead the work of the author of the *Kerygmata Petrou* and B here. With regard to B's additions, he is certainly right as concerns the baptismal formula in R 1.63.3 (see below in the section on B's redaction), and this element is in any event a clear indication that material older than R underlies R 1.63.

omitted R 1.22-74 because it was inconsistent with Acts.[25] Of a little more substantial weight is the suggestion that H omitted the section because he was offended by some of the Old Testament biblical material.[26] H 3.32-36 seems to be the philosophical account of creation H designed to replace R 1.27-28 (the parallels are striking, though they have received little attention; compare also R 8.22-33).

This observation points to a more decisive criterion for determining the literary history: detailed evaluation of parallels to this section particularly in H. Are there passages in H that disclose material clearly taken from the context as we have it in our section? Strecker deserves credit for having directly addressed this problem.[27] One such convincing instance is found in H 2.22.5 where it is said that Simon does not believe that the dead will be raised, denies Jerusalem, and introduces Mount Gerizim instead. Albrecht Ritschl already saw that the passage in H is a combination of the material in R 2.7 and R 1.54.2-5, 57.1.[28] This view has been approved by virtually all investigators,[29] for Simon's denial of Jerusalem is witnessed in no other source, whereas R 1.54.2-5 connects Dositheus with the Samaritans and Simon with Dositheus and R 1.57.1 permits identification of the Samaritan with Simon.

---

[25]John Chapman, "On the Date of the Clementines," *Zeitschrift für die neutestamentliche Wissenschaft* 9 (1908): 32, n. 1.

[26]Compare particularly H 2.52.2 on Noah and Abraham with R 1.30.2, 33.3-34.1. Contrast also R 1.29.1 and H 8.12-13.

[27]Strecker, *Das Judenchristentum in den Pseudoklementinen*, 41. The following discussion stands in reference to this page in Strecker's study. Compare also the statements by Waitz, *Die Pseudoklementinen, Homilien und Rekognitionen*, 22-23.

[28]Albrecht Ritschl, *Die Entstehung der altkatholischen Kirche: Eine kirchen- und dogmengeschichtliche Monographie* (Bonn: Adolph Marcus, 1850), 188-89.

[29]See Lehmann, *Die clementinischen Schriften*, 333-34, Waitz, *Die Pseudoklementinen, Homilien und Rekognitionen*, 20, Schmidt, *Studien*, 37, n. 2, Strecker, *Das Judenchristentum in den Pseudoklementinen*, 41, Karlmann Beyschlag, *Simon Magus und die christliche Gnosis*, Wissenschaftliche Untersuchungen zum Neuen Testament, vol. 16 (Tübingen: J. C. B. Mohr [Paul Siebeck], 1974), 54, and Lüdemann, *Untersuchungen zur simonianischen Gnosis*, 94-95. Rehm, "Entstehung," 137, is forced to say that the statement in H was spun out of the designation of Simon as a Samaritan. In view of the existence of R 1.54, 57, this explanation is hardly convincing.

The parallelism between R 1.29.3 and H 8.15.1, which is also cited by Strecker, is not convincing to the same degree. The possibility that R might be responsible for transferring this material from B to R 1.29.3 cannot be ruled out on the basis of the texts.[30] Otherwise, Strecker was able to cite only (quite broad) thematic parallels between this section and material he attributed only to B. He mentioned the view that the prophet travelled through the world and the annulment of sacrifice. While valuable, these observations do not form a strict proof, for it cannot be ruled out that R is responsible for taking up these views from B and creating this passage.

Are there other passages that provide insights into the literary history of R 1.27-71? Lehmann suggested that H 2.17.4 is dependent on the wording of R 1.64.2. H has secondarily changed the statement into a saying of Jesus and has placed it into relationship with Paul's false gospel.[31] This view of the literary relationship has been adopted by Schoeps and Strecker, though Rehm argued for precisely the inverse conclusion.[32] The discussion of this point has suffered from neglect of the Syriac, even though Waitz had pointed out that the parallel in the Syriac (R 3.61.2) corresponds much more closely with H 2.17.4.[33] While H 2.17.4 and R 1.64.2 (Syriac) do alone specifically share the mention of the rectification of the heresies, it cannot be excluded that this statement stood in B in the passage on the syzygies. Thus, H 2.17.4 (along with its parallel in the Syriac of R 3.61.2) cannot be said to be clearly dependent on R 1.64.2. This passage in R does, however, reflect an idea that was definitely present in B.

A similar case is offered by the unusual citation in H 3.53.3 and R 1.36.2 (especially the Syriac).[34] While it is possible that H has cited

---

[30]Strecker himself assumes that H 8.15-17 reflects the original order of B (*Das Judenchristentum in den Pseudoklementinen*, 71).

[31]Lehmann, *Die clementinischen Schriften*, 458-59.

[32]Schoeps, *Theologie und Geschichte des Judenchristentums*, 404-5, Strecker, *Das Judenchristentum in den Pseudoklementinen*, 190, 245, Rehm, "Entstehung," 162, n. 243.

[33]Waitz, "Lösung," 319.

[34]Compare the synoptic presentation in Leslie L. Kline, *The Sayings of Jesus in the Pseudo-Clementine Homilies*, Society of Biblical Literature Dissertation Series,

the saying from the context reflected in R 1.36.2 and has added "from your (or our) brothers" in accommodation to Acts, there is no way to establish this with certainty. The saying does, however, seem somewhat better anchored in its context in R than in H. Furthermore, this perspective provides a ready explanation for how H came to conceive of this citation as a saying of Jesus: In B, the historical overview was presented as the teaching of the prophet of truth (see R 1.26.3, 5 [Syriac]); thus H understood the material of R 1.36.2 as a saying of Jesus.

Another such case is found in H 2.33.3, which is perhaps dependent on R 1.34.4, 6. The shared references to the "people beloved by God" and the prayers of Moses are particularly striking. If H is directly responsible for H 2.33.3, then it seems most likely that he is paraphrasing the passage in B as reflected in R 1.34. A strict proof is, however, not possible here. The same applies to H 9.7.2, where the notion expressed in R 1.37.4, that the Jewish nation was often driven into exile so that it might learn to worship God without sacrifices, seems to have been expanded to a general historical phenomenon, namely, that humans are deprived of their kingdom for false worship. Similarly, the law given by an angel to the souls of the giants in H 8.18.2 seems to be a modification of R 1.30.1, 4.13.1, and 1.32.4; the first two of these passages state that a "law" was given to humans after the flood, while the last one refers to an intermediary angel.

A final way of approaching the question of whether this section formed a part of B is to ask if any of the ancient witnesses who used B demonstrate knowledge of this material. This approach is somewhat precarious because there are no undisputed fragments of B, nor is any witness universally acknowledged as being dependent on B. Nevertheless, three witnesses should not go unmentioned at this point: the *Apostolic Constitutions*, Epiphanius, and the *Chronicon Paschale*.

---

no. 14 (Missoula, Mont.: Scholars' Press, 1975), 147. Kline's failure to use the Syriac in this instance is particularly unfortunate.

If the *Chronicon Paschale* knew B,[35] then the citation in *Chronicon Paschale* 1.50-51 seems to provide evidence that R 1.30.7 stood in B, for many elements here have parallels in this passage though not in R 4.29 and H 9.5.[36]

Since Epiphanius *Panarion* 30.16.4, where it is reported that Christ was viewed as an archangel, seems to derive from R 2.42.5,[37] which is without parallel in H, Epiphanius most likely used B and not H.[38]   It

---

[35]So, e.g., Hort, *Clementine Recognitions*, 61, Waitz, *Die Pseudoklementinen, Homilien und Rekognitionen*, 43-47, Cullmann, *Roman pseudo-clémentin*, 38, and Rehm, "Entstehung," 117. Dependence on the Greek R is advocated by, e.g., Bousset, *Hauptprobleme der Gnosis*, 371 with n. 1, Schoeps, *Aus frühchristlicher Zeit*, 20, n. 2, and Strecker, *Das Judenchristentum in den Pseudoklementinen*, 269. Contra Strecker it should be noted that the *Chronicon Paschale* 1.49 does indeed mention Zoroaster. Contra Bousset and Schoeps the equation of Nimrod with Zoroaster in H 9.4.1 probably does not derive from B; the disturbed syntax of H 9.3.2, which even Bousset noted (*Hauptprobleme der Gnosis*, 144, n. 2), is an indication of this. Dependence on B is particularly likely in view of the parallels to *Chronicon Paschale* 1.40, where the specific correspondences with H's wording (in contrast to R, at least as translated by Rufinus) are striking. The *Chronicon Paschale* here says this material was related by Peter to Clement. It is perhaps merely coincidental, however, that this is the case only in R 1.29.5. Waitz, *Die Pseudoklementinen, Homilien und Rekognitionen*, 43, conjectured the dative of "Clementines" instead of the dative of "Clement," but the Greek construction does not favor this reading.

[36]Waitz, *Die Pseudoklementinen, Homilien und Rekognitionen*, 46, however, assumes the passage is a "direct citation."

[37]See the remarks by Schmidtke, *Judenchristliche Evangelien*, 192-93, and Schoeps, *Theologie und Geschichte des Judenchristentums*, 462-63; compare Strecker, *Das Judenchristentum in den Pseudoklementinen*, 265.

[38]This is the opinion of most recent research. See, for example, Schmidtke, *Judenchristliche Evangelien*, 177, Waitz in Waitz und Veil, "Auszüge aus den Pseudo-Clementinen," 161, Cullmann, *Roman pseudo-clémentin*, 37, Schoeps, *Theologie und Geschichte des Judenchristentums*, 461, and Strecker, *Das Judenchristentum in den Pseudoklementinen*, 265. Rehm, "Entstehung," 153, 130, n. 157, viewed Epiphanius as dependent on H especially in view of *Panarion* 26.16.8 and H 4.16.2 (Metis was seed). R, however, is abbreviating in the parallel R 10.20, and thus he or Rufinus may well have left out this (offensive) statement (compare even Rehm, "Entstehung," 130; the same applies to the possible references to this view in H 6.18.1 and 6.20.1 if they are supposed to have been in B). Contra Wehnert's view (Jürgen Wehnert, "Literarkritik und Sprachanalyse: Kritische Anmerkungen zum gegenwärtigen Stand der Pseudoklementinen-Forschung," *Zeitschrift für die neutestamentliche Wissenschaft und die Kunde der älteren Kirche* 74 [1983]: 289), it is likely that Epiphanius also knew the *Epistula Clementis*. The mention of writings addressed to elders in *Panarion* 30.2.6 is most probably a reference to the address in *Epistula Clementis* 1.1, as Schmidtke,

is possible that the statement that Christ came to Abraham (*Panarion* 30.3.5) reflects R 1.32.4-33.2.[39] The same may be said of the view that the words "having come and instructed" at the end of *Panarion* 30.16.4 are based on R 1.39.1 and 1.54.1.[40] Similarly, the statement that the Ebionites confess Joshua the son of Nun to be the exclusive follower of Moses (*Panarion* 30.18.4) seems to derive from R 1.38.1.[41] Furthermore, *Panarion* 30.16.3 might possibly be dependent on R 1.48.4, where Jesus is named the Son at baptism.[42] Much less convincing is the case for dependence in the parallel between *Panarion* 30.33.3 and R 1.33.5 or R 8.53.2.[43] In sum, it may be said that Epiphanius seems to have known our section as a part of B.

Judenchristliche Evangelien, 178-79, noted. (In his zeal to refute Strecker's position, Wehnert overlooked this argument by Schmidtke. Indeed, Schmidtke goes completely unmentioned in Wehnert's article even though Strecker, *Das Judenchristentum in den Pseudoklementinen*, 265-66, n. 1, referred to him for support.) Furthermore, *Panarion* 27.6.4 seems to be based on nothing other than *Epistula Clementis* 3.1.

It is not certain whether Epiphanius knew the *Epistula Petri* and the *Contestatio*. *Panarion* 30.23.1 possibly refers to the *Contestatio*, though this passage might also have the *Anabathmoi Jakobou* in mind, if this writing was supposed to have been composed by James. The list of seven witnesses in *Panarion* 19.1.6a and 19.6.4 (compare 30.17.4) is, however, best explainable on the basis of influence from *Contestatio* 2.1 and 4.1.

[39]See Schmidtke, *Judenchristliche Evangelien*, 198. While only here is it expressly said that the angel or true prophet actually came to Abraham, one should also compare R 2.47, H 17.4, and H 18.13.

[40]See Schmidtke, *Judenchristliche Evangelien*, 193. Note that the Syriac gives this view additional support.

[41]Schmidtke, *Judenchristliche Evangelien*, 181, derived this statement from Sirach 46:1, but he offers no explanation as to why Epiphanius would have added this remark. Joshua appears only in this passage in the *Pseudo-Clementines*.

[42]So Schoeps, *Theologie und Geschichte des Judenchristentums*, 462, and Strecker, *Das Judenchristentum in den Pseudoklementinen*, 265. See Epiphanius *Panarion* 28.1.5-7.

[43]See Schoeps, *Theologie und Geschichte des Judenchristentums*, 465, and, similarly, Strecker, *Das Judenchristentum in den Pseudoklementinen*, 265. The wording, however, is not similar, and information about the circumcision of other nations was fairly widespread. See, for example, Alexander Polyhistor in Eusebius *Praeparatio Evangelica* 9.27, Celsus in Origen *Contra Celsum* 1.22 and 5.41, and Origen *Contra Celsum* 5.48.
Panarion 30.23.1 could reflect R 1.55.4-64.3, but this is far from certain.

Finally, that the *Apostolic Constitutions* used B is a widespread view[44] challenged essentially only by the opinion that R was instead the source.[45] But since the designation of Zachaeus as a publican (*Apostolic Constitutions* 6.9.1) has a parallel only in H 2.1.2, use of B seems virtually certain. Later, when the *Apostolic Constitutions* 6.20.1 say the golden calf represented Apis (a remark added by the *Apostolic Constitutions* to the basic text of the *Didascalia*), dependency on R

---

[44]So Bigg, "The Clementine Homilies," 186, Schoeps, *Theologie und Geschichte des Judenchristentums*, 183, and Strecker, *Das Judenchristentum in den Pseudo-klementinen*, 266. Compare Marcel Metzger, ed., *Les Constitutions Apostoliques*, Sources chrétiennes, vols. 320, 329, 336 (Paris: Les Éditions du Cerf, 1985-87), 1:25.

[45]So Schwartz, "Beobachtungen," 175, 178, 189, and Bernhard Rehm, "Clemens Romanus II (PsClementinen)," in *Reallexikon für Antike und Christentum*, ed. Theodor Klauser et al. (Stuttgart: Anton Hiersemann, 1957), 5:198. The reason one excludes H is that only R supposedly explains the reference (in the *Apostolic Constitutions* 6.9.1) to three disputations in Caesarea before Simon's flight to Italy (so already Lipsius, *Apostelgeschichten*, 2.1:60).
A novel view was propounded by Wehnert, "Literarkritik und Sprachanalyse," 289-90, and "Abriß der Entstehungsgeschichte," 232, who denied dependence on B and essentially implied dependence on some epitomic tradition. The statement that the list of four followers of Peter in the *Apostolic Constitutions* corresponds "exactly" (so Wehnert, "Literarkritik und Sprachanalyse," 290) with an epitomic tradition transmitted in the two Arabic epitomes implies that these epitomes contain a similar list, which they do not. The figures are mentioned in the same way that they are in the two larger versions of the *Pseudo-Clementines*. Wehnert could have just as well cited the older Greek epitome (henceforth E) 43; indeed, the second Arabic epitome was evidently made on the basis of the Metaphrastic epitome (or a Greek text derived from this epitome; see Rehm, "Entstehung," 81, n. 11, and Franz Paschke, *Die beiden griechischen Klementinen-Epitomen und ihre Anhänge: Überlieferungsgeschichtliche Vorarbeiten zu einer Neuausgabe der Texte*, Texte und Untersuchungen zur Geschichte der altchristlichen Literatur, vol. 90 [Berlin: Akademie, 1966], 76), and thus it is absurd to submit that this Arabic epitome, which was evidently rendered from the Greek in the year 1659 (see the colophon in Margaret Dunlop Gibson, ed. and trans., *Apocrypha Sinaitica*, Studia Sinaitica, no. 5 [London: C. J. Clay, 1896], 51) preserves an independent epitomic tradition witnessed also by the *Apostolic Constitutions*. The Sinai Arabic epitome is of uncertain date (the manuscript should be dated probably to the ninth or tenth century; see Georg Graf, *Geschichte der christlichen arabischen Literatur*, vol. 1, *Die Übersetzungen*, Studi e testi 118 [Vatican City: Biblioteca Apostolica Vaticana, 1944], 283, 303), but it was made on the basis of R (so also Rehm, "Entstehung," 81, Paschke, *Klementinen-Epitomen*, 76) and thus cannot explain the *Apostolic Constitutions*' designation of Zachaeus as the toll-collector--all this above and beyond the fact that this epitome does not contain a list of followers of Peter.

1.35.5 (as in B) is most likely,[46] and thus one must conclude that R 1.27-71 formed a part of B.[47]

LOCATION IN B

If it is thus most likely that R 1.27-71 stood in the basic writing, the question of its original location in B must next be raised. Previous research has offered four possibilities, which may be examined as a springboard for the present discussion.

Waitz placed the section during the first full day in Caesarea after the report about Simon, after Zachaeus announces the postponement (H 2.35-37 and R 1.20-21), and after instructions on the true prophet (H 2.4-12 and R 1.21-26). R 1.27-71 is then followed by the discussion of false pericopes.[48] Chapman, in contrast, followed the order of H 2, only inserting R 1.22-74 between H 2.37 and 2.38.[49] Strecker also has R 1.27-71 during the first full day in Caesarea, but according to him this day begins with the announcement of delay and a discussion of the true prophet. Then, after the section on false pericopes follows R 1.27-71. R 2.1 and H 2.1 introduce the next day, and it is during the early morning discussion of this day that the report about Simon occurs.[50] For Rius-Camps, the first full day in Caesarea began with a discussion of prophecy and the prophet (H 2.1-14, 3.11-21) followed by Zachaeus's intervention and then R 1.21-74.[51]

To evaluate these possibilities, one may start by collecting any apparent weaknesses in the arguments of these four investigators.

---

[46]So Schmidt, *Studien*, 263, n. 1, Schoeps, *Theologie und Geschichte des Judenchristentums*, 183 with n. 1, and Metzger, *Les Constitutions Apostoliques*, 1:25, 27. Contra Metzger, *Les Constitutions Apostoliques*, 1:27, the comments on the role of Moses in the *Apostolic Constitutions* 6.20.6 are not dependent on R 1.35 but are rather taken directly from the *Didascalia*.

[47]Compare also *Apostolic Constitutions* 8.35.1 (James appointed bishop by the Lord) with R 1.43.3.

[48]Waitz, *Die Pseudoklementinen, Homilien und Rekognitionen*, 38.

[49]John Chapman, "Clementines," in *The Catholic Encyclopedia*, ed. Charles G. Herbermann et al. (New York: Robert Appleton, 1908), 4:40.

[50]Strecker, *Das Judenchristentum in den Pseudoklementinen*, 92-93.

[51]Rius-Camps, "Las Pseudoclementinas," 108.

Waitz thought that the statement in R 2.19.3 that Zachaeus had gone out a little before shows that R has the report of Zachaeus's first appearance (R 1.20-21) in the wrong place.[52] This argument is not convincing, however, because it conflicts with the delay of the discussion for one day (or more), a point that Waitz tacitly circumvents.

One problem with Strecker's view is that he assumes that in the basic writing the consideration Peter shows for Clement's weariness from the voyage (H 2.2.1) followed H 2.1 on the second full day in Caesarea. In this arrangement, however, Peter's consideration comes one day too late.

It thus seems most likely then that H 2.1 (with its parallel R 2.1) stood at the beginning of the first full day in Caesarea and that this was followed by the early morning discussion of bodily wants (R 2.1-2 and its parallel H 2.2-3). As the debate with Simon was planned for the day, it is most likely that the early morning discussion then led directly into the discussion of Simon and, accordingly, also of pairs (R 2.3.1-19.2 and 3.59-61 and the parallels H 2.19-32, 15-18, 33-34). At this point, Zachaeus entered and announced the postponement of the debate (R 1.20 and its parallel H 2.35). The instruction of Clement for seven days followed (R 1.21-74).

It is thus apparent that R rearranged his materials at the end of his first book and the beginning of his second. His motivation for doing so seems to have been organizational: this rearrangement allowed all the material pertaining to the instruction of Clement to stand together and all of the material relating to Simon to stand together uninterrupted.

An outline of the beginning of B would thus be:
Preliminaries
> *Epistula Petri*
> *Contestatio*
> *Epistula Clementis* (the Ordination of Clement)

I. Beginning: Clement's Introduction to Christianity
    Clement in Rome and Caesarea [R 1.1-19 par. H 1.1-7a, 9-22]

---

[52]Waitz, *Die Pseudoklementinen, Homilien und Rekognitionen*, 24.

Clement's Non-Christian Life in Rome [R 1.1-5 par. H 1.1-5]
Clement Hears of Christ [R 1.6-11 par. H 1.6-7a, 9-14]
Clement Travels to Caesarea and Meets Peter [R 1.12-14 par. H 1.15-17]
Discussion of the True Prophet [R 1.15-19 par. H 1.18-22]
Next Day
The Followers of Peter [R 2.1a par. H 2.1]
Early Morning Discussion: Consideration for Bodily Wants [R 2.1b-2 par. H 2.2-3]
Discussion of Simon and Pairs [R 2.3-19a par. H 2.19-32, R 3.59-61 par. H 2.15-18, 33-34]
Delay of the Discussion Announced by Zachaeus [R 1.20-21 par. H 2.35-36]
Instruction of Clement [R 1.22-74]

II. Debate with Simon in Caesarea
First Day
Early Morning Discussion [H 3.1-28]
Zachaeus Announces Time for Commencement of Debate [R 2.19b par. H 3.29]
Beginning of the Debate
On Peace in Discussion [R 2.20-36a par. H 3.30-32]
On the One God [R 2.36b-69 par. H 16.5-15a, 18.4-22, 17.4-19]
Adjournment [R 2.70-72 par. H 17.20]

A SOURCE?

Up to this point it has been seen that R 1.27-71 originally stood in the basic writing, and its precise location in this writing has been discussed. The present section addresses the question of whether B created R 1.27-71 *ad hoc* or rather drew on a special source for this material.

The criterion to be applied to answer this question may be formulated as follows. Do the views expressed in this section correspond with what may reasonably be attributed to B, or do they reveal marked differences from the rest of the *Pseudo-Clementines*? The evidence stands in support of the latter alternative, and as an answer to the question it will suffice to list the points where marked contrasts with other Pseudo-Clementine passages are apparent.

Of points already noted by previous investigators mention may be made particularly of the figure of seventy-two disciples in R 1.40.4 (compare R 1.34.2).[53] This number, listed as established in imitation of Moses, stands in contrast to Moses' seventy followers recorded in *Epistula Petri* 1.2, 3.2, H 2.38.1, and 3.47.1 as well as to the "seventy brethren" in *Epistula Petri* 2.1 (contrast also H 18.4.3 with R 2.42.4; compare R 5.10.3).

A distinctive view is also found in R 1.29.1 where Gen. 6:2 is understood as referring to righteous men. This tradition stands in contrast to R 4.26.3 and H 8.12.1, which take Gen. 6:2 in reference to angels.[54]

Furthermore, the relationship of Jesus and Moses as reflected in R 1.59 (Jesus is not equal to Moses but rather greater) differs from H 8.5-6 and its parallel R 4.5 where the identity of their teaching is asserted and the equality of their status is assumed. These latter passages thus also stand in contrast to three of the most distinctive views of R 1.27-71, namely, that Jesus came to complete the teaching of Moses by abolishing the sacrifices that Moses still allowed (R 1.36-37, 39), that recognition of Jesus as the Christ is necessary to salvation (R 1.63.2-4), and that this recognition is the *only* difference between "Jews" and "Christians" (R 1.43.2, compare R 1.50.5, 68.2). At the same time, the parallel drawn between the miracles of Moses and those of Jesus (R 1.41.1-3, 57.5-58.3) is distinctive to this section.[55]

The attitude toward John the Baptist, which is thoroughly positive in R 1.27-71, similarly stands in sharp contrast to at least the *Homilies*,

---

[53]See Strecker, *Das Judenchristentum in den Pseudoklementinen*, 224-25, and Brown, *James*, 199-200.

[54]The precise history of this material is in need of further investigation.

[55]Compare Strecker, *Das Judenchristentum in den Pseudoklementinen*, 232.

where John is considered the evil forerunner of Jesus (H 2.23; compare H 2.17.1-2, R 3.61.2 Syriac).[56]

Somewhat less certain is whether a distinctive feature of this section is baptism in the name of Jesus alone (see R 1.39.2-3 Latin),[57] for the Syriac does not witness this phrase.

The type of anti-Paulinism expressed in R 1.70-71 is also unparalleled in the rest of the *Pseudo-Clementines* and actually stands in contrast to the anti-Pauline attitude in H 17.13-19, where reference is made not to the persecutions of the church but rather to visionary experience.

Another distinctive element in this section is the "chiliasm" of R 1.61.2-3. In distinction to R 2.28.3, 5 and H 15.10.4 the poor are here called blessed because they will inherit the earth literally.[58]

This section also seems to differ from the rest of the *Pseudo-Clementines* when it lists the scribes and the Pharisees alongside the other Jewish heresies (R 1.54.6-7).[59]

Above, in the history of research, it was mentioned that this section has a chronology that stands in contrast to at least the opening section of the *Pseudo-Clementines*. Whereas the initial part assumes that Christ had only recently made his proclamation (H 1.6.2 and its parallel R 1.6.2), the section currently under consideration states that at least seven years had passed since Christ's crucifixion (R 1.43.3). While this latter figure is mentioned again in R 9.29.1 (compare R 1.72.7), it is likely that its origin in the *Pseudo-Clementines* is the source of R 1.27-71.[60]

---

[56]Compare Strecker, *Das Judenchristentum in den Pseudoklementinen*, 242.

[57]So Strecker, *Das Judenchristentum in den Pseudoklementinen*, 229, and, following Strecker, Martyn, "Clementine Recognitions," 276, and Van Voorst, *The Ascents of James*, 99, 165.

[58]Compare Strecker, *Das Judenchristentum in den Pseudoklementinen*, 244. Compare the distinction of the kingdom of heaven from the resurrection of the dead and eternal life in R 1.55.4.

[59]Compare Strecker, *Das Judenchristentum in den Pseudoklementinen*, 239.

[60]Compare Schmidt, *Studien*, 23, n. 1, and Strecker, *Das Judenchristentum in den Pseudoklementinen*, 234-35.

Other doctrines in this section do not stand in direct contradiction to other sections of the *Pseudo-Clementines*, but their centrality here is so apparent that their absence in the other parts of the novel may be taken as a sign of a distinct source. Thus while the emphasis placed on the destruction of the temple as the beginning of the gentile mission (R 1.64.2) finds parallels in H 2.17.4 and R 3.61.2 (Syriac),[61] the repeated point that the destruction would come about because of continued sacrifices (R 1.37.2-5, 39.3, 64.2) is unique to this section.

Similarly, the emphasis that those who believe Christ will be saved from the war (R 1.37.2, 39.3) is found only in this section, as is also the related, marked concern for the land of Israel (R 1.30.3, 31.2, 32.4, 34.4, 37.2-4, 38.3, 39.3; compare R 1.35.1, 6). That gentiles would have to be called in order to complete the number that was shown to Abraham (R 1.42.1) is equally a notion found only here in the *Pseudo-Clementines*.

Unique, too, is the statement in R 1.43.3 that James was appointed by the Lord (Jesus) to be bishop of Jerusalem. Elsewhere in the *Pseudo-Clementines* it is stated that God established James as bishop (*Contestatio* 5.4; compare *Epistula Petri* 1.1 and H 11.35.4).[62]

Similarly distinctive is the designation "eternal Christ" (R 1.43.1, [44.2,] 63.1; compare R 1.52.3).[63] The discussion of the two comings of Christ is also found only in this section (R 1.69.4; compare

---

[61]Strecker, *Das Judenchristentum in den Pseudoklementinen*, 245, in contrast, says that this notion is peculiar to his AJ II.

[62]Compare Strecker, *Das Judenchristentum in den Pseudoklementinen*, 235, 195. Brown, *James*, 204-5, and Pratscher, *Jakobus und die Jakobustradition*, 135, understand the passages just mentioned as also implying that Jesus appointed James to be bishop. Only Pratscher offers arguments for this view, yet these are faulty. R 4.34.4-5 and H 11.35.3 contain nothing to support Pratscher's case, and he incorrectly summarizes the context of *Contestatio* 5.4. Here it is said that the one who foreknows all things, not just that there would be "daring men" as Pratscher writes, established James as bishop. In the *Pseudo-Clementines* this predicate is used properly only of God (see the concordance and compare, for example, H 2.50.2-3, 15.4.1, 16.13.4-5, 20.11.4). Thus, H 2.50.2, for example, states that the prophet *received* foreknowledge from God. It is therefore no surprise to see that the statement in *Contestatio* 5.4 is immediately followed by a prayer to the Father of all and God. Furthermore, for an illuminative parallel to the wording of *Contestatio* 5.4, see H 19.25.2; here God is expressly mentioned.

[63]See however below, n. 12 to chapter 5.

R 1.49.1-5).[64] Again, the attitude toward the prophets (R 1.59.4-6, 61.3, 69.1) is much more positive than in other parts of the *Pseudo-Clementines*,[65] as is also the attitude toward astrology.[66]

Another way of verifying whether R 1.27-71 is based on a source is to ask if there are conspicuous elements of redaction indicative of such a state of affairs. This is the case in R 1.54.3. Here Dositheus and Simon have been tacked on to the description of the Sadducees. The author of the basic writing is obviously trying to uphold both the statement of the source that the Sadducees were the first heresy as well as his own thesis that Dositheus and Simon were followers of John the Baptist who created the various heresies. That R 1.54.3 is a somewhat awkward gloss was already pointed out by Hilgenfeld.[67] Taken together, this sign of redaction and the distinctive elements listed above provide a strong case that R 1.27-71 is heavily based on material from a source that was employed by B.

DELIMITATION OF THE SOURCE

As was apparent in the history of research, contemporary investigation into the source of R 1 may be generally characterized as uncritical adoption of Strecker's views. The naivety of this procedure is particularly evident in the matter of delineating which material belongs to the source. The following will first expose this naivety for the delineation of the beginning of the material and will then proceed positively to delimiting the material of the source.

---

[64]Compare Strecker, *Das Judenchristentum in den Pseudoklementinen*, 248-49.

[65]Compare Strecker, *Das Judenchristentum in den Pseudoklementinen*, 241.

[66]See R 1.28.2, 32.3, and contrast these passages with R 9.12, 10.7-12, H 14.3-5.

One might compare the elements listed above with Van Voorst, *The Ascents of James*, 39-40, where eighteen distinctive features are enumerated, yet over a third here are contrived or represent false or loose readings of the texts (see, particularly, numbers 1, 9, 10, 12, 14, and 15).

[67]Hilgenfeld, *Recognitionen und Homilien*, 81, idem, *Die Ketzergeschichte des Urchristenthums urkundlich dargestellt* (Leipzig: Fues's Verlag [R. Reisland], 1884), 156, n. 259. Compare idem, *Judenthum und Judenchristenthum: Eine Nachlese zu der "Ketzergeschichte des Urchristenthums urkundlich dargestellt,"* (Leipzig: Fues's Verlag [R. Reisland], 1886), 46-47 with n. 91; see also Ritschl, *Entstehung*, 1st ed., 161, n. 1.

Strecker states that the beginning of the source should be set at R 1.33.[68] This position has been hence adopted by others with minor additions[69] or merely implicitly,[70] or Strecker's arguments have been cited with considerable distortion.[71] No one, however, has questioned or, evidently, even checked the bases of Strecker's claims.[72] This is particularly surprising because within the next three pages of Strecker's book, statements are made that blatantly contradict two of Strecker's three arguments.

As his first argument for setting the beginning of the source at R 1.33, Strecker notes that in R 1.32 an angel delivers revelations to Abraham, whereas in R 1.33 the prophet of truth suddenly appears and assumes this function.[73] When dealing with R 1.33 two pages later, however, Strecker decides that the source did not even know the figure of the true prophet at all. This figure, according to Strecker, was introduced by the author of the basic writing.[74] Strecker evidently failed to note that this decision totally invalidated his first argument for

---

[68]Strecker, *Das Judenchristentum in den Pseudoklementinen*, 221.

[69]So, e.g., Brown, *James*, 195-99.

[70]So Lüdemann, *Antipaulinismus*, 230-48 (*Opposition to Paul*, 171-85), who contra *Antipaulinismus*, 230, n. 17 (*Opposition to Paul*, 297, n. 17), presupposes that the section containing material relevant to his R 1-source begins in R 1.33 without ever discussing the problem.

[71]Martyn, "Clementine Recognitions," 268-69, belongs here. That R 1.27-32 contains material used elsewhere in the *Pseudo-Clementines* is not an argument against it belonging with R 1.33-71 (contra Martyn, who cites this as one of the two major arguments for marking the beginning of the section in R 1.33). While Strecker, to whom Martyn refers, mentions this fact, he does not use it as an argument for the separation of R 1.27-32 from R 1.33-71. Van Voorst, *The Ascents of James*, 32, has repeated Martyn's misconception and has added his own by stating that Strecker also mentioned in support of his thesis that "*R* 1.33-44 has no parallel in the rest of *R* or in *H*." Nothing of the sort is to be found in Strecker, *Das Judenchristentum in den Pseudoklementinen*, 221, which Van Voorst cites; see, to the contrary, Strecker, *Das Judenchristentum in den Pseudoklementinen*, 41, for example.

[72]Van Voorst, *The Ascents of James*, 32-33, has, however, recently used partially correct observations to mount an argument for beginning the section at R 1.33.3. On p. 33 Van Voorst has failed to notice the Syriac of R 1.32.3, which implies that Abraham was at first in error with everyone else.

[73]Strecker, *Das Judenchristentum in den Pseudoklementinen*, 221.

[74]Strecker, *Das Judenchristentum in den Pseudoklementinen*, 223.

the establishment of the beginning of the source in R 1.33, for if the true prophet did not appear in the source, then the sudden appearance of this figure in R 1.33 (an insertion by B) says nothing at all about the source. One must readily admit that it is surprising that no one--not even Strecker himself in the twenty-three years between the first and second editions--has noted this discrepancy. It will be difficult to decide if one should be more surprised or less shocked to find that the case is similar with Strecker's second argument.

Here Strecker states that in R 1.33 the Persians are said to stem from Eliesdros, whereas in R 1.30 they are brought into connection with Nimrod and are said to derive from the Hamite Mizraim.[75] Besides the fact that R 1.30 does *not* state that the Persians are descendants of Mizraim,[76] Strecker himself states three pages later that it is uncertain whether B got the information that Eliezer was the son of Abraham from the *Kerygmata Petrou* or from AJ II.[77] Thus, this second argument also seems to be drawn into doubt even by Strecker's own statements. Moreover, it will be seen below in the section on B's redaction that there are strong reasons for attributing the whole of R 1.33 to B.[78]

Strecker's third argument is twofold in nature. On the one hand, he states that the enumeration of generations stops in R 1.32. On the other hand, he notes that the parallelism to Acts 7:2-53 begins in R 1.33. With regard to the second part of this argument it must be said that R 1.33 is by no means closer to Acts 7:2-53 than is R 1.32. In his edition of the text, Rehm mentions no direct parallels from Acts 7:2-53 to either section, and if one were forced to make a decision, one would have to say that R 1.32 (mention of Chaldeans and cryptic reference to the exile in Egypt) is closer to Acts 7:2-53 than is R 1.33.

---

[75]Strecker, *Das Judenchristentum in den Pseudoklementinen*, 221.

[76]This is stated in H 9.3.2 with its parallel R 4.27.2, and Strecker is evidently assuming a traditional connection of this statement with the figure of Nimrod in a certain literary level of the *Pseudo-Clementines*. Nevertheless, his statement, as it stands, is false, and it has misled others such as Brown, *James*, 195.

[77]Strecker, *Das Judenchristentum in den Pseudoklementinen*, 224.

[78]This accounts for the discrepancy regarding the origin of the Persians.

As an argument for marking the beginning of the section in R 1.33 one remains with the fact that the last enumeration of generations is found in R 1.32. Nevertheless, it should be noted that in R 1.33 one does not expect a further enumeration, for one is still in the midst of the report about Abraham. Thus, the fact that the last enumeration of generations is found in R 1.32 is not an absolute indication that new material begins in R 1.33. While this fact might indicate that new material begins sometime after R 1.32, it is difficult to draw from this fact precise information about where the new material begins because generations had not been consecutively enumerated even in the material before R 1.32. For example, there is a gap between the ninth generation and the twelfth generation that is filled simply by the report on Noah. Hence, it would be hard to say when one expects a new enumeration after R 1.32. R 1.34.3 (certainly not R 1.33) is probably the most likely place. But in view of the sporadic occurrences of the enumerations, which become increasingly imprecise in their relations to parallel Jewish speculation,[79] it seems best to abandon this argument in delineating the source.

If one searches for other arguments for delineation of particular material in R 1, one is led back to the old view that R 1.27-71 sets itself apart from the context by its broad form as a historical account from creation to the present day in the novel's story.[80]

This observation can be supported by consideration of the theological tendency of the material. One finds in this section theological views that vary from the rest of the *Pseudo-Clementines* and that form a unified whole. At times one can clearly observe how these views have been subjected to redaction so that they might accord with the dominant perspectives of the *Pseudo-Clementines*. Thus, two criteria, form and theological observations, can aid in delineating the material of

---

[79]See, for example, Schoeps's commentary in *Aus frühchristlicher Zeit*, 17, n. 1.

[80]This form does not actually terminate in R 1.71. When "R 1.71" is nevertheless written at this point, the conclusions of the next few pages are anticipated.

the source. In the following, these criteria will be applied to the section R 1.27-71.

From the perspective of form, it has long been noted that R 1.44.4-52.6 differs strikingly from the surrounding material.[81] In this section, the person of Clement and the dialogical style are reintroduced. Since Clement is a main figure of the *Pseudo-Clementines* and since the dialogical style is common in this romance, the form of this section speaks against it belonging with the rest of R 1.27-71. Furthermore, the discussion ends very abruptly in 1.52.6, and 1.53.1 continues the train of thought of 1.44.

These formal observations can be supported by comparison of the theological slants of R 1.44-52 with the rest of R 1.27-71. The following theological views found in this section are extraneous to the rest of R 1.27-71 but internally connected with other sections of the *Pseudo-Clementines*: the figure of the prophet of truth, the identification of him with Adam, and the notion that he was anointed with the oil of the tree of life. The concern with the prophet of truth in this section suggests that this figure did not belong to the source of R 1.27-71 at all, especially since a differing christology can be perceived at other places in R 1.27-71.[82]

If the affinities with the other parts of the *Pseudo-Clementines* make it likely that B is responsible for this insertion, it remains to be asked where precisely his work begins and ends. The motif of the priests (the high priest or Caiaphas) requesting a discussion recurs several times before and after the insertion (R 1.43.1, 3, 44.2, 53.3, 4, 55.1; compare R 1.41.4), and this raises the question of whether the redactor is responsible for one or more of these repetitions.[83] The

---

[81]There are differences as to the exact limits of this material. Compare, e.g., Hilgenfeld, *Recognitionen und Homilien*, 70, Bousset, review of *Die Pseudoklementinen*, by H. Waitz, 438, Schmidtke, *Judenchristliche Evangelien*, 183, Schoeps, *Theologie und Geschichte des Judenchristentums*, 437, and Strecker, *Das Judenchristentum in den Pseudoklementinen*, 236.

[82]Compare, similarly, Strecker, *Das Judenchristentum in den Pseudoklementinen*, 223, and Van Voorst, *The Ascents of James*, 34-35.

[83]For example, Strecker, *Das Judenchristentum in den Pseudoklementinen*, 236, attributes 53.1-53.4a to the redactor.

most disturbing of these repetitions is doubtless R 1.44.2-3 for it has Caiaphas sending priests several times on one day and the apostles rejecting the offer and looking for a suitable time on the same day. The difficulties of the texts are reduced considerably if the insertion by B is considered to start in the middle of R 1.44.1 (with the statement about James) and to end in the middle of R 1.53.4 after the two repetitions in R 1.53.3-4. On this reading, the statement that the disciples had assembled with the congregation during the Passover is then consequently followed by the decision to go to the temple and testify.[84]

In view of the history of research, it nevertheless needs to be asked if certain material from this insertion derives from the source. Strecker has pointed out three elements that the author has apparently picked up from the source: the rejection of sacrifice (R 1.48), the characterization of the relationship to the Jews (R 1.50.5), and the doctrine of the twofold coming of Jesus (R 1.49-50).[85] Since Strecker has accurately observed that the last doctrine is developed in a different manner in this section (orientation toward the expectation of the gentiles)[86] and since the characterization of the relationship of Christians and Jews is here secondarily mixed with the doctrine of the twofold coming, these elements seem to be clear indications that the author is not employing additional material from the source but is rather only expounding on parts that he has already reproduced. Following this indication, this study must distinguish its reconstruction of the source from those of such scholars as Schmidtke, Schoeps, and Lüdemann who have drawn (explicitly or implicitly) on all or some of this section to reconstruct a long speech of James supposedly in the original source.

---

[84]The attempt by Van Voorst, *The Ascents of James*, 35-37, to assign R 1.54 to R is not convincing and is based on incorrect readings and distortions of the text. For example, it is false to say that R "1.54.7 traces baptism to John" (p. 36). Nor is it the case that R 1.60.1-4 presents "the entire group" of John's disciples proclaiming him to be the Christ (also p. 36); only one of John's disciples speaks in R 1.60.1.

[85]Strecker, *Das Judenchristentum in den Pseudoklementinen*, 236.

[86]Strecker, *Das Judenchristentum in den Pseudoklementinen*, 248.

That this insertion is so concerned with the figure of the prophet of truth leads one back to Strecker's observation, mentioned above, that the prophet of truth suddenly appears in R 1.33. Instead of considering this to be a sign of the beginning of the source, this examination is led to the view that this section presents redaction. Further support for this conclusion is found in the observation that whereas R 1.32 speaks positively of the fact that Abraham was an astrologer (compare Jubilees 12:16-25), R 1.33 seems to cast aspersions on Abraham's astrological insights. R 1.33 insists that Abraham was in ignorance until the prophet of truth came and "revealed everything to him."

That R 1.27-32 actually belongs to the source becomes more probable in the light of certain elements isolated in the preceding section as distinctive to R 1.27-71. The attitude toward astrology, which was just discussed, was one of these elements. Furthermore, whereas Strecker evidently assumed that R 1.27-32 is dependent on another source elsewhere employed in the *Pseudo-Clementines*,[87] this study disclosed material peculiar to this section. Particularly important is the different exegesis of the very important passage Gen. 6:2 (contrast R 1.29.1 with R 4.26.3 and H 8.12.1).

Brown also listed some features that seem to connect R 1.27-32 with the following chapters.[88] He mentioned as especially noteworthy the unusual description of water becoming like "frost" in R 1.27.3 and R 1.34.6-7. The concordance allows one to confirm that Rufinus used this expression (*quasi* or *ut gelu*) only in these passages. Equally distinctive is the concern for the promised land. This special interest (the passages were listed in the preceding section) clearly unites R 1.27-32 with the following. In sum, R 1.27-32 does indeed belong to the source material also present in R 1.33-71.

It remains to determine the point at which material from the source terminates. The history of research reveals that in recent times the limit is most often placed at the end of R 1.71. Strecker has succinctly stated the argument underlying this view: it is here that the novel of

---

[87]See Strecker, *Das Judenchristentum in den Pseudoklementinen*, 221.

[88]Brown, *James*, 195.

Clement and Peter sets in again (Peter in Caesarea).[89]   There is, indeed, little that can be said against this argument.   One senses both the new material as well as the uneasy transition created by B.   Thus, Zachaeus, for example, is abruptly introduced, and all interest for the "enemy," who had dominated the last few chapters, suddenly disappears in its pure form and appears again only filtered by the novelist into Simon.

Relations to Jewish and Other
Early Christian Writings

With the delineation of the material of the source complete, the question of the relationship of this source to Jewish and other early Christian writings may now be addressed.   While previous scholars have commented on this issue when discussing particular passages, no one has dealt with the problem in a comprehensive way.   In the context of the present study, treatment of this issue will be important not only for matters of date and location of the author but also for the establishment of his intentions.

Perhaps the most important source of this text was the Book of Jubilees.   The dependency of R 1 on this apocryphal writing has been seen by others.[90]   The more convincing instances of dependency are the following.   In the story of creation the statement referring to rivers and mountains (R 1.27.8), which is not found in Genesis, probably derives from Jubilees 2:7.   The remarks on the division of the world among the sons of Noah by lot (R 1.30.2-3) are dependent on Jubilees 8:8-30, where this notion was evidently first developed.[91]   The related view that the descendants of Ham later illicitly occupied Palestine (R 1.31.2) also derives from Jubilees 10:29-34, for this idea

---

[89]Strecker, *Das Judenchristentum in den Pseudoklementinen*, 221.

[90]See Hermann Rönsch, *Das Buch der Jubiläen oder die kleine Genesis* (Leipzig: Fues's Verlag [R. Reisland], 1874), 322-24, and Schoeps, *Aus frühchristlicher Zeit*, 16, n. 4.

[91]Compare Schoeps, *Aus frühchristlicher Zeit*, 17-18, n. 5, who says that the dependency at this point is absolutely certain.   The threefold division of the earth is also mentioned in the Sibylline Oracles 3:114.

is again unique to Jubilees.[92] R 1.31.1 seems to be dependent on Jubilees 11:2. Similarly, the remark that Hebrew was the first language and that it prevailed till the building of the tower of Babylon (R 1.30.5) was most likely abstracted from Jubilees 12:26.[93]

In other passages it is less certain that Jubilees is the source. Thus, while Schoeps stated that R 1.31.3 was referring to Jubilees 12:14,[94] the statement that someone died before his father could derive simply from Gen. 11:28. Similarly, it seems probable that the description of Abraham and his instruction by an angel in R 1.32.2-33.2 is dependent on Jubilees 12:16-27, but for lack of specific and absolutely distinctive agreements, it is difficult to establish this dependency with certainty.

While the use of Jubilees cannot be doubted, it should also be remarked that the dependency is by no means one of blind adoption. For example, Jubilees is markedly in favor of sacrifices (see, e.g., Jubilees 6:2, 14:11), while R 1 is definitely against sacrifices. When in the partitioning of the world the eastern and western lots are perhaps the inverse of the lots in Jubilees (contrast R 1.30.3 with Jubilees 8:8-30), this is not because, as Charles assumed,[95] there is a mistake in the Latin R, but as not only the Syriac but also R 1.31.2 confirm, because the author of our source is possibly consciously altering the version in Jubilees. Furthermore, while Jubilees appears to be against astrology or astronomy (Jubilees 8:3), R 1.32.3 views such observations as leading to recognition of the true God (contrast Jubilees 12:16-17). R 1.28.2 also assigns such significance to the moon, whereas Jubilees 2:9 conspicuously omits reference to the moon in its rendition of Gen. 1:14.[96]

---

[92]Compare R. H. Charles, trans., *The Book of Jubilees or the Little Genesis Translated from the Editor's Ethiopic Text and Edited, with Introduction, Notes, and Indices* (London: A. and C. Black, 1902), 84, who states that to the best of his knowledge this view is found only in Jubilees and writings dependent on Jubilees.

[93]See Rönsch, *Das Buch der Jubiläen*, 323. Compare Charles, *The Book of Jubilees*, 96, and Schoeps, *Aus frühchristlicher Zeit*, 18, n. 3.

[94]Schoeps, *Aus frühchristlicher Zeit*, 24, n. 1.

[95]Charles, *The Book of Jubilees*, 84. Compare Rönsch, *Das Buch der Jubiläen*, 323.

[96]Compare Charles, *The Book of Jubilees*, 15, who states that the omission in

These remarks lead on to the observation that the Old Testament itself was also a source for our writing. It was the Septuagint version that was employed (see the passages mentioned in Rehm's edition of the Latin).

There has been more discussion of the use of New Testament writings in this section of the *Pseudo-Clementines*.[97] The author apparently had access to several of the New Testament writings. While it is unlikely that one can determine absolutely the precise corpus of New Testament writings known to the author,[98] there is clear evidence for the use of the following ones.

That the Gospel of Matthew was employed is most apparent in the list of apostles in R 1.55-62, which is clearly derived from Matt. 10:2-4. The following verse in that gospel, Matt. 10:5, is referred to in R 1.57.3. R 1.37.2 similarly reflects a saying found only in Matt. 9:13 and 12:7; R 1.42.4 mentions the guarding of the tomb as in Matt. 27:62-66 and 28:11-15; and R 1.41.2 seems to be based on Matt. 4:23.[99]

Use of material specific to Luke seems to be reflected in the source's statement that there were seventy-two disciples after the Twelve (R 1.40.4 and Luke 10:1, 17; compare also R 1.34.2).[100] Passages specific to Mark have yet to be identified in this section of R.

Jubilees is intentional.

[97]See, for example, Strecker, *Das Judenchristentum in den Pseudoklementinen*, 253, Lüdemann, *Antipaulinismus*, 242-43 (*Opposition to Paul*, 181, 300), and Van Voorst, *The Ascents of James*, 79, n. 4.

[98]For example, the author may have known some New Testament writings but might not have employed them in his presentation. In general, it should be no surprise that the author's text was "Western" in quality; see, e.g., n. 100.

[99]Rufinus is perhaps responsible for making the last passage even closer to Matthew. On R 1.37.2 see, however, Kline, *The Sayings of Jesus*, 142. Compare further R 1.64.2 with Matt. 24:15; R 1.69.4 with Matt. 28:20; R 1.40.2 with Matt. 11:18-19 and its parallel in Luke 7:33-34; R 1.61.2 with Matt. 5:5-6 and its parallel in Luke 6:21.

[100]See, nevertheless, Hilgenfeld, *Recognitionen und Homilien*, 66-67. For possible dependency on Luke, compare also R 1.41.3 with Luke 23:45 and R 1.54.6-7 with the "Western" text of Luke 11:52.

Dependency on Acts is evident, or may be suspected, at many places in R 1.27-71.[101] A noteworthy case is R 1.36.2, which reflects Acts 3:22-23. While Rufinus has made the text even closer to Acts, the order of words shared between the *Pseudo-Clementines* and Acts against Deuteronomy, the common use of the second person plural again in contrast to Deuteronomy, and the apparent combination of Deut. 18:15-16, 19 with Lev. 23:29 (note the appearance of "soul" and words for destruction) removes suspicion that this passage could be dependent simply on the Old Testament.[102] Similarly, R 1.65.3 is quite conspicuously dependent on Acts 5:38-39, and R 1.71.3-4 is obviously based on Acts 9:1-2 or its parallels in Acts 22:5 and 26:12. The numbering of the Jerusalem Christians as 5,000 in R 1.71.2 also doubtless derives from Acts 4:4. These instances may suffice as concrete evidence of the employment of Acts.[103]

Yet the author's use of Acts is by no means a sign of his submission to this presentation as authoritative. Instead, the author's dependency seems to reflect rather something of an obsession with this presentation of early Christian history; he seems to be annoyed by

---

[101]Compare Brown, *James*, 225-30, Van Voorst, *The Ascents of James*, 79, n. 4, and Beyschlag, "Jakobusmartyrium," 155-65. Beyschlag's view that the source was dependent on a pre-Lukan form of the material has been refuted by Brown.

Dependency on Acts is affirmed also by Strecker, *Das Judenchristentum in den Pseudoklementinen*, 253, and Lüdemann, *Antipaulinismus*, 242-43 with n. 50 (*Opposition to Paul*, 181, 300, n. 50). Along with Hegesippus, this witness needs to be taken into consideration in treatments of the reception of Acts in ancient Christianity.

[102]Compare Kline, *The Sayings of Jesus*, 147-48, where the Syriac has unfortunately been neglected, Strecker, *Das Judenchristentum in den Pseudoklementinen*, 122, and Howard M. Teeple, *The Mosaic Eschatological Prophet*, Journal of Biblical Literature Monograph Series, vol. 10 (Philadelphia: Society of Biblical Literature, 1957), 88.

[103]Compare also R 1.43.3 with Acts 4:4, 6:7; R 1.60.5 with Acts 1:23, 26; R 1.62.1-2 with Acts 4:6, 13, 17-18, 21, 29; R 1.62.5 with Acts 4:13; R 1.65.4-5 with Acts 4:3; R 1.70.8-71.1 with Acts 14:19-20; the figure of Gamaliel in R 1.65.2-5, 66.4-67.7 with Acts 5:34-39; and the entire historical review in R 1.32-40 with Acts 7:2-53. Other passages may have Old Testament material from Acts. Compare, for example, R 1.34.2 with Acts 7:8 and R 1.34.3 with Acts 7:6.

Acts' presentation and attempts to pick out the true elements and set them aright.[104]

Material possibly from the Gospel of John was sought particularly by J. L. Martyn with uncertain results.[105]   It is difficult to move beyond this realm of uncertainty. Elements that render dependency on John probable are the discussion of Mount Gerizim in R 1.57.1 (see John 4:20) and the portrayal of Gamaliel as a "secret" Christian.[106] While the author thus seems to have known the Gospel of John, it seems that he did not accord it the same importance as the Gospel of Matthew.

Contrary to other sections in the *Pseudo-Clementines* that draw on Paul's own letters in order to attack this missionary,[107] the author of the source of R 1.27-71 never displays evidence of knowing the content of Paul's writings. It should not be doubted, however, that the author of the source knew of Paul's letters, though he might never have read them or taken their content seriously.[108]

Some of the most striking parallels in R 1.27-71 are not with the New Testament, but rather with other early Christian writings. It is particularly important to note that this material can provide valuable clues regarding the author and date of the source of R 1.

Of decisive significance for the investigation of the source of R 1 are the parallels in Hegesippus.[109] The most relevant texts have recently

---

[104]Compare Brown, *James*, 229-30.

[105]Martyn, "Clementine Recognitions," 273-91. His results were summarized above in the first chapter.

[106]See R 1.65.2, 66.4 (especially the Syriac), and 68.1-2, and compare John 12:42-43 and 19:38 and the remarks on Nicodemus in John 3:1-5, 7:50-52, and 19:39-40. This material will be discussed further in chapter five.

[107]See, for example, *Epistula Petri* 2.4, 6, which displays knowledge of Gal. 2:11-21.

[108]Dependence on other writings of the New Testament cannot be demonstrated with certainty. If Rufinus's rendering of R 1.27.3 were correct with its reference to "crystal," then one might assume dependency on Rev. 4:6. In view of R 1.34.6, 7, however, it seems likely that Rufinus is responsible for adding this word.

[109]The most pertinent fragment of Hegesippus is preserved in Eusebius *Historia Ecclesiastica* 2.23.4-18. Eduard Schwartz, "Zu Eusebius Kirchengeschichte," *Zeitschrift für die neutestamentliche Wissenschaft* 4 (1903): 48-57, thought that Eusebius had access to only an interpolated version of Hegesippus and presents a

been repeatedly subjected to thorough analysis and presented in synoptic form.[110] It is the consensus of these recent investigations that neither is Hegesippus dependent on the immediate source of R 1.27-71 nor is this source dependent on Hegesippus but rather that both Hegesippus and the source of R 1.27-71 are each dependent on an earlier source or tradition.[111] While this thesis must remain a possibility, it needs to be asked anew if the source of R 1.27-71 could just be directly dependent on Hegesippus.[112] Such a solution would

---

reconstruction of what he considered to be the original text of Hegesippus. This extremely hypothetical reconstruction has been given blanket approval by scholars such as Lüdemann, *Antipaulinismus*, 233, n. 24 (*Opposition to Paul*, 298, n. 24), and has thereby acquired the appearance of having some credibility (yet when even Lüdemann summarizes Hegesippus in *Antipaulinismus*, 235-36 [*Opposition to Paul*, 175-76] he has failed to follow all of Schwartz's suggestions, e.g., the elimination of the scribes and Pharisees from the report; see Schwartz, 54-55). Actual examination of Schwartz's article should be enough to convince any reader that this reconstruction is at most just a possibility. In fact, there is insufficient reason for supposing that the text of Hegesippus available to Eusebius had been interpolated. Eusebius *Historia Ecclesiastica* 4.8.2 explicitly states that Hegesippus wrote in a very simple manner, and thus repetitions probably belonged to Hegesippus's narrative style and should not be all mechanically eliminated. See Zahn, *Forschungen*, 6:252-53, n. 1, for a list of such repetitions and other elements of simple style. Compare also the criticism of Schwartz, for example, by Hengel, "Jakobus der Herrenbruder," 76, n. 19. Schwartz's thesis will thus not be adopted in the following.

[110]See the synopses in Pratscher, *Jakobus und die Jakobustradition*, 239-40, and Lüdemann, *Antipaulinismus*, 235-36 (*Opposition to Paul*, 175-76), and compare Brown, *James*, 214.

[111]See Schoeps, *Theologie und Geschichte des Judenchristentums*, 415, 438, Beyschlag, "Jakobusmartyrium," 154, Lüdemann, *Antipaulinismus*, 236-37 (*Opposition to Paul*, 176-77), Pratscher, *Jakobus und die Jakobustradition*, 244-48, 254-55. Pratscher, ibid., 247-48, states that the assumption of a common written source is not justified. Lüdemann, *Antipaulinismus*, 236-37, 245 (*Opposition to Paul*, 176-77, 183), writes of an archetype and redaction thereupon, thus implying a written source, as postulated also by Schoeps. Brown, *James*, 267-68, however, is hesitant about postulating any (literary) relationship between the two. Strecker, *Das Judenchristentum in den Pseudoklementinen*, 249-50, also minimized the correspondences.

[112]So Schmidt, *Studien*, 325, n. 2. Schmidtke, *Judenchristliche Evangelien*, 184-85, also stated that "the redactor" (evidently R) was influenced by Hegesippus in this section. Rehm, "Entstehung," 146, similarly thought that the author of R probably drew on Hegesippus in composing this section. Most recently, Rius-Camps, "Sucesión y ministerios en las Pseudoclementinas," 170, n. 12, has stated that B very probably was inspired by Hegesippus in this section.

have the clear advantage of not having to postulate a lost written source. It also accounts better for the numerous agreements between the two writings, some of which are quite literal.[113]   In fact, one of

---

For the following, compare my study "The Martyrdom of James in Hegesippus, Clement of Alexandria, and Christian Apocrypha, Including Nag Hammadi: A Study of the Textual Relations," in *Society of Biblical Literature 1990 Seminar Papers: One Hundred Twenty-Sixth Annual Meeting, November 17-20, 1990, The New Orleans Marriott, The Sheraton New Orleans, New Orleans, Louisiana*, ed. David J. Lull, Society of Biblical Literature Seminar Papers Series, vol. 29 (Atlanta: Scholars Press, 1990), 322-35.

[113]Note the following agreements: (1) the listing of the Jewish sects and discussion with them (*Historia Ecclesiastica* 4.22.7, 2.23.8; R 1.54-65); (2) the notion that these Jewish sects were constituted against the Messiah (*Historia Ecclesiastica* 4.22.7; R 1.54.1); (3) mention of Simon and Dositheus in connection with these sects (*Historia Ecclesiastica* 4.22.5; R 1.54.3, 5); (4) a "commotion" (*Historia Ecclesiastica* 2.23.10; R 1.70.3); (5) the summons to discuss Jesus' messiahship and to "persuade" (*Historia Ecclesiastica* 2.23.10-11; R 1.43.1, 44.2, 55.1); (6) the notion of being "deceived" (*Historia Ecclesiastica* 2.23.10, 11, 12; R 1.62.1); (7) the time is that of the Passover (*Historia Ecclesiastica* 2.23.10, 11; R 1.44.1); (8) leaders had become believers in Hegesippus, while in R Gamaliel is a Christian and the high priest is ready to be baptized (*Historia Ecclesiastica* 2.23.10; R 1.65.2, 69.8); (9) "all the people" were on the verge of believing in Jesus as the Christ (*Historia Ecclesiastica* 2.23.10; R 1.43.1, 69.8); (10) James is in a high place where he is "visible" "to all the people" (*Historia Ecclesiastica* 2.23.11; R 1.66.3); (11) "crying out" (*Historia Ecclesiastica* 2.23.12, 15, 17; R 1.70.1); (12) James speaks concerning the parousia of Jesus (*Historia Ecclesiastica* 2.23.13; R 1.69.4); (13) the positive effect of James's speech (*Historia Ecclesiastica* 2.23.14; R 1.69.8); (14) James is "thrown down" from a height (*Historia Ecclesiastica* 2.23.16; R 1.70.8); (15) (no) beating of James with a piece of wood (*Historia Ecclesiastica* 2.23.18; R 1.70.8); (16) the cry "Stop! What are you doing?" (*Historia Ecclesiastica* 2.23.17) and R 1.70.2 ("What are you doing?") as well as 1.70.5 ("What are you doing? Why are you delaying?"--the first question here is not witnessed by the Syriac); (17) the notion that the Roman war against the Jews was connected with the rejection of the Christian message (*Historia Ecclesiastica* 2.23.18; R 1.37.2 Syriac, 39.3); (18) mention of gravestone(s) (*Historia Ecclesiastica* 2.23.18; R 1.71.5).

Compare the lists of agreements in Brown, *James*, 214, and Pratscher, *Jakobus und die Jakobustradition*, 246-47.   Strecker did not give enough consideration to these parallels, and his remark to R 1.70 that the only common element between this text and the report of Hegesippus is the fall of James is a gross understatement (Strecker, *Das Judenchristentum in den Pseudoklementinen*, 249-50; strangely similar: Hengel, "Jakobus der Herrenbruder," 76-77).

Perhaps the strongest argument against the view that the source of R 1 is directly dependent on Hegesippus is the claim that Hegesippus is secondary in mentioning the pinnacle of the temple as the place of James's fall.   See, for example, Lipsius, *Apostelgeschichten*, 2.2:244, Schoeps, *Theologie und Geschichte des Judenchristentums*, 415, and Pratscher, *Jakobus und die Jakobustradition*, 245

the few points that has hindered the adoption of this solution is the supposed earlier date of the source of R 1.[114] Yet there is no sufficient reason for assuming that the source of R 1 was composed before Hegesippus, and thus there is no reason for not assuming that the source did indeed employ Hegesippus.

Previous research is generally agreed that the same relationship applies to the *Second Apocalypse of James* as is usually thought to be the case with Hegesippus and the source of R 1. All three are thus supposed to derive independently from a lost source or group of traditions.[115] The above result with respect to the relationship of Hegesippus and the source of R 1 raises the question anew. Examination of the texts and of previous arguments again reveals no reason for not assuming that the martyrdom in the *Second Apocalypse of James* 61.12-62.16 is directly or indirectly dependent on Hegesippus.[116] The correspondences are numerous also in this case,

---

("with certitude secondary"). Yet Pratscher's own stemma of the reports brings him (and others) into difficulty at this point, for two of his three independent witnesses to the source of the Jewish Christian tradition (Hegesippus and the *Second Apocalypse of James*) speak of the pinnacle as the place of James's fall. Pratscher is thus forced to invalidate his stemma by assuming that Hegesippus and the *Second Apocalypse of James* are also jointly dependent on another tradition later than the version reflected in R 1 (*Jakobus und die Jakobustradition*, 251). Brown, *James*, 182, in contrast, correctly drew the conclusion that the "pinnacle" must have been mentioned in the source.

See other possible points against the original quality of Hegesippus's report in Beyschlag, "Jakobusmartyrium," 151-53, none of which are substantial.

[114]See, for example, Brown, *James*, 268. It should be remembered that in earlier research this section was often considered to be book seven of the *Kerygmata Petrou*.

[115]See Lüdemann, *Antipaulinismus*, 231-33, 236-37 (*Opposition to Paul*, 171-73, 176-77), and Pratscher, *Jakobus und die Jakobustradition*, 241-44, 248-51, 254-55. Compare Brown, *James*, 267-68, and Wolf-Peter Funk, ed., trans., and comm., *Die Zweite Apokalypse des Jakobus aus Nag-Hammadi-Codex V*, Texte und Untersuchungen zur Geschichte der altchristlichen Literatur, vol. 119 (Berlin: Akademie, 1976), 173.

[116]Pratscher, *Jakobus und die Jakobustradition*, 251, lists merely one element common to the source of R 1 and the *Second Apocalypse of James* that is not found in Hegesippus: mention of "stairs." Yet in the framework of Pratscher's own deliberations this observation can carry no weight, for on p. 167 he has followed W.-P. Funk in separating (traditionally) the section mentioning "stairs" from the report of the martyrdom. Brown's arguments in *James*, 173-87, similarly prove

and literary dependency is again made likely in view of several literal agreements.[117]

Since the question of the relationship to Hegesippus (and the *Second Apocalypse of James*) is often involved with the further question of the relationship of the source of R 1.27-71 to the *Anabathmoi Jakobou* mentioned by Epiphanius, it is appropriate to turn now to this issue. There are two elements of this problem that should be clearly distinguished: first, exegesis of Epiphanius's remarks to determine precisely what information he provides, and second, a comparison of this information with R 1.27-71.

With regard to the first aspect, when Epiphanius writes in *Panarion* 30.16.6 that the Ebionites "call other acts 'of the apostles,'" it is likely that all that Epiphanius had available to him was the material of R 1 and the *Anabathmoi Jakobou*, which he immediately describes in *Panarion* 30.16.7-9. Since it is very unlikely that Epiphanius would have

---

nothing.

The narrative framework in the first part of the *Second Apocalypse of James* does indeed seem to stem from a source different from the martyrdom. Several features (the secret priest, the stairs, the descriptions of the crowd, the prediction of the destruction of the temple) make it probable that this part is loosely dependent on the material of R 1 as found either in its original source, in B, or perhaps even in R.

[117]Compare especially *Second Apocalypse of James* 61.13-15 ("Come, let us stone the Just One") with Eusebius *Historia Ecclesiastica* 2.23.16 ("Let us stone James the Just")--Pratscher, *Jakobus und die Jakobustradition*, 254, has to dismiss this as *independent* contamination from Josephus--, the play on Isa. 3:10 in *Second Apocalypse of James* 61.16-19 ("Yes, let us kill this man so that he might be removed from among us, for he will be of no use to us") with the citation of Isa. 3:10 in *Historia Ecclesiastica* 2.23.15 ("Let us take away the Just One, for he is of no use to us"), and *Second Apocalypse of James* 62.7 ("You have erred") with *Historia Ecclesiastica* 2.23.15 ("Even the Just One erred"). For the many other correspondences, which need not be further listed here, see Brown, *James*, 173, Lüdemann, *Antipaulinismus*, 231-32 (*Opposition to Paul*, 171-72)--Lüdemann fails to list a single reason for not assuming that the *Second Apocalypse of James* is directly dependent on Hegesippus; this remark pertains to his n. 20 on p. 232 (*Opposition to Paul*, 298, n. 20)--, Pratscher, *Jakobus und die Jakobustradition*, 239-40, 248-51, and Jones, "The Martyrdom of James," 332. The view that the *Second Apocalypse of James* presupposes Hegesippus has been recently promoted by Cirillo, "L'antipaolinismo nelle Pseudoclementine," 136.

There is also no reason to deny that the *First Apocalypse of James* is indebted to Hegesippus. Brown, *James*, 108-9, does this, without any substantial basis.

invented a name for Ebionite writings,[118] it must be considered most probable that the *Anabathmoi Jakobou* did in fact exist and was available to Epiphanius. The text reads best when it is understood as indicating that all of the material in *Panarion* 30.16.7-9, and not merely *Panarion* 30.16.7, was in the *Anabathmoi Jakobou*.[119]

When the details of *Panarion* 30.16.7-9 are compared with R 1.27-71, the differences are more striking than the similarities.[120] Thus, R 1.27-71 contains nothing of either the deprecation of Paul on the basis of his supposed Greek descent or the tale of his attempt to marry the daughter of a priest (*Panarion* 30.16.8-9). Nor, for example, does *James* preach against the temple, sacrifices, and fire on the altar in R 1.68.3-69.8, though R 1.70.6 does mention the fire on the altar, and sacrifices are declared outdated in a speech by Peter in R 1.64.1 (compare R 1.36.1, 37.2). Furthermore, Peter says that the temple will be destroyed because of the continued sacrifices in R 1.64.2 (compare R 1.37.2-4).[121] Yet these elements seem to represent little more

---

[118]Contra Schmidtke, *Judenchristliche Evangelien*, 182-83.

[119]See, for example, Hort, *Clementine Recognitions*, 41-42, Strecker, *Das Judenchristentum in den Pseudoklementinen*, 252, Brown, *James*, 202, Pratscher, *Jakobus und die Jakobustradition*, 134, n. 43.

[120]This, of course, has been pointed out by a number of scholars from Lehmann, *Die clementinischen Schriften*, 344-45, onwards.
Here is a translation of the entire passage in the *Panarion*:
(30.16.6) "They call other acts 'of the apostles.' In these there is much that is full of impiety. There they armed themselves against the truth in no minor way. (7) Now they set out certain steps and guides in the *Steps of James* (*Anabathmoi Jakobou*) as if he expounds against the temple and sacrifices and against the fire on the altar and many other things full of babble. (8) Hence, they are not ashamed of denouncing even Paul here through certain contrived falsehoods of their pseudoapostles' villainy and deceit. They say, on the one hand, that he was a Tarsian, as he himself declares and does not deny. On the other hand, they assert that he was from the Greeks by taking a pretext in the passage spoken by him through love of the truth, 'I am a Tarsian, a citizen of no ignoble city' (Acts 21:39). (9) Then they say that he was a Greek, the child of both a Greek mother and a Greek father, that he went to Jerusalem and remained there a while, that he desired to marry a priest's daughter, that for this reason he became a proselyte and was circumcised, that when he still did not receive such a girl he became angry and wrote against circumcision and against the Sabbath and the law."

[121]It is also possible to see a common element in the references to the stairs of the temple in R 1.55.2 and 1.70.8 and the first word in the title *Anabathmoi Jakobou*. Yet it is far from certain that ἀναβαθμά here means "stairs" or even

than common themes that were not limited to these writings but that rather had a much broader currency in Jewish Christian traditions.[122] This observation means that the postulation of a main common written source for R 1.27-71 and the *Anabathmoi Jakobou* mentioned by Epiphanius[123] does not rest on sufficient evidence in the texts; the marked differences between the two accounts actually speak with a fairly clear voice against this thesis.[124]

It remains to be asked more broadly if the source of R 1 shows signs of dependency on any other known patristic or apocryphal literature.

While the evidence for usage of the *Anabathmoi Jakobou* is insufficient, there are some striking agreements with another Jewish Christian writing mentioned by Epiphanius, the *Gospel of the Ebionites*.[125] Unfortunately, only a few small fragments of this gospel have survived; this state of affairs will severely hamper any attempt to determine literary relationships with other writings. Nevertheless, the source of R 1 and certain of the preserved excerpts from the *Gospel of the Ebionites* concur in points that render the literary dependency of this source on the gospel probable. The most remarkable common element is the explicit statement that the Pharisees were baptized by John (Epiphanius *Panarion* 30.13.4, R 1.54.6-7).[126]

"ascents."

[122]See, for example, Epiphanius *Panarion* 19.3.6, where Elchasai is said to have condemned sacrifices, rites, altar, and fire as foreign to God, and the citation from the *Gospel of the Ebionites* in *Panarion* 30.16.5, where Christ says that he has come to abolish sacrifices.

[123]So, for example, Strecker, *Das Judenchristentum in den Pseudoklementinen*, 252-53, and those who have followed him, such as Martyn, "Clementine Recognitions," 270. Van Voorst, *The Ascents of James*, 45, has vulgarized even this position to make R 1 directly dependent on the *Anabathmoi Jakobou*; he simultaneously feels no compulsion to explain the differences or how the material in Epiphanius fits together with the material in R 1.

[124]Nevertheless, absolute certainty is not attainable at this point not least because such a small portion of the *Anabathmoi Jakobou* is represented in Epiphanius's report.

[125]By "*Gospel of the Ebionites*" I intend the fragments of the apocryphal gospel preserved in Epiphanius *Panarion* 30.13.2-8, 14.5, 16.5, and 22.4.

[126]In the New Testament the baptism of the Pharisees is never explicitly

Furthermore, the connection between the continuation of sacrifices and divine destruction (R 1.37.2-4; compare R 1.39.3) and the understanding of the purpose of Christ's coming as admonition to discontinue sacrifices (R 1.39.1, 54.1) agree strikingly with the excerpt from the *Gospel of the Ebionites* in Epiphanius *Panarion* 30.16.5 ("I have come to abolish sacrifices, and unless you desist from sacrificing, wrath will not desist from you"). One may also ask if the vegetarianism of the *Gospel of the Ebionites* (Epiphanius *Panarion* 30.22.4) was not of influence on the source of R 1 (see R 1.30.1). However that may be, it seems that the first two points of agreement are substantial enough to support the thesis that the source of R 1 used the *Gospel of the Ebionites*.[127]

Another writing with which the source of R 1 shows several agreements is Justin's *Dialogue with Trypho*. Thus, the notion that sacrifices were allowed in accommodation to the Israelites in order to hinder idolatry (R 1.36.1) is also found in Justin *Dialogue* 19.6.[128] This parallel is particularly striking if the Syriac's mention of the "name of God" is original. The objection that Jesus was a magician (R 1.42.3, 58.1, 70.2) is similarly found in *Dialogue* 69.7. Furthermore, the notion of "perishing" by believing in Christ is found both in the *Dialogue* 8.4 and R 1.62.1. Other agreements with Justin are found in the descriptions of the two comings of Christ (see *Dialogue* 14.8, 32.2, 40.4, 49.2, 7-8 and R 1.69.4).[129] Both sources agree that the first coming was one of humiliation while the second is one of glory. Taken together, these elements of agreement are perhaps not strong enough to confirm absolutely literary dependency on Justin's *Dialogue,* but neither can such dependency be absolutely ruled out.

---

affirmed. For the closest parallel, see Matt. 3:7. Compare also the "Western" text of Matt. 21:32.

It is nevertheless possible that B is responsible for adding the remark that the scribes and Pharisees were baptized by John.

[127]Another possible point of influence of this gospel on the source of R 1 will be mentioned below in the section on B's redaction.

[128]Compare also, however, the Jewish material collected in Schoeps, *Theologie und Geschichte des Judenchristentums,* 227-28.

[129]See also R 1.49.2-4, 50.5 and Justin *First Apology* 52.3.

Such are the literary relationships of the source of R 1 with Jewish and other early Christian writings. These observations will be of importance later in the discussion of the date of the source and also now in the following discussion of the original structure of this lost writing.

Towards the Original Structure of the Source

A RELEVANT CONSEQUENCE ARISING FROM THE PRECEDING SECTION

The decision above pertaining to the lack of an immediate relationship to the *Anabathmoi Jakobou* means that the *Anabathmoi Jakobou* cannot be employed to reconstruct the original source of R 1.27-71. Since the *Anabathmoi Jakobou* has so often been drawn upon for precisely such purposes, a consequent rejection of this procedure places the investigator before something of a tabula rasa.

To start with just one large skeleton left standing when this thesis is consequently abandoned, the assumption that in the source of R 1 James originally held a much longer speech than R 1.68.3-69.8 and that this speech may be recovered by pasting together (parts of) the apostles' speeches in R 1.55-64 as well as much of R 1.44.4-52.6 now dissolves into the question of why the author of the basic writing should have eliminated a longer speech by James. Did not James form the hinge of his entire story?[130] Even in the present version of R 1.27-71, James obviously presents the high point of the entire report. It would thus be strange for the author of the basic writing (hereafter called "basic author") to preserve and massively reinforce such a narrative structure and simultaneously to plunder all but a few lines of one of the two speeches of this virtually ethereal character. Such considerations throw an even greater shadow on the thesis that R 1.27-71 and the *Anabathmoi Jakobou* derive from a common source. But they also lead to positive insights: the structure of the story in the source of R 1.27-71 was, at least on this not negligible point, similar to the structure as preserved in the present *Recognitions*.

---

[130]Consider the framing motif of Clement sending his report to James (see, for example, *Epistula Clementis* 20, H 1.20.2-3 and its parallel in R 1.17.2-3, and R 3.74.4).

B'S REDACTION

In the section above on "delimiting the source" redaction by B was already discussed in order to isolate the blocks of material that belong to the source. In the present section the tool of redaction criticism will be taken up again and applied to the delimited material itself (the axe will be exchanged for the scalpel, so to speak), the goal being to proceed toward the disclosure of the original structure of the source by removing the later layers. First, the most apparent accretions will be removed and examined. Further clues might then be found as to what else is secondary.

One element that immediately catches the eye of the reader is the unusual baptismal formula that is also found throughout other parts of the *Pseudo-Clementines*. While both translators apparently had difficulty in rendering the Greek of the formula or modified it on purpose, the original wording seems clear enough from a comparison of the two translations and from the parallel passages. The Greek in R 1.63.3 and 69.5 undoubtedly spoke of the τρισμακαρία ἐπονομασία.[131] This unusual phrase and its accompanying remark about baptism in "living" water should doubtless be attributed to B.[132] B is concerned to emphasize that this particular baptism is absolutely necessary for salvation,[133] and he seems to have felt that in his source this point was not sufficiently made.[134]

Another element that reflects B's redaction is the figure of the true prophet.[135] This figure presents one of B's main doctrines and also appears in R 1.27-71, though not as often as one might expect. Instead, R 1.27-71 speaks more often of Jesus just as the Christ and

---

[131]See, for example, H 9.19.4 and its parallel in R 4.32.2 and H 11.23.3 and its parallel in R 6.9.3. For the translation of this phrase by Rufinus and the Syriac translator, compare also R 3.67.4. For other examples, see the concordance.

[132]Compare, for example, Strecker, *Das Judenchristentum in den Pseudo-klementinen*, 249.

[133]See, for example, H 11.25-26 and its parallel and H 13.21.2-3.

[134]See the slightly ambivalent statement on the origin of baptism in R 1.39.2 (which the Syriac translator felt obliged to correct).

[135]See the comments on this subject above in the section on the "delimitation of the source."

as the prophet predicted by Moses. It is remarkable that in the debates of the disciples with the Jewish sects "the prophet of truth" plays no role at all,[136] whereas at the insertion by B (R 1.44.1-53.4) this figure immediately reappears (R 1.44.5-6).

Careful study of the texts will undoubtedly reveal further such doctrinal corrections; more important at this point in the present study is the question of how much of the larger framework of the narrative should be attributed to B.

One element of the framework that reveals how B redacted the material to fit his larger story is the statement in R 1.70.8 that the "enemy" did not smite James again after his fall. James's survival is crucial to B's narrative, according to which Peter sends his reports to James in Jerusalem. By letting James survive the fall B simultaneously transforms the story of James's martyrdom into a preliminary encounter.[137]

Another part of B's framework is found in the summarizing phrases pertaining to what Peter had said at other places (when this material is not contained in R 1.27-71). R 1.33.3 is such an instance.[138]

---

[136]In R 1.27-44.3, 53-71, this figure is mentioned only in R 1.33.1, 3 (Syriac), 34.4, 37.3 (Latin), 54.5 (Latin), and 69.5. This observation again speaks strongly against the attribution of this material (either in form or content) to B's redaction.

[137]The chronological placement of these events in the seventh year after the passion might thus possibly be attributable to B and not to the source. Nevertheless, it is quite possible that the source presupposed a late date for the death of Jesus. Alexander of Jerusalem, for example, evidently dated Jesus' death to 58 C.E. See Ernst von Dobschütz, *Das Kerygma Petrou kritisch untersucht*, Texte und Untersuchungen zur Geschichte der altchristlichen Literatur, vol. 11, no. 1 (Leipzig: J. C. Hinrichs, 1893), 136-50. See the discussion of other early Christian witnesses to this type of view in Walter Bauer, *Das Leben Jesu im Zeitalter der neutestamentlichen Apokryphen* (Tübingen: J. C. B. Mohr [Paul Siebeck], 1909), 290-95. B apparently did not share this chronology; see H 1.6.1 and its parallel R 1.6.1, and see above, p. 129.

One telltale sign of B's alteration at this point is the difficulty that results from having the congregation flee from Jerusalem in R 1.71.2 while wanting James still to remain there (R 1.72.1 Syriac). Rufinus evidently tried to smooth over the discrepancy in the last mentioned passage, and this has led some research to the view that R thought James, too, fled to Jericho. See, for example, Bousset, review of *Die Pseudoklementinen*, by H. Waitz, 427, and Pratscher, *Jakobus und die Jakobustradition*, 133, n. 41.

[138]See also R 1.29.3 (Syriac).

This insight into the redactional nature of R 1.33.3 leads to the question of how much of the surrounding material seems to need to be attributed to B. It was noted above that B introduced the figure of the true prophet into his source material. This figure is found at this point (R 1.33.3) in the Syriac as well as at R 1.33.1. Thus, it seems likely that B is responsible for having introduced a larger block of material at R 1.33. Indeed, R 1.33 as a whole is a doublet, for a revelation to Abraham has already occurred in R 1.32.3-4[139] and his two sons are introduced again in R 1.34.1 as if they had not been discussed in R 1.33.3-5. Furthermore, since R 1.34.1 joins onto the end of R 1.32.4 without difficulty, the conclusion lies at hand that R 1.33 as a whole is an insertion by B. The material of R 1.33.2, in particular, strikes one as perhaps the best short summary of B's views found anywhere in the *Pseudo-Clementines*.[140]

Another element of the framework that is sometimes attributed to the work of B (or R) is the stereotype phrase employed at the end of each of the apostles' speeches.[141] Indeed, Lüdemann took this as a major sign that all of R 1.55-65 should be attributed to B or R.[142] Yet it is at least just as likely that this phrase, or a similar one, stood in the source, where it might have been formulated in dependence on a similar phrase in Hegesippus.[143] While the Pseudo-Clementine

---

[139]Thus, the statement concerning Abraham's ignorance in R 1.33.1 takes the reader by surprise.

[140]The parallels in B at this point overwhelm even Strecker, *Das Judenchristentum in den Pseudoklementinen*, 224, and are also noticed and discussed by Van Voorst, *The Ascents of James*, 32. See, in particular, H 1.17.2-4 and its parallel R 1.14.2-4 and H 8.10.2 and its parallel R 4.9.2.
Furthermore, the parallels of R 1.33.3b-5 with Bardaisan's *Book of the Laws of the Countries* 27-29, 43 (Arabs, Persians, Brahmins, Indians, Egypt, circumcision) are also indicative of B's hand. The view of Eliezer as the son of Abraham (R 1.33.3, 34.1) similarly seems to stem from B's redaction (see H 2.16.5, 52.2).

[141]See, e.g., the last words of R 1.55.4, 56.3, and 57.5. For isolation of this phrase as redactional, see Lüdemann, *Antipaulinismus*, 239-40 (*Opposition to Paul*, 179).

[142]Lüdemann, *Antipaulinismus*, 240 with n. 41 (*Opposition to Paul*, 179 with n. 41 on p. 299).

[143]Eusebius *Historia Ecclesiastica* 2.23.18, 3.32.3, 6. See Beyschlag, "Jakobusmartyrium," 154.

concordance reveals many parallels to the first words of the phrase,[144] it is remarkable that the connection of these words with the concluding statement "he was silent" occurs only in R 1.55-65.[145] This finding renders it likely that the source of R 1.27-71 had a similar concluding phrase after each disciple's speech. Furthermore, there is no reason for assuming that B (or R) inserted the list of sects and the disciples' disputes with them, for the origin of the idea for this narrative is evidently Hegesippus in Eusebius *Historia Ecclesiastica* 2.23.8, where Hegesippus states that some of the seven sects, whom he had mentioned earlier, posed questions to James. The author of the source of R 1.27-71 did little more than expand the narrative on the basis of Hegesippus's own remarks.

A more fundamental question relating to the framework of R 1.27-71 is whether Peter was originally the narrator of the account or, indeed, whether there was any narrator at all. Peter is, of course, a main figure of the *Pseudo-Clementines*, and it is thus very plausible that B would have introduced him as the narrator if the original source had another personage filling this role, especially one who played little or no role in the Pseudo-Clementine story. Are there any clues as to how this narrative was originally related?[146]

As noted in the history of research, Hans Waitz expressed the view that R 1.53-71 was originally a writing composed under the name of Thomas. Waitz reached this conclusion on the basis of the disturbed

---

[144]See the separate listing of this phrase in Georg Strecker, *Die Pseudoklementinen III: Konkordanz zu den Pseudoklementinen*, Die griechischen christlichen Schriftsteller der ersten Jahrhunderte (Berlin: Akademie, 1986-89), s.v. *similis*; see also s.v. ὅμοιος.

[145]See Strecker, *Konkordanz*, s.v. *sileo* and σιωπάω.

[146]Since the time of Uhlhorn, *Homilien und Recognitionen*, 365-66, it has been supposed that the third person reference to Peter in R 1.71.4 demonstrates not only that the material derives from a source but that the source was not originally related in the first person (of Peter). See Lehmann, *Die clementinischen Schriften*, 345-46, Waitz, *Die Pseudoklementinen, Homilien und Rekognitionen*, 109, and recently and emphatically Van Voorst, *The Ascents of James*, 159, n. 70. This argument was shown to be faulty, however, already by Schmidt, *Studien*, 22, n. 3, who pointed out that in the narrative R 1.71.4 is presenting the report of someone who had come from Jerusalem.

order of the apostles in R 1.55-62 (compared with Matt. 10:2-4).[147] The observation that the pair Thomas and Matthew has been displaced is correct, but for the following reasons it seems more likely that the original writing was composed under the name of Matthew rather than under the name of Thomas.

First of all, Waitz assumes that the author not only displaced the pair Thomas and Matthew but also divided it to place Matthew at the beginning and Thomas at the end. A simpler assumption would be that the author merely displaced the pair to have Thomas and Matthew come last. The basic author would then have only exchanged the first and last speakers. This assumption would imply that the original narrator in the source of R 1.27-71 was Matthew.

Additional weight comes to this view when it is considered that the source employed the *Gospel of the Ebionites*, which was also composed in the name of Matthew,[148] and that Jewish Christians in general held Matthew and his gospel(s) in high regard. It thus seems likely that the source of R 1.27-71 was originally composed as a writing of Matthew. This conclusion allows the first person plural pronoun, which occurs throughout this section,[149] to remain as part of the source.

All of these observations on the original structure of the source may now be extended in the final chapter of this study, which will directly address the source's author and his intentions.

---

[147]Waitz, *Die Pseudoklementinen, Homilien und Rekognitionen*, 168.

[148]See Epiphanius *Panarion* 30.13.2-3.

[149]See, e.g., R 1.55.3, 63.1, 66.1.

V

Conclusion

The Author's Identity and Perspective on the Nature and History of Christianity

The preceding investigations may now be all drawn together to construct a portrait of the author of the source of R 1.27-71.

It has been seen that the source of R 1 was a writing composed probably under the name of Matthew. This writing offered a survey of history from the time of the creation onwards. While B has the survey extending only to the seventh year after the death of Christ, the original source, in contrast, told of the death of James[1] and possibly ended with the flight of the congregation from Jerusalem to Jericho.[2]

---

[1]Probably also his burial was discussed. See Hegesippus in Eusebius *Historia Ecclesiastica* 2.23.18. The chronology of the source cannot be determined with certainty.

[2]In any event, B stops excerpting material at this point. Whether--and, if so, how--the source continued is a matter of pure speculation.

157

This ending point sheds light on a structuring element of the entire narrative, namely, the concern with the land of Israel.[3] This concern is evident from the report on the early history of humankind, through the debates with the Jewish sects, and even in the very last remarks from the source, for Jericho lies within the land. While the author has adopted some of this material from the Book of Jubilees, he has added and combined other elements in such a way that his own interest is quite apparent. In view of this material, it is strange to find the suggestion that the author is the earliest witness, or one of the earliest witnesses, to the tradition about Pella and indeed thus betrays his own origin in Pella.[4] When the author speaks of refuge to "a fortified place of the land" (R 1.37.2 Syriac), Strecker states that though Pella is not mentioned one can think of no other locality.[5] Yet it must be objected that the text clearly speaks against this assumption because Pella does not lie "in the land" at all but is rather a city of the Decapolis. For the author of the source, the flight of the Christians is to some locality *within* the land, and Jericho was probably conceived as a first stopping point along the way.[6]

---

[3]See the passages listed in the section on "A Source?" in chapter 4.

[4]See Strecker, *Das Judenchristentum in den Pseudoklementinen*, 230, 253, Lüdemann, *Antipaulinismus*, 243, 278 (*Opposition to Paul*, 182, 208), Pratscher, *Jakobus und die Jakobustradition*, 131, n. 36, 134, n. 45, and Van Voorst, *The Ascents of James*, 78. For the origin of this view, see Schmidt, *Studien*, 292-93.

Jozef Verheyden, *De Vlucht van de Christenen naar Pella: Onderzoek van het Getuigenis van Eusebius en Epiphanius*, Verhandelingen van de Koninklijke Academie voor Wetenschappen, Letteren en schone Kunsten van België, Klasse der Letteren, year 50, no. 127 (Brussels: Paleis der Academiën, 1988), 23-28, and "The Flight of the Christians to Pella," *Ephemerides Theologicae Lovanienses* 66 (1990): 371-75, lists more literature on this point and argues for a theological interpretation of the texts that excludes a geographical reference. This argument overlooks the recurrent concern of the source with "the land."

[5]Strecker, *Das Judenchristentum in den Pseudoklementinen*, 230. Compare Koester, "Flight to Pella Tradition," 101, and Wehnert, "Auswanderung der Jerusalemer Christen," 244.

[6]The extent to which this conception was influenced by Hegesippus cannot be determined precisely. It is not clear where Hegesippus thought the election of Simeon took place. What speaks for a locality outside of Jerusalem is the simple statement that there was an assembly "at one place" (ἐπὶ ταὐτόν), where Jerusalem is not explicitly mentioned, in Eusebius *Historia Ecclesiastica* 3.11, which is possibly dependent on Hegesippus, and the fact that the other relatives of Jesus

How this material should be evaluated in respect to the identity of
the author is a difficult question. Stötzel, it will be recalled, thought
that the author represents a Jewish Christian congregation outside of
Jerusalem that hoped to reestablish itself in the city; he consequently
dated the source between 70 and 135 C.E.[7] Since it has been seen,
however, that the author employs Hegesippus and since the edict of
Hadrian also seems to be presupposed (R 1.39.3), Stötzel's configura-
tion cannot be sustained.

Above, the supposed link of this source to the tradition about Pella
was also shown to be a misconception. Thus, if one asks where the
author's home is likely to have been, his theology of the land points in
the direction of Judaea (Syria Palaestina), and a location of the author
actually in Jerusalem itself (Aelia Capitolina) is also not out of the
question.[8] The author sees his religion as generally[9] what God desired
from the beginning. He evidently experiences the (unbelieving) Jews
being forced to endure worshipping without sacrifices (R 1.39.3). For
the author, Christianity is thus a Judaism purified of the sacrifices (and

---

Hegesippus mentions (except James) evidently lived on the land (i.e., outside of
Jerusalem; see Eusebius *Historia Ecclesiastica* 3.20.2; 3.32.6 indicates that they
then led the church[es]). In any event, Hegesippus is hardly responsible for the
theology of the land that occupied the author of the source of R 1.27-71.

[7]Stötzel, "Die Darstellung der ältesten Kirchengeschichte," 32.

[8]Does R 1.71.5 ultimately reflect some sort of local tradition?

Jerusalem (and Judaea) seems sometimes to be excluded as a possible origin
for this writing because, on the assumption of the author's supposed Jewish
Christianity, it is thought that the edict of Hadrian would have banned him from the
area. Yet it must be recalled that during the uprising of Bar Cosiba a strict line of
distinction was drawn between Jews and Christians. Christians could not assent
to viewing Bar Cosiba as the Messiah and were consequently persecuted. See
Justin *First Apology* 31.6. While passages such as Tertullian *Adversus Judaeos*
13.3-4 indicate that Jews still did not reside in the area later, it cannot be excluded
that Christians of a Jewish Christian slant survived in this vicinity after gentiles
took over the bishopric of Jerusalem (Eusebius *Historia Ecclesiastica* 4.6.4, 5.12.1).

[9]It is not clear, for example, how the author precisely understood an assertion
such as R 1.30.5, which he took over from the Book of Jubilees. It must be
remembered that the author of the source was not the only one to transmit this
tradition; see, for example, the texts collected in a note to the Book of Jubilees
3:28 by Charles, *The Book of Jubilees*, 27-28. Furthermore, it is possible that the
author also had some competence in Aramaic, which he considered to be roughly
equivalent to Hebrew.

temple) that acknowledges Jesus as the Messiah. For him, Christianity (a term he does not use) is true Judaism (another term he does not employ).

The author accordingly views Christianity as the religion originally intended by Moses. The ten commandments are accepted as the law that Moses originally received (R 1.35.2), and this view implies that the later legislation was all given to the Israelites only because they had become accustomed to the ways of the Egyptians. Moses himself had indicated that another prophet would come to abolish the legislation that was only provisionally given, and the author saw in the destruction of the temple and the expulsion of the unbelieving Jews an important historical confirmation of the truth of Christianity.

Since Christianity is considered by the author to be the true Judaism, he finds it necessary to explain the discontinuity with respect to race. He explains in R 1.42.1 that gentiles *had* to be called (into "Judaism") in the place of those Jews who had not believed in order that the number that had been shown to Abraham might be filled. The designation of this state of affairs in the Syriac as "confusion" seems to be original, and if it is, it is perhaps a clue that the author himself was of "Jewish" descent.[10] Thus, when Peter speaks of "our race, the Hebrews," he seems to express the author's own standpoint. The author was well aware of the gentile mission (see, other than R 1.42.1, R 1.63.2 and 64.2) and had no objections to its legitimacy without circumcision, yet he had also not forgotten the past and the roots of the church in "Judaism."

Some of the above remarks have simultaneously also disclosed the essence of the author's christology. It consists of two main elements: (1) that Jesus was the prophet proclaimed by Moses who would come for the abolition of sacrifices and (2) that Jesus is the Christ who has both already come and who will come again. The first coming of Christ

---

[10]The statement on circumcision in R 1.33.5 could theoretically be used to bolster the claim that the author of the source is Jewish Christian (see Lehmann, *Die clementinischen Schriften*, 94, Pratscher, *Jakobus und die Jakobustradition*, 132, and Martyn, "Clementine Recognitions," 271, in the light of Strecker, *Das Judenchristentum in den Pseudoklementinen*, 251). Yet it was seen above (in the section on B's redaction) that all of R 1.33.5 is an interpolation by B.

was made necessary, so to speak, by the fact that Moses could not propagate the proper type of religion in its total truth.

Whether the author presupposes the preexistence of Christ[11] is not quite clear. The meaning of the phrase "eternal Christ" (R 1.43.1, 63.1; compare R 1.44.2), if this should be assumed for the source,[12] is never explicated within the delimited material. In this regard, it is noteworthy that the revelation to Abraham is delivered not by Christ but rather by some indeterminate angel (R 1.32.4).[13] B felt obliged to correct his source at this point so that it was apparent that this angel was actually the prophet of truth. The source, in contrast, seems to have spoken of just two advents of the Christ (R 1.69.3-4). Though it is said that he "took a Jewish body" when he came (R 1.60.7), he is not mentioned in the creation story. R 1.64.3 (Syriac) is another correction by B (see *Epistula Clementis* 2.6, H 2.33.2 par. R 3.59.5).

A final element of the author's christology is reflected in what appears to be his baptismal formula. The Latin of R 1.39.2-3 twice preserves a reference to baptism "in the name of Jesus."[14] The Latin of R 1.73.4, which is part of a retrospect of R 1.55-72, also mentions baptism in the name of Jesus. Since reasons for Rufinus to have added these phrases have not yet been adduced and are not apparent, it should probably be assumed that the Syriac translator omitted this notion each time.[15] In any event, baptism in the name of Jesus would

---

[11]So Strecker, *Das Judenchristentum in den Pseudoklementinen*, 243, who draws a parallel to Aristo of Pella at this point (see also p. 253: "parallels with the theology of Aristo of Pella"); repeated by Lüdemann, *Antipaulinismus*, 243-44 (*Opposition to Paul*, 182). Nevertheless, the source of R 1.27-71 does not witness Aristo's reading of Gen. 1:1 as "in the Son," to which Strecker and Lüdemann refer (see R 1.27.1). This difference actually speaks against Strecker and Lüdemann's localization of this source in Pella.

That the source presupposes the preexistence of Christ is also argued (in a more nuanced manner) by Van Voorst, *The Ascents of James*, 112, 134-35, 164.

[12]Teeple, *The Prophet in the Clementines*, 10, stated that the term is a later insertion. He may well be right because R 1.44.2 is redactional and the closing phrases of R 1.43.1 and R 1.63.1 have the appearance of glosses.

[13]This angel ultimately stems from the Book of Jubilees 12:22 (cf. 2:1).

[14]It should be noted that Strecker, *Konkordanz*, s.v. *nomen*, failed to list the occurrence in R 1.39.3.

[15]It is possible that the Syriac translator suspected the phrase might be

seem to accord with other statements in the source that emphasize
that Christ came in order to reveal baptism (R 1.54.1) and that mention
"the baptism of Christ" (R 1.54.9), the "baptism of Jesus" (R 1.55.4
Latin), or the "baptism of our Jesus" (R 1.55.3 Latin; Syriac: "our
baptism, which was given by Jesus").

A remarkable feature of the source is its confirmation of the value
of astrology. A comparison of one relevant text, R 1.32.3-4, with what
was probably its model, the Book of Jubilees 12:16-27, highlights the
peculiarly strong astrological beliefs of the author. The author of the
source of R 1.27-71 goes beyond the Book of Jubilees in stating that
in the days of Abraham the whole world was in ignorance and was on
the verge of being destroyed. It was at this dark moment in human
history that Abraham *recognized* God through his study of the stars.
This last statement is also a revelatory expansion of the Book of
Jubilees. The author is thus assigning astrology a crucial role both in
the history of humankind and in the very founding of the trajectory of
true religion that extends to his own Christianity. Rufinus by no means
failed to recognize the radicality of this text and accordingly ameliorated
in his rendition.[16]

Another passage that confirms the author's astrological proclivities
is his interpretation of Gen. 1:14 in R 1.28.1-2. Origen, of course,
struggled with precisely this verse in his remarks on astrology in his
Commentary on Genesis (preserved in Eusebius *Praeparatio Evangelica*
6.11 and elsewhere). A comparison with Origen, whose point of view

---

amenable to Eunomianism. On Eunomian baptism see Kopecek, *A History of Neo-
Arianism*, 160-61, 398-400, Thomas A. Kopecek, "Neo-Arian Religion: The
Evidence of the Apostolic Constitutions," in *Arianism, Historical and Theological
Reassessments: Papers from the Ninth International Conference on Patristic
Studies, September 5-10, 1983, Oxford, England*, ed. Robert C. Gregg, Patristic
Monograph Series, no. 11 (n.p.: Philadelphia Patristic Foundation, 1985), 166-68,
and Rowan Williams, "Baptism and the Arian Controversy," in *Arianism after Arius:
Essays on the Development of the Fourth Century Trinitarian Conflicts*, ed. Michel
R. Barnes and Daniel H. Williams (Edinburgh: T. & T. Clark, 1993), 171-75.

[16]For example, he avoids stating that Abraham was in ignorance with everyone
else in R 1.32.3. Yet in R 1.33.3 he left a telltale sign of his alteration.

For the notion that Abraham recognized God from the pattern of the stars,
compare Plato *Timaios* 47; this idea was echoed in later texts such as Timaios of
Locri *On the Nature of the World and the Soul* 50.

was considered extreme enough, reveals how serious the author's interest apparently is. The author of the material preserved in R 1.27-71 affirms, in contrast to Origen, that the indications of the sun and moon are comprehensible to the diligent.

This evaluation of astrology reminds one of certain eastern streams of Christianity. Bardaisan, it will be recalled, assigned a limited significance to astrology.[17] It is also known that at least certain brands of Jewish Christianity accorded astrology crucial importance.[18] The author of the source of R 1.27-71 was thus not alone in his emphasis on the significance of the heavenly bodies.

A further doctrine that lies just below the surface of the present text is the author's chiliasm. This doctrine perhaps links up with the author's concern for the Holy Land and comes to expression, for example, in R 1.55.4, where the kingdom of heaven is clearly differentiated from the resurrection of the dead and eternal life. The high priest objects to such earthly hopes in R 1.61.1-2, yet R 1.61.3 by no means defuses them. A messianic kingdom will be established with the second advent of Christ (R 1.69.4).

The preceding remarks thus provide a good insight into the beliefs of the author. It remains to draw some conclusions as to the historical place of this writer.

The date of his composition must fall between Hegesippus's work (between 173 and 190 C.E.)[19] and the composition of the Pseudo-Clementine basic writing (probably circa 220 C.E.). A date of about 200 C.E. would accord with these indications as well as with the fact that the first and second Jewish wars against Rome have coalesced in the mind of the author.[20]

---

[17]See, for example, *Book of the Laws of the Countries* 19-22.

[18]See, for example, Hippolytus *Refutatio Omnium Haeresium* 9.16.2-4 on Alcibiades of Apamaea and the *Book of Elchasai*. I deal with this tradition in my study "The Astrological Trajectory in Ancient Syriac-Speaking Christianity (Elchasai, Bardaisan, and Mani)," presented at the Third International Conference on Manichaean Studies.

[19]See, for example, Adolf Harnack, *Geschichte der altchristlichen Literatur bis Eusebius*, 2d ed., enl. (Leipzig: J. C. Hinrichs, 1958), 2.1:311-12.

[20]See R 1.39.3, where the conditions of Hadrian's edict after the second war

A final question is whether the author should be classified as a Jewish Christian.[21]   The guideline for the decision is found in the author's theology of the land combined with his remarks on the history of the people of God, both of which were discussed above in this chapter. The author sees himself as a member of the legitimate heir of earliest Christianity in Jerusalem. He is also aware of a licit gentile mission that he seems to distinguish from earlier work in this area (Paul). It is highly unlikely that he would have demanded circumcision of the gentile believers, for the very notion of calling the *nations* to complete the number shown to Abraham (R 1.42.1; compare R 1.63.2, 64.2) contradicts the view that these gentiles should first have to convert to Judaism (e.g., submission to circumcision) before entering Christianity. Indeed, the author sees the mission to the gentiles resulting in the "separation" of the unbelieving Jews.[22] It would not be

---

are indiscriminately associated with "the war" that would come upon the unbelievers, and compare Strecker, *Das Judenchristentum in den Pseudo-klementinen*, 231. For a similar dating of the source, see Hort, *Clementine Recognitions*, 115-19.

[21]Research has had notorious difficulties in defining "Jewish Christianity." The following understanding of early Jewish Christianity will be adopted in the following remarks.

"Earliest Jewish Christianity" is equivalent to the body of Jews who soon confessed Jesus as the Messiah and thus to all of earliest Christianity. Earliest Christianity contained various undeveloped points of view on the precise nature of Christianity.

"Early Jewish Christianity" stands for *one* development out of earliest Christianity. Its characteristics are: (1) confession of Christ, (2) Jewish observance (where relevant: to a degree that separated it from the evolving Great Church, particularly including one or more of the following elements: [a] observance of the sabbath, [b] observance of the commands regarding sexual purity, [c] observance of circumcision, and [d] attendance at a synagogue), and (3) some sort of direct genetic relationship to earliest Jewish Christianity.

This definition is tolerably close to the one developed by Simon C. Mimouni, "Pour une définition nouvelle du judéo-christianisme ancien," *New Testament Studies* 38 (1992): 183-84. In June 1992, the author informed me orally that by "Jews" he understands (evidently in contrast to L. Marchal, whom he cites) anyone who observes the Torah as defined there p. 183, n. 85.

[22]R 1.64.2 (Syriac). The Latin does not witness the word placed in quotation marks above, and it is thus uncertain if this word goes back to the original text (above in chapter 2 it was decided that the anti-Jewish remark in R 1.40.2 [Syriac] should probably be attributed to the Syriac translator). Nevertheless, the thought of a separation of the unbelieving Jews from the true people of God is also implied

impossible for a gentile author to subscribe to any of these views, yet the remark that the gentile mission resulted in "confusion" (R 1.42.1) reveals a self-consciousness of (Jewish) race that should probably not be imputed to a gentile writer. The author thus seems aware both of his separation from (unbelieving) Judaism and of his distinct position with respect to the evolving gentile church. The most probable conclusion that may be drawn from these considerations is that the author stood in some sort of direct genetic relationship to earliest Jewish Christianity and thus that he should indeed be classified as a Jewish Christian.

This conclusion may be corroborated by observations on the author's portrayal of "secret" Jewish Christians and on his anti-Paulinism. To begin with the first set of comments, it should be noted that the author displays an unusual degree of interest for figures who secretly believe in Jesus but attempt to remain among the unbelieving Jews in order both to influence "Jewish" opinion and to protect the Christians from "Jewish" plots. This interest is expressed particularly in the portrayal of Gamaliel (R 1.65.2, 66.4 [especially the Syriac]; compare R 1.68.1-2). Though the notion of Jews secretly believing in Christ is also found in the Gospel of John,[23] the author of the source of R 1.27-71 does not share the criticism of these figures as expressed in John 12:43. It is furthermore unlikely that his interest is merely a literary development of John (and Acts 5:34-40) because such "secret" Jewish Christians are witnessed in the history of Jewish Christianity by Epiphanius. Epiphanius not only knows of such persons from the report of Joseph of Tiberias,[24] but also actually met such a "Jew" on his way up from Jericho in the desert of Bethel and Ephraim.[25] Furthermore, the *Book of Elchasai* and Origen witness to the Jewish Christian Elchasaite belief that denial with the lips was indeed permissible for an

---

in Rufinus's rendering of R 1.64.2, which states that their unbelief would be judged (or condemned) by the faith of the gentiles.

[23]See John 12:42-43 and 19:38 and the remarks on Nicodemus in John 3:1-5, 7:50-52, and 19:39-40.

[24]See his account in *Panarion* 30.4.5-7, 9.3.

[25]See *Panarion* 30.9.4-5. This "Jew" is also a witness to other such "Jews" (see the final words of *Panarion* 30.9.5).

Elchasaite Christian when he was threatened with persecution.[26] It thus seems that the author of the source of R 1.27-71 reflects a genuine Jewish Christian concern in his remarks on "secret" Christians among the Jews. At no point does he condemn such behavior, and he is likely to have condoned denial with the lips in certain circumstances.

The author's Jewish Christianity is also corroborated by his anti-Paulinism. Paul is given responsibility not only for the death of James[27] but also for the disruption of the baptism of *all* the people and the high priest (R 1.69.8). Paul is furthermore said to have started the massacre of Christians in Jerusalem (R 1.70.6-7) and to have undertaken a mission to destroy Christians elsewhere (R 1.71.3-5).[28] This type of anti-Paulinism, which does not attack Paul's later criticism of the law, seems best explainable as a development out of earlier (Jewish Christian) anti-Paulinism.[29] It is perhaps a remarkable indication of this secondary anti-Paulinism that the author apparently did not use the letters of Paul at all in his presentation. Not improbably, he took no account of them because he considered these writings to be the product of a ruthless murderer.

In conclusion, the present study has managed to gain a profile of a Jewish Christian writing circa the year 200 C.E. quite possibly in Judaea or Jerusalem. The author's attention to James the bishop, particularly if he called him "archbishop,"[30] might lead to the suspicion

---

[26]See Epiphanius *Panarion* 19.1.8, 2.1, 3.2 and Origen *Homily on Psalm 82* in Eusebius *Historia Ecclesiastica* 6.38.

[27]It was noted in chapter 4 that B altered the narrative in R 1.70.8 to allow James to survive for his novel.

[28]None of this material seems to have been contained in Hegesippus (see Eusebius *Historia Ecclesiastica* 4.22.4, 2.23.9-18); it should thus be attributed to creative work of the author of the source (employing Acts).

[29]Compare Lüdemann, *Antipaulinismus*, 246-47 (*Opposition to Paul*, 184-85).

[30]See R 1.68.2 and compare R 1.73.3 (Latin). Strecker, *Das Judenchristentum in den Pseudoklementinen*, 235, Brown, *James*, 204, n. 25, and Pratscher, *Jakobus und die Jakobustradition*, 148, however, assign this title to B's redaction. See, furthermore, Rehm, "Entstehung," 162, n. 243. Schmidt, *Studien*, 108, 329-30, seems to assume, to the contrary, that the title was found in the source. He, as well as Strecker and Pratscher, believes the title was formed in imitation of the "high priest," with whom James is about to dispute.

that the author was a Jewish Christian "bishop" or presbyter.[31] He will probably have submitted to the authority of the "archbishop" at his time (the leading gentile Christian bishop in Jerusalem [Narcissus?]), but he does not look at the current development of incorporation into the larger church without some trepidation.

Epilogue

The present study has investigated a section of the *Pseudo-Clementine* R in hope of ascertaining traditions of early Syrian Jewish Christianity. The broader objective of the investigation has been to make a contribution to the study of early Jewish Christianity and ancient Christianity generally.

The methodologically required steps have involved (1) detailed study and critique of the current state of research, (2) description of the procedures that enable recovery of the original text of the lost Greek R from the extant Latin and Syriac versions, (3) translation of the complete Syriac into English for the first time and provision of a new parallel translation from the Latin, (4) investigation of the text of R 1.27-71 using established analytical methods to separate and identify three different literary layers, and (5) critical sifting of these results to piece together a picture of the author of the source of R 1.27-71 and to isolate his perspective on the nature and history of Christianity.

For those unfamiliar with the investigation of early Jewish Christianity, the results of the examination may be somewhat bewildering. The necessary procedural steps both were complicated and led to conclusions that may at best be characterized as probable. Traditions that might claim an antiquity equal to the Pauline letters could only rarely be identified in a pure form. Nevertheless, the study will be considered

---

[31]On the list of Jerusalem bishops, see, for example, Harnack, *Geschichte der altchristlichen Literatur*, 2.1:218-30. On p. 221 Harnack decides that the earlier portion of this list reflects "presbyter-bishops in office alongside each other." "The first gentile Christian monarchic bishop in Jerusalem was probably Alexander" (ibid.).

significant by those acquainted both with the difficulties of reconstructing the history of early Christianity and with the light that the larger
Jewish Christian development sheds on the history of the early church.

Early Jewish Christians have a claim to the heritage of primitive
Christianity that places the victorious path of the evolving (gentile)
Great Church in a new perspective.   Toward the end of the second
century Jewish Christians had not given up hope of maintaining some
of their distinctive emphases in the new faith.   This study has
unearthed the thoughts and struggles of at least one of these Jewish
Christians.   To integrate him further (1) into the larger history of early
Jewish Christianity and (2) into a comprehensive history of the early
church is a task that promises to be fruitful for future studies.

BIBLIOGRAPHY

Sources

Apocrypha. Charles, R. H., trans. *The Book of Jubilees or the Little Genesis Translated from the Editor's Ethiopic Text and Edited, with Introduction, Notes, and Indices*. London: A. and C. Black, 1902.

_____. Charlesworth, James H., ed. *The Old Testament Pseudepigrapha*. 2 vols. Garden City, N.Y.: Doubleday, 1983-85.

_____. Funk, Wolf-Peter, ed., trans., and comm. *Die Zweite Apokalypse des Jakobus aus Nag-Hammadi-Codex V*. Texte und Untersuchungen zur Geschichte der altchristlichen Literatur, vol. 119. Berlin: Akademie, 1976.

_____. Geffcken, Johannes, ed. *Die Oracula Sibyllina*. Die griechischen christlichen Schriftsteller der ersten drei Jahrhunderte, vol. 8. Berlin: J. C. Hinrichs, 1902.

_____. Gibson, Margaret Dunlop, ed. and trans. *Apocrypha Sinaitica*. Studia Sinaitica, no. 5. London: C. J. Clay, 1896.

_____. James, Montague Rhodes, trans. *The Apocryphal New Testament: Being the Apocryphal Gospels, Acts, Epistles, and Apocalypses with Other Narratives and Fragments*. Corrected ed. Oxford: Clarendon, 1953.

Apologists. Goodspeed, Edgar J., ed. *Die ältesten Apologeten: Texte mit kurzen Einleitungen*. Göttingen: Vandenhoeck & Ruprecht, 1914.

Athanasius. Opitz, Hans-Georg, ed. *Athanasius: Werke*. Vol. 3, pt. 1, *Urkunden zur Geschichte des arianischen Streites 318-328*. 2 issues. Berlin and Leipzig: Walter de Gruyter, 1934-35.

169

Bardaisan. Nau, F., ed. "Bardesanes: Liber Legum Regionum." In *Patrologia Syriaca*, ed. R. Graffin, pt. 1, vol. 2, 490-658. Paris: Didot, 1907.

Bible. Aland, Kurt et al., eds. *Novum Testamentum Graece*. 26th rev. ed. Stuttgart: Deutsche Bibelstiftung, 1979.

_____. Erzabtei Beuron, ed. *Vetus Latina: Die Reste der altlateinischen Bibel*. Vol 2, *Genesis*, ed. Bonifatius Fischer. Freiburg: Herder, 1951-54.

_____. Peshitta Institute Leiden, ed. *The Old Testament in Syriac according to the Peshitta Version*. Pt. 1, fasc. 1, *Preface, Genesis-Exodus*. Leiden: E. J. Brill, 1977.

_____. Rahlfs, Alfred, ed. *Septuaginta Id Est Vetus Testamentum Graece iuxta LXX Interpretes*. 2 vols. Stuttgart: Württembergische Bibelanstalt, 1935.

_____. Soden, Hermann Freiherr von. *Die Schriften des Neuen Testaments in ihrer ältesten erreichbaren Textgestalt*. Pt. 2, *Text mit Apparat*. Göttingen: Vandenhoeck & Ruprecht, 1913.

_____. Tischendorf, Constantinus, ed. *Novum Testamentum Graece*. 8th larger ed. 2 vols. Leipzig: Giesecke & Devrient, 1869-72.

_____. Weber, Robert, ed. *Biblia Sacra iuxta Vulgatam Versionem*. Edited by Bonifatius Fischer. 3d ed., rev. 2 vols. Stuttgart: Deutsche Bibelgesellschaft, 1983.

Chronicon Paschale. Edited by Ludwig Dindorf. 2 vols. Corpus Scriptorum Historiae Byzantinae. Bonn: Ed. Weber, 1832.

Clement of Rome [pseud.]. Metzger, Marcel, ed. *Les Constitutions Apostoliques*. Sources chrétiennes, vols. 320, 329, 336. 3 vols. Paris: Les Éditions du Cerf, 1985-87.

_____. Cotelier, Jean Baptiste, ed. *Ss. Patrum Qui Temporibus Apostolicis Floruerunt; Barnabæ, Clementis, Hermæ, Ignatii, Polycarpi; Opera Edita et Inedita, Vera et Suppositicia. Unà cum Clementis, Ignatii, Polycarpi Actis atque Martyriis*. 2 vols. Paris: Typis Petri le Petit, 1672.

_____. Dressel, Albert Rud. Max., ed. *Clementinorum Epitomae Duae*. 2d, unchanged ed. Leipzig: J. C. Hinrichs, 1873.

_____. Frankenberg, Wilhelm. *Die syrischen Clementinen mit griechischem Paralleltext: Eine Vorarbeit zu dem literargeschichtlichen Problem der Sammlung*. Texte und Untersuchungen zur Geschichte der altchristlichen Literatur, vol. 48, no. 3. Leipzig: J. C. Hinrichs, 1937.

_____. Gersdorf, E. G., ed. *S. Clementis Romani Recognitiones Rufino Aquilei. Presb. Interprete*. Bibliotheca Patrum Ecclesiasticorum Latinorum Selecta, vol. 1. Leipzig: Bernh. Tauchnitz Jun., 1838.

_____. Lagarde, Paul Anton de, ed. *Clementis Romani Recognitiones Syriace*. Leipzig: F. A. Brockhaus; London: Williams & Norgate, 1861.

_____. Rehm, Bernhard, ed. *Die Pseudoklementinen I: Homilien*. Edited by Georg Strecker. 3d ed., rev. Die griechischen christlichen Schriftsteller der ersten Jahrhunderte, vol. 42. Berlin: Akademie, 1992.

_____. Rehm, Bernhard, ed. *Die Pseudoklementinen II: Rekognitionen in Rufins Übersetzung.* Edited by Georg Strecker. 2d ed., rev. Die griechischen christlichen Schriftsteller der ersten Jahrhunderte, vol. 51. Berlin: Akademie, 1994.

_____. Renoux, Charles. "Fragments arméniens des Recognitiones du Pseudo-Clément." *Oriens Christianus* 62 (1978): 103-13.

_____. Smith, Thomas, trans. "Pseudo-Clementine Literature." In *The Ante-Nicene Fathers: Translations of the Writings of the Fathers down to A.D. 325,* ed. Alexander Roberts and James Donaldson, American reprint rev. A. Cleveland Coxe, vol. 8, *The Twelve Patriarchs, Excerpts and Epistles, the Clementina, Apocrypha, Decretals, Memoirs of Edessa and Syriac Documents, Remains of the First Ages,* 67-346. Reprint ed. Grand Rapids, Mich.: William B. Eerdmans, 1978.

_____. Strecker, Georg. *Die Pseudoklementinen III: Konkordanz zu den Pseudoklementinen.* Die griechischen christlichen Schriftsteller der ersten Jahrhunderte. Berlin: Akademie, 1986-89.

Epiphanius. Holl, Karl, ed. *Epiphanius (Ancoratus und Panarion).* Edited by Jürgen Dummer. 2d ed., rev. 3 vols. Die griechischen christlichen Schriftsteller der ersten Jahrhunderte. Berlin: Akademie, 1980-.

Eusebius. Schwartz, Eduard, and Mommsen, Theodor, eds. *Eusebius: Werke.* Vol. 2, *Die Kirchengeschichte.* Die griechischen christlichen Schriftsteller der ersten drei Jahrhunderte, vol. 9. Leipzig: J. C. Hinrichs, 1903-9.

_____. Mras, Karl, ed. *Eusebius: Werke.* Vol. 8, *Die Praeparatio Evangelica.* Die griechischen christlichen Schriftsteller der ersten Jahrhunderte, vol. 43. Berlin: Akademie, 1954-56.

Hippolytus. Wendland, Paul, ed. *Hippolytus: Werke.* Vol. 3, *Refutatio Omnium Haeresium.* Die griechischen christlichen Schriftsteller der ersten drei Jahrhunderte, vol. 26. Leipzig: J. C. Hinrichs, 1916.

Origen. Koetschau, Paul, ed. *Origenes: Werke.* Vols. 1-2, *Die Schrift vom Martyrium, Buch I-VIII gegen Celsus, die Schrift vom Gebet.* Die griechischen christlichen Schriftsteller der ersten drei Jahrhunderte, vols. 2-3. Leipzig: J. C. Hinrichs, 1899.

Plato. Burnet, Ioannes, ed. *Platonis Opera.* Scriptorum Classicorum Bibliotheca Oxoniensis. 5 vols. Oxford: Clarendon, 1900-1907.

Rufinus. Simonetti, Manlius, ed. *Tyrannii Rufini Opera.* Corpus Christianorum Series Latina, vol. 20. Turnhout: Brepols, 1961.

Tertullian. *Quinti Septimi Florentis Tertulliani Opera.* Pt. 2, *Opera Montanistica.* Corpus Christianorum Series Latina, vol. 2. Turnhout: Brepols, 1954.

Timaios of Locri. Marg, Walter, ed. and trans. *De Natura Mundi et Animae: Überlieferung, Testimonia, Text und Übersetzung.* Philosophia Antiqua, vol. 24. Leiden: E. J. Brill, 1972.

Secondary Literature

Abramowski, Rudolf. "Pseudoclemens: Zu W. Frankenbergs Clemensausgabe," review of *Die syrischen Clementinen mit griechischem Paralleltext: Eine Vorarbeit zu dem literargeschichtlichen Problem der Sammlung*, by Wilhelm Frankenberg. *Theologische Blätter* 18 (1939): 147-51.

Backhaus, Knut. *Die "Jüngerkreise" des Täufers Johannes: Eine Studie zu den religionsgeschichtlichen Ursprüngen des Christentums*. Paderborner theologische Studien, vol. 19. Paderborn, Munich, Vienna, and Zurich: Ferdinand Schöningh, 1991.

Bacon, Benjamin W. *Studies in Matthew*. London: Constable & Co., 1930.

Bardsley, Herbert James. *Reconstructions of Early Christian Documents*. Vol. 1. London: S.P.C.K., 1935.

Barnes, Michel R., and Williams, Daniel H., eds. *Arianism after Arius: Essays on the Development of the Fourth Century Trinitarian Conflicts*. Edinburgh: T. & T. Clark, 1993.

Bauer, Walter. *Das Leben Jesu im Zeitalter der neutestamentlichen Apokryphen*. Tübingen: J. C. B. Mohr (Paul Siebeck), 1909.

Beyschlag, Karlmann. "Das Jakobusmartyrium und seine Verwandten in der frühchristlichen Literatur." *Zeitschrift für die neutestamentliche Wissenschaft und die Kunde der älteren Kirche* 56 (1965): 149-78.

_____. *Simon Magus und die christliche Gnosis*. Wissenschaftliche Untersuchungen zum Neuen Testament, vol. 16. Tübingen: J. C. B. Mohr (Paul Siebeck), 1974.

⅄ Bigg, Charles. "The Clementine Homilies." In *Studia Biblica et Ecclesiastica: Essays Chiefly in Biblical and Patristic Criticism*, by members of the University of Oxford, 2:157-93. Oxford: Clarendon, 1890.

Bousset, Wilhelm. "Die Wiedererkennungs-Fabel in den pseudoklementinischen Schriften, den Menächmen des Plautus und Shakespeares Komödie der Irrungen." *Zeitschrift für die neutestamentliche Wissenschaft* 5 (1904): 18-27.

_____. Review of *Die Pseudoklementinen, Homilien und Rekognitionen: Eine quellenkritische Untersuchung*, by Hans Waitz. *Göttingische gelehrte Anzeigen* 167 (1905): 425-47.

_____. *Hauptprobleme der Gnosis*. Forschungen zur Religion und Literatur des Alten und Neuen Testaments, vol. 10. Göttingen: Vandenhoeck & Ruprecht, 1907.

Brown, Scott Kent. *James: A Religio-Historical Study of the Relations between Jewish, Gnostic, and Catholic Christianity in the Early Period through an Investigation of the Traditions about James the Lord's Brother*. Ann Arbor, Mich.: University Microfilms, 1972.

Bruce, F. F. *Peter, Stephen, James, and John: Studies in Early Non-Pauline Christianity*. Grand Rapids, Mich.: William B. Eerdmans, 1979.

⅄ Bussell, F. W. "The Purpose of the World-Process and the Problem of Evil as Explained in the Clementine and Lactantian Writings in a System of Subordinate Dualism." In *Studia Biblica et Ecclesiastica: Essays Chiefly in Biblical and*

Patristic Criticism, by members of the University of Oxford, 4:133-88. Oxford: Clarendon, 1896.

Calzolari, Valentina. "La tradition arménienne des *Pseudo-Clémentines*: État de la question." *Apocrypha* 4 (1993): 263-93.

Chapman, John. "Clementines." In *The Catholic Encyclopedia*, ed. Charles G. Herbermann et al., 4:39-44. New York: Robert Appleton, 1908.

_____. "On the Date of the Clementines." *Zeitschrift für die neutestamentliche Wissenschaft* 9 (1908): 21-34, 147-59.

Christensen, Torben. "Rufinus of Aquileia and the *Historia Ecclesiastica, lib. VIII-IX,* of Eusebius." *Studia Theologica* 34 (1980): 129-52.

_____. *Rufinus of Aquileia and the* Historia Ecclesiastica, *Lib. VIII-IX, of Eusebius*. Det Kongelige Danske Videnskabernes Selskab, historisk-filosofiske Meddelelser, vol. 58. Copenhagen: Munksgaard, 1989.

Cirillo, Luigi. *Évangile de Barnabé: Recherches sur la composition et l'origine*. Beauchesne religions. Paris: Éditions Beauchesne, 1977.

_____. "L'antipaolinismo nelle Pseudoclementine." *Richerche Storico Bibliche*, 1989, fasc. 2 (July-December), 121-37.

Cullmann, Oscar. *Le problème littéraire et historique du roman pseudo-clémentin: Étude sur le rapport entre le gnosticisme et le Judéo-Christianisme*. Études d'histoire et de philosophie religieuses publiées par la faculté de théologie protestante de l'Université de Strasbourg, no. 23. Paris: Librairie Félix Alcan, 1930.

Dobschütz, Ernst von. *Das Kerygma Petrou kritisch untersucht*. Texte und Untersuchungen zur Geschichte der altchristlichen Literatur, vol. 11, no. 1. Leipzig: J. C. Hinrichs, 1893.

Graf, Georg. *Geschichte der christlichen arabischen Literatur*. Vol. 1, *Die Übersetzungen*. Studi e testi, vol. 118. Vatican City: Biblioteca Apostolica Vaticana, 1944.

Gunkel, Hermann. *Zum religionsgeschichtlichen Verständnis des Neuen Testaments*. Forschungen zur Religion und Literatur des Alten und Neuen Testaments, vol. 1. Göttingen: Vandenhoeck & Ruprecht, 1903.

Hammond, Caroline P. "The Last Ten Years of Rufinus' Life and the Date of His Move South from Aquileia." *Journal of Theological Studies*, n.s., 28 (1977): 372-429.

Hanson, R. P. C. *The Search for the Christian Doctrine of God: The Arian Controversy 318-381*. Edinburgh: T. & T. Clark, 1988.

Harnack, Adolf. *Geschichte der altchristlichen Literatur bis Eusebius*. 2d ed., enl. 2 pts. Leipzig: J. C. Hinrichs, 1958.

Harter, William H. *The Causes and the Course of the Jewish Revolt against Rome, 66-74 C. E., in Recent Scholarship*. Ann Arbor, Mich.: University Microfilms, 1984.

Hausrath, Adolf. *Neutestamentliche Zeitgeschichte*. Pt. 4, *Das nachapostolische Zeitalter*. 2d ed. Heidelberg: Fr. Bassermann, 1877.

Hengel, Martin. "Jakobus der Herrenbruder--der erste 'Papst'?" In *Glaube und Eschatologie: Festschrift für Werner Georg Kümmel zum 80. Geburtstag*, ed. Erich Gräßer and Otto Merk, 71-104. Tübingen: J. C. B. Mohr (Paul Siebeck), 1985.

Hilgenfeld, Adolf. *Die clementinischen Recognitionen und Homilien, nach ihrem Ursprung und Inhalt dargestellt.* Jena: J. G. Schreiber; Leipzig: Chr. E. Kollmann, 1848.

_____. *Die Ketzergeschichte des Urchristenthums urkundlich dargestellt.* Leipzig: Fues's Verlag (R. Reisland), 1884.

_____. *Judenthum und Judenchristenthum: Eine Nachlese zu der "Ketzergeschichte des Urchristenthums."* Leipzig: Fues's Verlag (R. Reisland), 1886.

Hoppe, Heinrich. "Rufin als Uebersetzer." In *Studi dedicati alla memoria di Paolo Ubaldi*, 133-50. Pubblicazioni della Università Cattolica del Sacro Cuore, 5th ser., vol. 16. Milan: Società editrice "Vita e pensiero," 1937.

Hort, Fenton John Anthony. *Judaistic Christianity*. Cambridge, London, and New York: Macmillan, 1894.

_____. *Notes Introductory to the Study of the Clementine Recognitions: A Course of Lectures*. London and New York: Macmillan, 1901.

Jones, F. Stanley. "The Pseudo-Clementines: A History of Research." *The Second Century* 2 (1982): 1-33, 63-96. Reprinted in *Studies in Early Christianity*, ed. Everett Ferguson, vol. 2, *Literature of the Early Church*, 195-262. New York and London: Garland, 1993.

_____. "The Martyrdom of James in Hegesippus, Clement of Alexandria, and Christian Apocrypha, Including Nag Hammadi: A Study of the Textual Relations." In *Society of Biblical Literature 1990 Seminar Papers: One Hundred Twenty-Sixth Annual Meeting, November 17-20, 1990, The New Orleans Marriott, The Sheraton New Orleans, New Orleans, Louisiana*, ed. David J. Lull, 322-35. Society of Biblical Literature Seminar Papers Series, vol. 29. Atlanta: Scholars Press, 1990.

_____. Review of *The Ascents of James: History and Theology of a Jewish-Christian Community*, by Robert E. Van Voorst. *Critical Review of Books in Religion*, 1991, 344-46.

_____. "Evaluating the Latin and Syriac Translations of the Pseudo-Clementine *Recognitions*." *Apocrypha* 3 (1992): 237-57.

Klijn, A. F. J., and Reinink, G. J. *Patristic Evidence for Jewish-Christian Sects*. Supplements to Novum Testamentum, vol. 36. Leiden: E. J. Brill, 1973.

Kline, Leslie L. *The Sayings of Jesus in the Pseudo-Clementine Homilies*. Society of Biblical Literature Dissertation Series, no. 14. Missoula, Mont.: Scholars' Press, 1975.

Koester, Craig. "The Origin and Significance of the Flight to Pella Tradition." *Catholic Biblical Quarterly* 51 (1989): 90-106.

Köstlin, Karl Reinhold. Review of *Die clementinischen Recognitionen und Homilien, nach ihrem Ursprung und Inhalt dargestellt*, by Adolf Hilgenfeld. *Allgemeine Literatur-Zeitung* (Halle), 1849, cols. 577-78, 585-608, 612-16.

Kopecek, Thomas A. *A History of Neo-Arianism.* Patristic Monograph Series, no. 8. 2 vols. Cambridge, Mass.: Philadelphia Patristic Foundation, 1979.

_____. "Neo-Arian Religion: The Evidence of the Apostolic Constitutions." In *Arianism, Historical and Theological Reassessments: Papers from the Ninth International Conference on Patristic Studies, September 5-10, 1983, Oxford, England*, ed. Robert C. Gregg, 153-79. Patristic Monograph Series, no. 11. N.p.: Philadelphia Patristic Foundation, 1985.

Kutsch, Wilhelm. Review of *Die syrischen Clementinen mit griechischem Paralleltext: Eine Vorarbeit zu dem literargeschichtlichen Problem der Sammlung*, by Wilhelm Frankenberg. *Orientalia*, n.s., 8 (1939): 184-86.

Lagarde, Paul de. Review of *Die clementinischen Schriften mit besonderer Rücksicht auf ihr literarisches Verhältniss*, by Johannes Lehmann. In *Symmicta*, 2-4, 108-12. Göttingen: Dieterichsche Verlagsbuchhandlung, 1877.

_____. "Clementina herausgegeben von Paul de Lagarde, 1865." In *Mittheilungen*, 26-54. Göttingen: Dieterichsche Sortimentsbuchhandlung (A. Hoyer), 1884.

Langen, Joseph. *Die Klemensromane: Ihre Entstehung und ihre Tendenzen aufs neue untersucht.* Gotha: Friedrich Andreas Perthes, 1890.

Legasse, Simon. "La polémique antipaulinienne dans le judéo-christianisme hétérodoxe." *Bulletin de Littérature Ecclésiastique* 90 (1989): 5-22, 85-100.

Lehmann, Johannes. *Die clementinischen Schriften mit besonderer Rücksicht auf ihr literarisches Verhältniss.* Gotha: Friedrich Andreas Perthes, 1869.

Lightfoot, John Barber. *St. Paul's Epistle to the Galatians with Introductions, Notes, and Dissertations.* 10th ed. London and New York: Macmillan, 1890; reprint ed., Lynn, Mass.: Hendrickson Publishers, 1981.

Lindemann, Andreas. *Paulus im ältesten Christentum: Das Bild des Apostels und die Rezeption der paulinischen Theologie in der frühchristlichen Literatur bis Marcion.* Beiträge zur historischen Theologie, vol. 58. Tübingen: J. C. B. Mohr (Paul Siebeck), 1979.

Lipsius, Richard Adelbert. Review of *Die clementinischen Schriften mit besonderer Rücksicht auf ihr literarisches Verhältniss*, by Johannes Lehmann. *Protestantische Kirchenzeitung für das evangelische Deutschland* 16 (1869): 477-82.

_____. *Die Quellen der römischen Petrus-Sage kritisch untersucht.* Kiel: Schwers'sche Buchhandlung, 1872.

_____. "Petrus nicht in Rom." *Jahrbücher für protestantische Theologie*, 1876, 561-645.

_____. *Die apokryphen Apostelgeschichten und Apostellegenden: Ein Beitrag zur altchristlichen Literaturgeschichte.* Vol. 2, 2 halves. Braunschweig: C. A. Schwetschke und Sohn (Wiegandt & Appelhans; M. Bruhn), 1884-87.

Lüdemann, Gerd. *Untersuchungen zur simonianischen Gnosis.* Göttinger theologische Arbeiten, vol. 1. Göttingen: Vandenhoeck & Ruprecht, 1975.

_____. *Paulus, der Heidenapostel.* Vol. 2, *Antipaulinismus im frühen Christentum.* Forschungen zur Religion und Literatur des Alten und Neuen Testaments, vol. 130. Göttingen: Vandenhoeck & Ruprecht, 1983. Translated by M. Eugene

Boring, under the title *Opposition to Paul in Jewish Christianity*. Minneapolis: Fortress, 1989.

Marti, Heinrich. *Übersetzer der Augustin-Zeit: Interpretation von Selbstzeugnissen*. Studia et Testimonia Antiqua, vol. 14. Munich: Wilhelm Fink, 1974.

⚔ Martyn, J. Louis. "Clementine Recognitions 1,33--71, Jewish Christianity, and the Fourth Gospel." In *God's Christ and His People: Studies in Honour of Nils Alstrup Dahl*, ed. Jacob Jervell and Wayne A. Meeks, 265-95. Oslo, Bergen, and Tromsö: Universitetsforlaget, 1977.

Meeks, Wayne A., ed. *The Writings of St. Paul: Annotated Text, Criticism*. Norton Critical Editions. New York: W. W. Norton, 1972.

Meyboom, H. U. *De Clemens-roman*. Vol. 2, *Wetenschappelijke Behandeling*. Groningen: J. B. Wolters, 1904.

Mimouni, Simon C. "Pour une définition nouvelle du judéo-christianisme ancien." *New Testament Studies* 38 (1992): 161-86.

Murphy, Francis X. *Rufinus of Aquileia (345-411): His Life and Works*. The Catholic University of America Studies in Mediaeval History, n.s., vol. 6. Washington, D.C.: Catholic University of America Press, 1945.

Paschke, Franz. *Die beiden griechischen Klementinen-Epitomen und ihre Anhänge: Überlieferungsgeschichtliche Vorarbeiten zu einer Neuausgabe der Texte*. Texte und Untersuchungen zur Geschichte der altchristlichen Literatur, vol. 90. Berlin: Akademie, 1966.

Patrick, William. *James the Lord's Brother*. Edinburgh: T. & T. Clark, 1906.

Pratscher, Wilhelm. *Der Herrenbruder Jakobus und die Jakobustradition*. Forschungen zur Religion und Literatur des Alten und Neuen Testaments, vol. 139. Göttingen: Vandenhoeck & Ruprecht, 1987.

⚑ Quarry, J. "Notes, Chiefly Critical, on the Clementine Homilies and the Epistles Prefixed to Them." *Hermathena* 7 (1890): 67-104, 239-67; 8 (1893): 91-112, 133-60, 287-300.

Rehm, Bernhard. "Zur Entstehung der pseudoclementinischen Schriften." *Zeitschrift für die neutestamentliche Wissenschaft und die Kunde der älteren Kirche* 37 (1938): 77-184.

_____. "Clemens Romanus II (PsClementinen)." In *Reallexikon für Antike und Christentum*, ed. Theodor Klauser et al., 5:197-206. Stuttgart: Anton Hiersemann, 1957.

Richard, Marcel. "Quelques nouveaux fragments des pères anténicéens et nicéens." In *Opera Minora*, vol. 1, no. 5. Turnhout: Brepols; Leuven: University Press, 1976.

Ritschl, Albrecht. *Die Entstehung der altkatholischen Kirche: Eine kirchen- und dogmengeschichtliche Monographie*. Bonn: Adolph Marcus, 1850.

_____. *Die Entstehung der altkatholischen Kirche: Eine kirchen- und dogmengeschichtliche Monographie*. 2d ed., rev. Bonn: Adolph Marcus, 1857.

Rius-Camps, Josep. "Las Pseudoclementinas: Bases filológicas para una nueva interpretación." *Revista Catalana de Teologia* 1 (1976): 79-158.

_____. "Sucesión y ministerios en las Pseudoclementinas." In *La potestad de orden* ⟩
en los primeros siglos, by Mons. Capmany et al., 163-215. Teología del sacerdocio, vol. 9. Burgos: Ediciones Aldecoa, 1977.

Rönsch, Hermann. *Das Buch der Jubiläen oder die kleine Genesis.* Leipzig: Fues's
Verlag (R. Reisland), 1874.

Salmon, George. "Clementine Literature." In *A Dictionary of Christian Biography,
Literature, Sects and Doctrines*, ed. William Smith and Henry Wace, 1:567-78.
London: John Murray, 1877.

Schliemann, Adolph. "Die clementinischen Recognitionen eine Ueberarbeitung der
Clementinen." *Theologische Mitarbeiten* 4, no. 4 (1843): 1-72.　　　ʃ

Schmidt, Carl. *Studien zu den Pseudo-Clementinen nebst einem Anhange: Die
älteste römische Bischofsliste und die Pseudo-Clementinen.* Texte und
Untersuchungen zur Geschichte der altchristlichen Literatur, vol. 46, no. 1.
Leipzig: J. C. Hinrichs, 1929.

Schmidtke, Alfred. *Neue Fragmente und Untersuchungen zu den judenchristlichen
Evangelien: Ein Beitrag zur Literatur und Geschichte der Judenchristen.* Texte
und Untersuchungen zur Geschichte der altchristlichen Literatur, vol. 37, no.
1. Leipzig: J. C. Hinrichs, 1911.

Schoeps, Hans Joachim. *Theologie und Geschichte des Judenchristentums.*
Tübingen: J. C. B. Mohr (Paul Siebeck), 1949.

_____. *Aus frühchristlicher Zeit: Religionsgeschichtliche Untersuchungen.*
Tübingen: J. C. B. Mohr (Paul Siebeck), 1950.

_____. *Urgemeinde, Judenchristentum, Gnosis.* Tübingen: J. C. B. Mohr (Paul
Siebeck), 1956.

_____. *Jewish Christianity: Factional Disputes in the Early Church.* Translated by
Douglas R. A. Hare. Philadelphia: Fortress, 1969.

Schonfield, Hugh J. *The History of Jewish Christianity from the First to the
Twentieth Century.* London: Duckworth, 1936.

_____. *According to the Hebrews.* London: Duckworth, 1937.

Schwartz, Eduard. "Zu Eusebius Kirchengeschichte." *Zeitschrift für die
neutestamentliche Wissenschaft* 4 (1903): 48-66.

_____. "Unzeitgemäße Beobachtungen zu den Clementinen." *Zeitschrift für die
neutestamentliche Wissenschaft und die Kunde der älteren Kirche* 31 (1932):
151-99.

Scott, James Julius, Jr. *The Church of Jerusalem, A.D. 30-100: An Investigation
of the Growth of Internal Factions and the Extension of Its Influence in the
Larger Church.* Ann Arbor, Mich.: University Microfilms, 1969.

Seeberg, Reinhold. *Lehrbuch der Dogmengeschichte.* Vol. 1, *Die Anfänge des
Dogmas im nachapostolischen und altkatholischen Zeitalter.* 3d ed., enl. and
rev. Sammlung theologischer Lehrbücher. Leipzig and Erlangen: A. Deichertsche
Verlagsbuchhandlung Dr. Werner Scholl, 1920.

Simon, Marcel. "La migration à Pella: Légende ou réalité?" *Recherches de Science
Religieuse* 60 (1972): 37-54.

Skarsaune, Oskar. *The Proof from Prophecy, A Study in Justin Martyr's Proof-Text Tradition: Text-Type, Provenance, Theological Profile.* Supplements to Novum Testamentum, vol. 56. Leiden: E. J. Brill, 1987.

Stötzel, Arnold. "Die Darstellung der ältesten Kirchengeschichte nach den Pseudo-Clementinen." *Vigiliae Christianae* 36 (1982): 24-37.

Strecker, Georg. *Das Judenchristentum in den Pseudoklementinen.* 2d ed., rev. Texte und Untersuchungen zur Geschichte der altchristlichen Literatur, vol. 70. Berlin: Akademie, 1981.

_____. "Das Land Israel in frühchristlicher Zeit." In *Das Land Israel in biblischer Zeit: Jerusalem-Symposium 1981 der Hebräischen Universität und der Georg-August-Universität,* ed. Georg Strecker, 188-200. Göttinger theologische Arbeiten, vol. 25. Göttingen: Vandenhoeck & Ruprecht, 1983.

Tardieu, Michel. "Une diatribe antignostique dans l'interpolation eunomienne des *Recognitiones.*" In *ΑΛΕΞΑΝΔΡΙΝΑ: Hellénisme, judaïsme et christianisme à Alexandrie: Mélanges offerts au P. Claude Mondésert,* 325-37. Paris: Les Éditions du Cerf, 1987.

Teeple, Howard M. *The Mosaic Eschatological Prophet.* Journal of Biblical Literature Monograph Series, vol. 10. Philadelphia: Society of Biblical Literature, 1957.

_____. *The Prophet in the Clementines.* Introduction by F. Stanley Jones. Religion and Ethics Institute Occasional Papers 2. Evanston, Ill.: Religion and Ethics Institute, 1993.

Thomas, Joseph. "Les ébionites baptistes." *Revue d'Histoire Ecclésiastique* 30 (1934): 257-96.

_____. *Le mouvement baptiste en Palestine et Syrie (150 av. J.-C.-300 ap. J.-C.).* Universitas Catholica Lovaniensis Dissertationes, 2d ser., vol. 28. Gembloux: J. Duculot, 1935.

Tosolini, Fabrizio. "Paolo in *Atti* e nelle Pseudoclementine (*Recognitiones* I, 33-71)." *Augustinianum* 26 (1986): 369-400.

Uhlhorn, Gerhard. *Die Homilien und Recognitionen des Clemens Romanus nach ihrem Ursprung und Inhalt dargestellt.* Göttingen: Verlag der Dieterichschen Buchhandlung, 1854.

_____. "Clementinen I." In *Realencyklopädie für protestantische Theologie und Kirche,* ed. Albert Hauck, 4:171-79. 3d ed., rev. and enl. Leipzig: J. C. Hinrichs, 1898.

Van Voorst, Robert E. *The Ascents of James: History and Theology of a Jewish-Christian Community.* Society of Biblical Literature Dissertation Series, no. 112. Atlanta: Scholars Press, 1989.

Verheyden, Jozef. *De Vlucht van de Christenen naar Pella: Onderzoek van het Getuigenis van Eusebius en Epiphanius.* Verhandelingen van de Koninklijke Academie voor Wetenschappen, Letteren en schone Kunsten van België, Klasse der Letteren, year 50, no. 127. Brussels: Paleis der Academiën, 1988.

_____. "The Flight of the Christians to Pella." *Ephemerides Theologicae Lovanienses* 66 (1990): 368-84.

_____. Review of *The Ascents of James: History and Theology of a Jewish-Christian Community*, by Robert E. Van Voorst. *Ephemerides Theologicae Lovanienses* 66 (1990): 417-18.

Wagner, M. Monica. *Rufinus, the Translator: A Study of His Theory and His Practice as Illustrated in His Version of the* Apologetica *of St. Gregory Nazianzen*. The Catholic University of America Patristic Studies, vol. 73. Washington, D.C.: The Catholic University of America Press, 1945.

Waitz, Hans. *Die Pseudoklementinen, Homilien und Rekognitionen: Eine quellenkritische Untersuchung*. Texte und Untersuchungen zur Geschichte der altchristlichen Literatur, n.s., vol. 10, no. 4. Leipzig: J. C. Hinrichs, 1904.

_____. "Clementinen." In *Realencyklopädie für protestantische Theologie und Kirche*, ed. Albert Hauck, 23:312-16. 3d ed., rev. and enl. Leipzig: J. C. Hinrichs, 1913.

_____. "Die Pseudoklementinen und ihre Quellenschriften." *Zeitschrift für die neutestamentliche Wissenschaft und die Kunde der älteren Kirche* 28 (1929): 241-72.

_____. "Die Lösung des pseudoclementinischen Problems?" *Zeitschrift für Kirchengeschichte* 59 (1940): 304-41.

_____, and Veil, Heinrich. "Auszüge aus den Pseudo-Clementinen." In *Neutestamentliche Apokryphen*, ed. Edgar Hennecke, 151-63, 212-26. 2d ed., rev. and enl. Tübingen: J. C. B. Mohr (Paul Siebeck), 1924.

Webber, Martin I. Ἰάκωβος ὁ Δίκαιος: *Origins, Literary Expression and Development of Traditions about the Brother of the Lord in Early Christianity*. Ann Arbor, Mich.: University Microfilms, 1985.

Wehnert, Jürgen. "Literarkritik und Sprachanalyse: Kritische Anmerkungen zum gegenwärtigen Stand der Pseudoklementinen-Forschung." *Zeitschrift für die neutestamentliche Wissenschaft und die Kunde der älteren Kirche* 74 (1983): 268-301.

_____. "Die Auswanderung der Jerusalemer Christen nach Pella--historisches Faktum oder theologische Konstruktion? Kritische Bemerkungen zu einem neuen Buch." *Zeitschrift für Kirchengeschichte* 102 (1991): 231-55.

_____. "Abriß der Entstehungsgeschichte des pseudoklementinischen Romans." *Apocrypha* 3 (1992): 211-35.

Williams, Rowan. *Arius: Heresy and Tradition*. London: Darton, Longman and Todd, 1987.

_____. "Baptism and the Arian Controversy." In *Arianism after Arius: Essays on the Development of the Fourth Century Trinitarian Conflicts*, ed. Michel R. Barnes and Daniel H. Williams, 149-80. Edinburgh: T. & T. Clark, 1993.

Winkelmann, Friedhelm. "Einige Bemerkungen zu den Aussagen des Rufinus von Aquileia und des Hieronymus über ihre Übersetzungstheorie und -methode." In *Kyriakon: Festschrift Johannes Quasten*, ed. Patrick Granfield and Josef A. Jungmann, 532-47. Munster: Aschendorff, 1970.

Zahn, Theodor. Review of *Die clementinischen Schriften mit besonderer Rücksicht auf ihr literarisches Verhältniss*, by Johannes Lehmann. *Göttingische gelehrte Anzeigen*, 1869, 905-17.

_____. *Forschungen zur Geschichte des neutestamentlichen Kanons und der altkirchlichen Literatur*. Pt. 6, *I. Apostel und Apostelschüler in der Provinz Asien, II. Brüder und Vettern Jesu*. Leipzig: A. Deichert'sche Verlagsbuchhandlung Nachf. (Georg Böhme), 1900.

_____. *Die Apostelgeschichte des Lucas*. 3d and 4th ed. Kommentar zum Neuen Testament, vol. 5. 2 pts. Leipzig and Erlangen: A. Deichertsche Verlagsbuchhandlung Dr. Werner Scholl, 1922-27.

INDEXES

Passage Index

Specific references to the Armenian, Greek, Latin, Syriac, or "Western" versions of a passage are indicated in parentheses before the page number.

CLASSICAL AUTHORS
Alexander Polyhistor. *See under* ANCIENT CHRISTIAN WRITINGS, Eusebius
Celsus. *See under* ANCIENT CHRISTIAN WRITINGS, Origen
Plato *Timaios*: 47, 162n. 16
Timaios of Locri *On the Nature of the World and the Soul*: 50, 162n. 16

OLD TESTAMENT
Genesis: 1, 47; 1:1, 161n. 11; 1:14, 139, 162; 6:2, 128, 137; 11:28, 139
Leviticus: 23:29, 141
Deuteronomy: 18:15-16, 141; 18:19, 141
Isaiah: 3:10, 146n. 117

INTERTESTAMENTAL WRITINGS
Book of Jubilees: 2:1, 161n. 13; 2:7, 138; 2:9, 139; 3:28, 159n. 9; 6:2, 139; 8:3, 139; 8:8-30, 138-39; 10:29-34, 138; 11:2, 139; 12:14, 139; 12:16-17, 139; 12:16-25, 137; 12:16-27, 139, 162; 12:22, 161n. 13; 12:26, 139; 14:11, 139
Sibylline Oracles: 3:114, 138n. 91

INTERTESTAMENTAL WRITINGS (*continued*)
Sirach: 46:1, 123n. 41

NEW TESTAMENT
The Gospels
Matthew: 3:7, 148-49n. 126; 4:23, 140; 5:5-6, 48n. 24, 140n. 99; 9:13, 140; 10:2-4, 12, 140, 155; 10:5, 140; 11:18-19, 140n. 99; 12:7, 140; 21:32 ("Western" text), 148-49n. 126; 24:15, 140n. 99; 27:62-66, 140; 28:11-15, 140; 28:20, 140n. 99
Luke: 6:21, 140n. 99; 7:33-34, 140n. 99; 10:1, 140; 10:17, 140; 11:52 ("Western" text), 140n. 100; 23:45, 140n. 100
John: 3:1-5, 142n. 106, 165n. 23; 4:20, 142; 7, 25; 7:50-52, 142n. 106, 165n. 23; 9, 25; 12:42-43, 142n. 106, 165n. 23; 12:43, 165; 16, 25; 19:38, 142n. 106, 165n. 23; 19:39-40, 142n. 106, 165n. 23
Acts of the Apostles: 1-15, 15; 1:23, 141n. 103; 1:26, 141n. 103; 3:22-23, 141; 4:3, 141n. 103; 4:4, 141, 141n. 103; 4:6, 141n. 103; 4:13, 141n. 103;

181

R 1, specific references to (*continued*)
158-59n. 6, 161n. 11, 162-63, 165-
67; R 1.27-72, 4-5, 16; R 1.27-74,
14n. 54, 17, 24, 116-18; R 1.27.1,
161n. 11; R 1.27.1-2, (Latin and
Syriac) 48; R 1.27.1-44.1, 53.4-71.6,
3; R 1.27.2, (Latin and Syriac) 48; R
1.27.3, (Syriac) 48, 137, (Latin) 142n.
108; R 1.27.6, (Syriac) 48; R 1.27.7,
(Syriac) 48; R 1.27.8, (Latin) 48, 138;
R 1.28.1-2, 162; R 1.28.2, 131n. 66,
139; R 1.29.1, 119n. 26, 128, 137; R
1.29.3, 120, (Syriac) 152n. 138; R
1.29.5, 122n. 35; R 1.30, 133; R
1.30.1, 121, 149; R 1.30.2, 119n. 26;
R 1.30.2-3, 138; R 1.30.3, 130, (Latin
and Syriac) 139; R 1.30.5, 27n. 124,
139, 159n. 9; R 1.30.7, 122; R
1.31.1, 139; R 1.31.2, 130, 138-39; R
1.31.3, 139; R 1.32, 132-34, 137; R
1.32-40, 141n. 103; R 1.32.1, 27n.
124; R 1.32.2-33.2, 139; R 1.32.3,
131n. 66, (Syriac) 132n. 72, 139,
(Latin) 162n. 16; R 1.32.3-4, 153,
162; R 1.32.4, 13n. 51, 121, 130,
153, 161; R 1.32.4-33.2, 123; R 1.33,
20, 23, 25n. 113, 132, 132nn. 70-71,
133-34, 137, 153; R 1.33-43, 28; R
1.33-44, 132n. 71; R 1.33-54, 28,
28n. 131; R 1.33-71, 25, 28-29, 33,
132n. 71, 137; R 1.33.1, 152n. 136,
153, 153n. 139; R 1.33.2, 153; R
1.33.3, 132n. 72, 152, (Syriac) 152n.
136, 153, 153n. 140, (Latin) 162n.
16; R 1.33.3-5, 153; R 1.33.3-34.1,
119n. 26; R 1.33.3-44.3, 32; R
1.33.3b-5, 153n. 140; R 1.33.5, 123,
160n. 10; R 1.34, 121; R 1.34.1, 153,
153n. 140; R 1.34.2, 128, 140, 141n.
103; R 1.34.3, 134, 141n. 103; R
1.34.3-35.1, (Armenian) 45, (Armenian, Latin, and Syriac) 46; R 1.34.4,
121, 130, 152n. 136; R 1.34.6, 31n.
144, 121, 142n. 108; R 1.34.6-7,
137; R 1.34.7, (Armenian and Syriac)
46, 142n. 108; R 1.35, 125n. 46; R
1.35.1, (Armenian and Latin) 46,
(Armenian and Syriac) 46, 130; R
1.35.2, 160; R 1.35.5, 124-25; R
1.35.6, 130; R 1.36-37, 128; R 1.36-
42, 19; R 1.36-71, 6; R 1.36.1, 147,
149, (Syriac) 149; R 1.36.2, 120,
(Syriac) 120, 121, 141; R 1.37, 27;
R 1.37-39, 33; R 1.37.2, 130, 140,
140n. 99, (Syriac) 144n. 113, 147,
(Syriac) 158; R 1.37.2-4, 130, 147,

R 1, specific references to (*continued*)
149; R 1.37.2-5, 130; R 1.37.3, 31n.
144, (Latin) 152n. 136; R 1.37.4, 121;
R 1.38.1, 123; R 1.38.3, 130; R
1.38.5, 31n. 144; R 1.39, 14, 27,
128; R 1.39.1, 123, 149; R 1.39.2,
151n. 134, (Syriac) 151n. 134; R
1.39.2-3, (Latin) 129, (Latin) 161,
(Syriac) 161; R 1.39.3, 130, 144n.
113, 149, 159, (Latin) 161n. 14,
163n. 20; R 1.40.2, (Syriac) 49, 140n.
99, (Syriac) 164n. 22; R 1.40.4, 128,
140; R 1.41.1-3, 128; R 1.41.2, 140;
R 1.41.3, 140n. 100; R 1.41.4, 135; R
1.42.1, 130, 160, 164-65; R 1.42.3,
149; R 1.42.4, 140; R 1.43, 11; R
1.43-44a, 18; R 1.43-44.3, 24n. 108;
R 1.43-52, 14; R 1.43-72, 14n. 53; R
1.43b-53a, 11; R 1.43.1, 130, 135,
144n. 113, 161, 161n. 12; R 1.43.2,
23, 23n. 100, 128; R 1.43.3, 118,
125n. 47, 129-30, 135, 141n. 103; R
1.44, 14n. 54, 135; R 1.44-52, 135; R
1.44-54, 5; R 1.44-71, 8; R 1.44a, 33;
R 1.44b-52, 13, 18; R 1.44b-53, 19; R
1.44.1, 31n. 144, 136, 144n. 113; R
1.44.1-53.4, 152; R 1.44.2, 130, 135,
144n. 113, 161, 161n. 12; R 1.44.2-
3, 136; R 1.44.3-53.4a, 20, 28, 28n.
131; R 1.44.4-52.6, 135, 150; R
1.44.5-6, 152; R 1.45.3-5, (Armenian)
45; R 1.45.5, (Syriac) 112n. 2; R
1.47.3, 8n. 29; R 1.48, 14, 19, 136; R
1.48.4, 123; R 1.49-50, 136; R
1.49.1-5, 131; R 1.49.2-4, 149n. 129;
R 1.50.5, 128, 136, 149n. 129; R
1.52.3, 130; R 1.52.6, 135; R 1.53-
71, 11-12, 152n. 136, 154; R 1.53-
72, 11; R 1.53-74, 24n. 108; R 1.53c-
62, 33; R 1.53.1, 135; R 1.53.1-
53.4a, 135n. 83; R 1.53.1-74.2, 112;
R 1.53.3, 135; R 1.53.3-4, 136; R
1.53.4, 135-36; R 1.54, 7, 28, 119n.
29, 136n. 84; R 1.54-65, 12, 18, 18n.
73, 144n. 113; R 1.54-71, 15; R
1.54.1, (Syriac) 112n. 2, 123, 144n.
113, 149, 162; R 1.54.2-5, 119; R
1.54.3, 131, 144n. 113; R 1.54.4, 7n.
24; R 1.54.5, 144n. 113, (Latin) 152n.
136; R 1.54.6-7, 129, 140n. 100,
148; R 1.54.7, 136n. 84; R 1.54.9,
162; R 1.55, 19; R 1.55-62, 32, 140,
155; R 1.55-64, 150; R 1.55-65, 28,
153-54; R 1.55-70, 14; R 1.55-71, (or
73) 14n. 54, 16; R 1.55-72, 161; R
1.55.1, 31n. 144, 135, 144n. 113;

Modern Authors Index

Subject Index

God (*continued*)

Abraham through the pattern of the stars, 59, 162, 162n. 16; recognition of the true, 139; reconciliation with, 98; reverence for, 108; rule of, over the final judgment, 83-85; sacrifices, rites, altar, and fire condemned as foreign to, 148n. 122; sacrifices to, 65-66; Son of (*see* Son of God); the Lord your, 66; translation of humans by, 84-85; what is pleasing to, 57, 59, 70, 75; will of, 52-53, 70, 97, 100, 112; wisdom of, 66, 69-70; worship of, without sacrifices, 64, 121

gods, rulers (heads of nations) worshipped as, 57

gospel: proclamation of the, to the gentiles, 29n. 134, 99

Gospel according to John, 25-26, 142, 165, 165n. 23; as possible source material, 142, 142n. 106; motifs in the, 26

Gospel according to Luke, 3, 20n. 82; use of the, in the source document, 3, 140, 140nn. 99-100

Gospel according to Mark, 140

Gospel according to Matthew, 3, 48n. 24, 148-49n. 126; use of the, in the source document, 3, 140, 140n. 99, 142, 155, 157. *See also* Matthew

Gospel according to the Hebrews, 15-16, 16-17n. 66

Gospel of the Ebionites, 3, 148, 148nn. 122, 125; as a Jewish Christian writing, 148; as an apocryphal writing, 148n. 125; as composed under the name of Matthew, 155; in the *Panarion*, 148nn. 122, 125, 149; use of the, in the source document, 3, 148-49, 149n. 127; vegetarianism in the, 149

gravestone(s), 109, 144n. 113

Great Church, 164n. 21, 168

Greek epitome. See under *Pseudo-Clementines*

Greek myths, 55

Greek version. See under *Recognitions*

Greek Old Testament, use of, in source document, 3, 140

H. See *Homilies*

Hadrian: edict of, 21, 159, 159n. 8, 163n. 20

Ham: descendants of, 56, 138; −, Palestine illicitly occupied by, 57-58, 138

Hamite. *See* Mizraim

heaven(s) 98; and earth, 52-53, 55; −, as one house, 52-53; expanse of the, 64; firmament called, 53; first, 48, 53; manna supplied by, 64; stars in the, 54; ten plagues sent to Egypt from the, 61; twofold, 53. *See also* kingdom(s) of heaven(s)

heavenly bodies, significance of the, 163. *See also* astrology

Hebrew(s) (also *Hebrews*): descent of the, from Abraham, 58; escape by the, from the Egyptians, 61-63; in the desert, 63-66; in Egypt, 61, 65; language, 57; −, Aramaic as roughly equivalent to the, 159n. 9; −, as pleasing to God, 57; −, as the first, 139; race of the, 58, 160; ruled by judges, 68; ruled by kings, 68

Hegesippus, 3, 10, 14-15, 24, 27, 31, 35, 141n. 101, 142, 142-43n. 109, 143, 143n. 111, 143-44n. 112, 144, 144-45n. 113, 145, 145n. 116, 146n. 117, 153-54, 157n. 1, 158-59n. 6, 166n. 28; writings of, 142-46, 166n. 28; −, dating of the, 163; −, dependency of the, on earlier source or tradition, 27, 143, 143n. 111, 144-45n. 113, 145; − −, viz., the *Anabathmoi Jakobou*, 10, 32; − −, viz., the Ebionite *Acts*, 19; − −, viz., the *Gospel of the Hebrews*, 15; −, leaders had become believers in the, 144n. 113; −, lost written source of the, 144; −, on presentation of James's martyrdom, 15, 21, 144n. 113, 145; −, original version of the, 142-43n. 109; −, narrative style of the, 142-43n. 109; −, parallels in the, with the source of R 1 and R 1.27-71, 15, 142-43, 143n. 111, 144-45n. 113, 145, 145n. 116, 146; −, relationship of the, to the *Second Apocalypse of James*, 144-45n. 113, 145, 145n. 116, 146, 146n. 117; −, supposedly interpolated version of the, 142-143n. 109; −, used in source R of 1, 3, 17, 24n. 108, 34-35, 142-43, 143-44n. 112, 144, 144-45n. 113, 145, 153-54, 159. *See also* Eusebius, *Historia Ecclesiastica*, Hegesippus in

hell, 85

high priest (*also* chief priest *and* high priesthood), 78-80, 88-89; Aaron as the first, 77, 80; as ready to be baptized, 106, 144n. 113, 166; Caiaphas as the, 74, 86, 104, 108, 135; disruption of the baptism of the, by Paul, 166; James named "archbishop" in imitation of the, 166n. 30; views of the, on the earthly messianic kingdom, 163

Hippolytus, *Refutatio Omnium Haeresium* by, 163n. 18

Holy Land, author's concern for the, 163. *See also* land

Holy Spirit (*also* holy spirit, Paraclete), 77, 98, 106

Homilies (H), 1, 5-6, 8-9, 11, 15, 18, 22n. 95, 24, 26, 36-37, 40n. 2, 44n. 16, 112, 114-17, 117n. 22, 118-19, 119nn. 26, 29, 120, 120n. 30, 121-22, 122nn.

Recognitions (R) (*continued*)
  R 1.27-71 (*continued*)
    author of (*continued*)
      159; as standing at a great historical
      distance from the events he is
      describing, 6; attention of the, to
      James the bishop, 166; awareness by
      the, of the gentile mission, 160, 164-
      65; baptismal formula of the, 161;
      beliefs of the, 163; chiliasm of the,
      163; christology of the, 160-61; co-
      alescence of the first and second Jew-
      ish wars against Rome in the mind of
      the, 163; concern of the, for the Holy
      Land, 163; consideration of the, that
      Christianity is the true Judaism, 160;
      date of composition by the, 163; his-
      torical place of the, 163; home of the,
      as Judaea, 159, 166; identity of the,
      159; interest of the, in those who
      secretly believe in Jesus, 165-66; lack
      of use of the letters of Paul by the,
      166; location of the, in Jerusalem,
      159, 166; on the submission of the, to
      the authority of the "archbishop," 167;
      possible competence in Aramaic by the,
      159n. 9; regarding supposed presuppo-
      sition of preexistence of Christ by the,
      160-61; religion of the, 159-60; re-
      marks by the, on the history of the
      people of God, 164; theology of the
      land of the, 158-59, 164; use of Hege-
      sippus by the, 159. *See also under*
      Matthew and *Recognitions*, R 1.27-71,
      source of
    author's views on: astrology, 3, 162-63;
      inheritance of the land of Israel, 3,
      158, 164; religion, 3, 165; the gentile
      mission, 164-65
    baptismal formula in, 117-18n. 24, 151,
      161
    biblical account in, 47-48
    characterizations of, 37-38
    chronological references in (chronology
      of), 17, 37, 118, 129, 152n. 137
    comparison of R 1.27 and Genesis 1 in,
      47-48
    dating of, 166
    dialogical style in, 135
    disputation of the apostles with the Jews
      concerning the true Christ in, 11
    Eunomian interpolator of, supposed, 113-
      14, 114n. 14, 115, 115n. 17
    Greek text of, 2, 151; compared with the
      Latin and Syriac versions of, 48; Latin
      and Syriac as the two extant ancient
      translations of the lost, 2-3, 38-40
    historical account from creation to pres-
      ent day in, 134, 141n. 103, 157

Recognitions (R) (*continued*)
  R 1.27-71 (*continued*)
    history of material in, 35-36
    history of traditions in, 27, 27n. 127,
      28, 28-29n. 131, 29, 35-36, 159n. 9,
      167
    Latin version of, 2-3, 25n. 116, 31-32n.
      144, 32, 38-39, 46, 51, 112, 129,
      152n. 136, 161-62, 164-65n. 22,
      166n. 30, 167 (*see also under* Rufi-
      nus); accommodation to biblical text in,
      47-48; compared to the Armenian
      fragments of, 45-46, 46nn. 22-23, 47;
      English translation(s) of the, 3, 31-32n.
      144, 32, 51, 52, 52n. 3, 53-109, 167;
      relative value of the, 3, 38, 42, 44-46,
      46n. 23, 47-49, 51
    list of apostles in, 89-97, 140, 154-55
    literary character (criteria *or* layers) of, 2-
      3, 32, 35, 37, 167; analysis of the,
      27-28n. 128, 28, 32-33, 35, 37, 111-
      38, 167
    Matthew, composed under the name of,
      3, 155, 157
    redactional work of B and R in, 3, 6-7,
      7n. 22, 8, 11, 13, 16, 20, 24, 24n.
      108, 28, 33, 37, 113-16, 116n. 19,
      117, 117-18n. 24, 118, 120-21, 126,
      131, 135, 135n. 83, 137, 143n. 112,
      151-52, 152nn. 136-37, 153, 153nn.
      140-41, 154, 160n. 10, 161n. 12,
      166n. 30
    relationship of, to the Ebionite *Acts*, 6,
      17-19, 146
    research on, historical, 2-3, 35-38, 48,
      154, 167; —, survey of previous, 4-34,
      37 (*see also under specific authors in
      the* Modern Authors Index)
    source of, 2-9, 9n. 34, 10-19, 19n. 76,
      20-23, 24n. 108, 25-28, 28-29n. 131,
      29-34, 34n. 153, 35-36, 127-32,
      132n. 70, 133-41, 141n. 101, 142-
      44, 144-45n. 113, 145, 145-46n.
      116, 146, 148-51, 152n. 137, 153-
      54, 154n. 146, 155, 157, 157n. 2,
      158-61, 161n. 11, 162-67; *Anabath-
      moi Jakobou* as the supposed, 3, 6-9,
      12-16, 18-19, 22n. 95, 23, 25-26, 29-
      32, 35, 146-48; anti-Paulinism of the,
      9, 11, 21, 29, 29n. 131, 30, 33, 129,
      166; as supposedly sharing a common
      source or tradition with Hegesippus,
      27, 143, 143n. 111; author of the, 3-
      4, 12, 29n. 134, 139-40, 140n. 98,
      141-43, 154-55, 157-58, 158-59n. 6,
      159n. 9, 161-66, 166n. 28, 167 (*see
      also under* Matthew and *Recognitions*,
      R 1.27-71, author of); —, as a Jewish
      Christian, 3-4, 33, 159n. 8, 160n. 10,